HEBREWS
VOLUME TWO

PREACHING THE WORD

HEBREWS
VOLUME TWO

An Anchor for the Soul

R. Kent Hughes

CROSSWAY BOOKS • WHEATON, ILLINOIS
A DIVISION OF GOOD NEWS PUBLISHERS

Hebrews, Volume Two.

Copyright © 1993 by R. Kent Hughes.

Published by Crossway Books
                a division of Good News Publishers
                1300 Crescent Street
                Wheaton, Illinois 60187.

Cover banner: Marge Gieser

Art Direction/Design: Mark Schramm

First printing, 1993

Printed in the United States of America

ISBN 0-89107-723-5

Unless otherwise noted, all Bible quotations are taken from *Holy Bible: New International Version,* copyright © 1978 by the New York International Bible Society. Used by permission of Zondervan Bible Publishers.

01	00	99	98	97	96	95	94	93
15	14	13	12	11	10	9	8	7	6	5	4	3	2	1

To
Dr. Charles Lee Feinberg

We have this hope as an anchor for the soul,
firm and secure. It enters the inner sanctuary
behind the curtain, where Jesus, who went before us,
has entered on our behalf. He has become a
high priest forever, in the order of Melchizedek.

(Hebrews 6:19, 20)

Table of Contents

Acknowledgments

I must express appreciation to my secretary, Mrs. Sharon Fritz, for her patience and care in typing the manuscript of these studies; also to Mr. Herbert Carlburg for his cheerful, weekly proofreading, and Rev. Jeff Buikema, pastor of Covenant Presbyterian Church, LaCrosse, Wisconsin, for his reading of the manuscript and helpful suggestions. Lastly, special thanks to Dr. Lane Dennis, president of Crossway Books, for his vision for this undertaking and consistent encouragement.

A Word to Those Who Preach the Word

There are times when I am preaching that I have especially sensed the pleasure of God. I usually become aware of it through the unnatural silence. The ever-present coughing ceases and the pews stop creaking, bringing an almost physical quiet to the sanctuary — through which my words sail like arrows. I experience a heightened eloquence, so that the cadence and volume of my voice intensify the truth I am preaching.

There is nothing quite like it — the Holy Spirit filling one's sails, the sense of his pleasure, and the awareness that something is happening among one's hearers. This experience is, of course, not unique, for thousands of preachers have similar experiences, even greater ones.

What has happened when this takes place? How do we account for this sense of his smile? The answer for me has come from the ancient rhetorical categories of *logos*, *ethos*, and *pathos*.

The first reason for his smile is the *logos* — in terms of preaching, God's Word. This means that as we stand before God's people to proclaim his Word, we have done our homework. We have exegeted the passage, mined the significance of its words in their context, and applied sound hermeneutical principles in interpreting the text so that we understand what its words meant to its hearers. And it means that we have labored long until we can express in a sentence what the theme of the text is — so that our outline springs from the text. Then our preparation will be such that as we preach, we will not be preaching our own thoughts about God's Word, but God's actual Word, his *logos*. This is fundamental to pleasing him in preaching.

The second element in knowing God's smile in preaching is *ethos* — what you are as a person. There is a danger endemic to preaching, which is having your hands and heart cauterized by holy things. Phillips Brooks illustrated it by the analogy of a train conductor who comes to believe that he has been to the places he announces because of his long and loud heralding of them. And that is why Brooks insisted that preaching must be "the bringing of truth through personality." Though we can never *perfectly* embody the truth we preach, we must be subject to it, long for it, and make it as much a part of our ethos as possible. As the Puritan William Ames said, "Next to the

Scriptures, nothing makes a sermon more to pierce, than when it comes out of the inward affection of the heart without any affectation." When a preacher's ethos backs up his *logos*, there will be the pleasure of God.

Last, there is *pathos* — personal passion and conviction. David Hume, the Scottish philosopher and skeptic, was once challenged as he was seen going to hear George Whitefield preach: "I thought you do not believe in the gospel." Hume replied, "I don't, but *he does*." Just so! When a preacher believes what he preaches, there will be passion. And this belief and requisite passion will know the smile of God.

The pleasure of God is a matter of *logos* (the Word), *ethos* (what you are), and *pathos* (your passion). As you *preach the Word* may you experience his smile — the Holy Spirit in your sails!

R. Kent Hughes
Wheaton, Illinois

HEBREWS
VOLUME TWO

The law is only a shadow of the good things that are coming — not the realities themselves. For this reason it can never, by the same sacrifices repeated endlessly year after year, make perfect those who draw near to worship. If it could, would they not have stopped being offered? For the worshipers would have been cleansed once for all, and would no longer have felt guilty for their sins. But those sacrifices are an annual reminder of sins, because it is impossible for the blood of bulls and goats to take away sins. Therefore, when Christ came into the world, he said: "Sacrifice and offering you did not desire, but a body you prepared for me; with burnt offerings and sin offerings you were not pleased. Then I said, 'Here I am — it is written about me in the scroll— I have come to do your will, O God.'" First he said, "Sacrifices and offerings, burnt offerings and sin offerings you did not desire, nor were you pleased with them" (although the law required them to be made). Then he said, "Here I am, I have come to do your will." He sets aside the first to establish the second. And by that will, we have been made holy through the sacrifice of the body of Jesus Christ once for all. Day after day every priest stands and performs his religious duties; again and again he offers the same sacrifices, which can never take away sins. But when this priest had offered for all time one sacrifice for sins, he sat down at the right hand of God. Since that time he waits for his enemies to be made his footstool, because by one sacrifice he has made perfect forever those who are being made holy. The Holy Spirit also testifies to us about this. First he says: "This is the covenant I will make with them after that time, says the Lord. I will put my laws in their hearts, and I will write them on their minds." Then he adds: "Their sins and lawless acts I will remember no more." And where these have been forgiven, there is no longer any sacrifice for sin. (10:1-18)

1

Covenant and Perfection

HEBREWS 10:1-18

As we said in our first volume on the epistle to the Hebrews, no New Testament book has had more background research than Hebrews, and none has spawned a greater diversity of opinion, though there is broad agreement that the grand theme of this epistle is the supremacy and finality of Jesus Christ.

A consensus also exists regarding the general identity of the recipients: they were a group of Jewish Christians who had never seen Jesus in person, yet had believed. Their conversion had brought them hardship and persecution with the result that some had slipped back into Judaism. And, thus, the purpose for the letter was to encourage them to not fall away, but to press on (cf. 2:1ff.; 3:12ff.; 6:4ff.; 10:26ff.; and 12:15ff.).

There is also universal agreement, first expressed by Origen, that "only God knows certainly" who wrote this letter. There is also agreement that the author, whoever he was, was a magnificent stylist with an immense vocabulary and a vast knowledge of the Greek Old Testament.

Despite general agreement on these matters, no scholar has yet proven the exact destination or occasion of the letter — though many contemporary scholars tentatively propose that the letter was written to a small house-church of beleaguered Jewish Christians in the mid-sixties before the destruction of the Jerusalem Temple. Hebrews was evidently written to a group of Jewish Christians whose world was falling apart. The author's conveying the greetings of several Italian Christians who were with him (13:24)

17

supports the idea that the harried little church was on Italian soil — very likely in or around Rome.

Their Christianity had not been a worldly advantage. Rather, it set them up for persecution and the loss of property and privilege, and now could possibly even cost them their lives.

We know they had already paid a price for their initial commitment to Christ. As the writer recalls in 10:32-34:

> Remember those earlier days after you had received the light, when you stood your ground in a great contest in the face of suffering. Sometimes you were publicly exposed to insult and persecution; at other times you stood side by side with those who were so treated. You sympathized with those in prison and joyfully accepted the confiscation of your property, because you knew that you yourselves had better and lasting possessions.

This description of their earlier sufferings fits well into the picture of the hardships that came to Jewish Christians under Claudius in A.D. 49. Suetonius' *Life of the Deified Claudius* records that "there were riots in the Jewish quarter at the instigation of Chrestus. As a result, Claudius expelled the Jews from Rome" (25.4). "Chrestus," historians believe, is a reference to Christ, and the riots and expulsion occurred when Jewish Christians were banished from the synagogue by the Jewish establishment.

Now, as the author of Hebrews writes, fifteen years have gone by since the Claudian persecution, and a new persecution looms. No one has been killed yet, but 12:4 raises the possibility that martyrdom may soon come — "In your struggle against sin, you have *not yet* resisted to the point of shedding your blood."

The writer of Hebrews was writing to admonish and encourage his friends, a small group of Jewish Christians who were scared stiff! Some had begun to avoid contact with outsiders. Some had even withdrawn from the worshiping community altogether (10:25). The author feared there might be those who, if arrested, would succumb to the conditions of release — a public denial of Christ (6:6; 10:29). The tiny home-church was asking some hard questions: Did God know what was going on? If so, how could this be happening to them? Did he care? Only God could protect them, but where was he? Why did he not answer? Why the silence of God?

The letter arrived, and word was sent out. The congregation gathered. Perhaps no more than fifteen or twenty were seated or standing around the house. All were quiet.Through these magnificent words the beleaguered church was brought face to face with the God who speaks, and this God — through his superior Son, Jesus Christ — would bring them comfort in the midst of life's troubles.

Now we will continue our study of this remarkable Biblical document, beginning with chapter 10.

Soon after I began to date my future wife, Barbara, I obtained her picture — a beautiful black-and-white 8 x 10 photograph taken the year before we met — and it immediately became an item of pre-nuptial "worship." It was one of those bare-shouldered, sorority-style pictures so popular at the time. She looked like an angel floating in the clouds. It became my portable hope, most often sitting on my desk, sometimes in my car, at other times propped in front of my plate and my love-struck eyes.

However, the day came when we stood before God and our families and friends and pledged our lives to each other as she became mine. Suddenly I had gone from the possession of a one-dimensional portrait to the possession of the real thing, who smiled, talked, and laughed — a real, three-dimensional wife — a living, life-loving soul! And the picture? It remained just as beautiful, but from then on it received relatively scant attention.

But imagine that one day I appear before my wife holding the black-and-white photograph, and I say, "My dear, I've missed your picture, and I'm going back to it. I really am attached to the silhouette and the monochrome shading and the matte finish." Then I passionately kiss the glass protecting the photograph, clutch it to my chest, and exit mumbling my devotion to the picture — "I love you, O photograph of my wife. You're everything to me."

People's suspicions that pastors are weird would be confirmed. Time to call for the men in the white jackets!

How absurd for anyone, once having the substance, to go back to the shadow. Yet, some in the early church were forsaking the Covenant of Grace for the Old Covenant of the Law. And this is what the author of Hebrews wants to steel his people against as he concludes his comparison of the Old and New Covenants in 10:1-18.

THE PROBLEM OF IMPERFECTION (vv. 1-4)

The author/pastor begins with a forthright statement of the facts: "The law is only a shadow of the good things that are coming — not the realities themselves" (v. 1a). As a "shadow," the Law is only a pale reflection, a mere outline or silhouette, and is thus unsubstantial.[1] The Ten Commandments, the Book of the Covenant, and the Tabernacle cultus only foreshadow the reality of Christ. And as a shadow, the Law had substantial imperfections that the writer proceeds to spell out:

> For this reason it can never, by the same sacrifices repeated endlessly year after year, make perfect those who draw near to worship. If it could, would they not have stopped being offered? For the wor-

shipers would have been cleansed once for all, and would no longer have felt guilty for their sins. But those sacrifices are an annual reminder of sins, because it is impossible for the blood of bulls and goats to take away sins. (vv. 1b-4)

Imperfect Cleansing

Of course, the author of Hebrews was not the first to understand that animal blood would not atone for sins. Scriptural writers had been alert to this for hundreds of years. David's repentant words head the list: "You do not delight in sacrifice, or I would bring it; you do not take pleasure in burnt offerings. The sacrifices of God are a broken spirit; a broken and contrite heart, O God, you will not despise" (Psalm 51:16, 17). Consider also Samuel's words to King Saul: "Does the Lord delight in burnt offerings and sacrifices as much as in obeying the voice of the Lord? To obey is better than sacrifice, and to heed is better than the fat of rams" (1 Samuel 15:22). And Isaiah said:

> "The multitude of your sacrifices — what are they to me?" says the Lord. "I have more than enough of burnt offerings, of rams and the fat of fattened animals; I have no pleasure in the blood of bulls and lambs and goats. When you come to appear before me, who has asked this of you, this trampling of my courts? Stop bringing meaningless offerings!" (Isaiah 1:11-13a)

Later Isaiah expressed God's displeasure at offerings when one's heart is not right:

> But whoever sacrifices a bull is like one who kills a man, and whoever offers a lamb, like one who breaks a dog's neck; whoever makes a grain offering is like one who presents pig's blood, and whoever burns memorial incense, like one who worships an idol. They have chosen their own ways. . . . For when I called, no one answered, when I spoke, no one listened. (66:3, 4)

Similarly, Jeremiah inveighed against sacrifices presented without an obedient heart:

> "This is what the Lord Almighty, the God of Israel, says: Go ahead, add your burnt offerings to your other sacrifices and eat the meat yourselves! For when I brought your forefathers out of Egypt and spoke to them, I did not just give them commands about burnt offerings and sacrifices, but I gave them this command: Obey me, and I will be your God and you will be my people." (Jeremiah 7:21-23)

God said through Hosea, "For I desire mercy, not sacrifice, and acknowledgment of God rather than burnt offerings" (Hosea 6:6). And Amos shared God's thoughts about wrong-hearted sacrifices:

"I hate, I despise your religious feasts; I cannot stand your assemblies. Even though you bring me burnt offerings and grain offerings, I will not accept them. Though you bring choice fellowship offerings, I will have no regard for them. Away with the noise of your songs! I will not listen to the music of your harps. But let justice roll on like a river, righteousness like a never-failing stream!" (Amos 5:21-24)

Lastly, we include the famous words of Micah:

With what shall I come before the Lord and bow down before the exalted God? Shall I come before him with burnt offerings, with calves a year old? Will the Lord be pleased with thousands of rams, with ten thousand rivers of oil? Shall I offer my firstborn for my transgression, the fruit of my body for the sin of my soul? He has showed you, O man, what is good. And what does the Lord require of you? To act justly and to love mercy and to walk humbly with your God. (Micah 6:6-8)

It is a fact that at the time of Christ many pious Jews honored the sacrificial system and even offered sacrifices, but realized that those sacrifices could not remove sin. This is why, when the Temple was destroyed and the sacrifices ended, the people so easily adapted. They understood that animal sacrifice was insufficient to obtain forgiveness.[2]

An Imperfect Conscience

Because the old system could not take away their sin, it produced a second imperfection — a guilty conscience (cf. v. 2). Of course one's conscience can be seared or defaced, as C. S. Lewis noted in joking with a friend when he wrote:

We were talking about cats and dogs the other day and decided that both have consciences but the dog being an honest, humble person, always has a bad one, but the cat is a Pharisee and always has a good one. When he sits and stares you out of countenance he is thanking God that he is not as these dogs, or these humans, or even as these other cats![3]

But assuming that one didn't have a cat's non-conscience, one's conscience under the Old Covenant always had a pervasive sense of dis-ease. One's inner moral discernment[4] always registered a floating guilt, and in some, this was a raging, unquenchable guilt.

> Not all the blood of beasts
> On Jewish altars slain,
> Could give the guilty conscience rest
> Or wash away one stain.

Memorialized Imperfection

The result was, as verse 3 points out, that the sacrifices remained as "an annual reminder of sins." As a matter of fact, the Day of Atonement increased the burden of those with sensitive hearts. The Day's well-defined ritual was constructed to aggravate one's conscience. The shadow of the Old Covenant Law and sacrifice inflamed the unrequited need for *forgiveness* and a *clear conscience*. The photograph, so to speak, pictured what could be and activated an ache for the reality.

The Old Covenant simply could not "make perfect those who draw near to worship" (v. 1). It was good, as far as it went. But it was frustratingly inadequate.

THE SOLUTION FOR IMPERFECTION (vv. 5-9)

Of course, the Godhead was not unaware of this, and beginning in verse 5 we have a brief synopsis of the conversation that took place there when Jesus elected to come into the world as a man.

The Divine Dialogue

"Therefore, when Christ came into the world, he said [Christ's pre-incarnate words]: 'Sacrifice and offering you did not desire, but a body you prepared for me; with burnt offerings and sin offerings you were not pleased. Then I said, "Here I am — it is written about me in the scroll — I have come to do your will, O God"'" (vv. 5-7). Actually, Christ's words here were a quotation from King David taken from a paraphrased Greek version of Psalm 40:6-8 (LXX, Psalm 39:7-9). David had spoken it one thousand years earlier, but Christ in Heaven took it and reapplied it, so as to describe his own inner thinking and dialogue with the Father when he came into the world.

What a high place this gives Scripture! Our pre-incarnate Savior quoted Psalm 40 as being prophetic of his thoughts at his human birth. Interestingly, the Hebrew of Psalm 40:6 literally reads, "ears you have dug for me," but the Greek paraphrase of it that Christ and the author quoted in Hebrews is, "a body you prepared for me." This may be because the Greek translator regarded the creation of ears as part of fashioning a whole human body.[5]

Whatever the explanation may be, Christ said in essence, "My Father, the Old Testament sacrifices have proven unsatisfactory, so you have prepared a body for me, that I might become a pleasing sacrifice." (The author reiterates this idea in verse 8, noting that the Father was not pleased with the old sacrifices "although the law required them to be made.") The fact was, though God had instituted blood animal sacrifices (Exodus 24), he had never been pleased with them and did not see them as ends. He had established them as object lessons to instruct his people about the sinfulness of their hearts, his hatred of sin, the fact that sin leads to death, the need of an atonement, and his delight in those whose hearts were clean and obedient and faithful. But there was nothing appealing to him in the sight of a dying animal. God had no pleasure in the moans and death-throes of lambs or bulls. What he did find pleasure in was those who offered a sacrifice with a contrite, obedient heart.

The Divine Disposition

Having verbalized what the Father wanted — Jesus Christ's sacrificial death — our Lord now states his joyous resolve: "Then I said, 'Here I am — it is written about me in the scroll — I have come to do your will, O God'" (v. 7). On the verge of the Incarnation, the Lord Jesus stopped to pay tribute to the Old Testament Scripture and to proclaim that what he was about to do had been fully written of in advance in the scroll.

Hours could be spent here inspecting the familiar Old Testament prophecies and types that point so fully to the incarnate Messiah. But the great emphasis here, one we must not miss, is Christ's exuberant determination and eagerness to *obey* the Father — "Then I said, 'Here I am . . . I have come to do your will, O God.'" Our Lord did not obey the Father grudgingly or under duress but with joy! Later, in 12:2, the writer tells us that Jesus endured the cross "for the joy set before him." The angels sang at the Incarnation (Luke 2:13ff.) because they were reflecting and expressing Christ's joy. He had come to die, and that could logically have produced an angelic dirge. But the angels gave out an anthem instead, because of the anthem of Christ's heart — "Then I said, 'Here I am . . . I have come to do your will, O God.'" There is "in Deity Itself the joy of obedience: obedience which is a particular means of joy and the only means of that particular joy."[6] Jesus willed to be subordinate to God!

What is the application for us? Jesus' joyous resolve to obediently do God's will is the essence of the true sacrifice and worship that God desires. Jesus does what God desired from every worshiper in the Old Covenant. God did not want animal sacrifices. What he wanted and still wants is obedience! That is the *only* sacrifice that is acceptable to God.

Everything is ashes if we are not living in conscious obedience to God.

Is there something you know God wants you to do, but you have been unwilling? Perhaps it is a kindness to perform — a confession to make — a gift to give — a commitment to fulfill — a task to perform. If you know what it is, say reverently to him, "Here I am . . . I have come to do your will, O God."

THE RESULTS OF PERFECTION (vv. 10-18)

The author introduces the results of Christ's willingness to do God's will by saying, "And by that will, we have been made holy through the sacrifice of the body of Jesus Christ once for all" (v. 10). Jesus' sacrifice "once for all" is emphatic, and the writer wants us to see that its results are equally final, for "we have been made holy" refers to an enduring, continuous state (perfect tense). Our salvation is a completed thing — a "done deal."[7]

From the writer's perspective, the comparative postures of Jesus (our Melchizedekian priest) and the Aaronic priests make the point. He explains:

> Day after day every priest stands and performs his religious duties; again and again he offers the same sacrifices, which can never take away sins. But when this priest had offered for all time one sacrifice for sins, he sat down at the right hand of God. Since that time he waits for his enemies to be made his footstool, because by one sacrifice he has made perfect forever those who are being made holy. (vv. 11-14)

Significantly, there were no chairs in the Tabernacle — no provision whatsoever to sit down. Priests stood or kept moving, because their imperfect work was never over. But Jesus, in exact fulfillment of the Melchizedekian prophecies in Psalm 110:1 — "The Lord says to my Lord, 'Sit at my right hand until I make your enemies a footstool for your feet'" — sat down forever at the right hand of honor and power (cf. 1:3, 13; 8:1). Jesus rests. Our salvation, as we have said, is a "done deal." Our perfection is accomplished. And in the timelessness of eternity our holiness will go on and on.[8]

The preacher to the Hebrews finishes this great section with a brief recap of two perfections of the New Covenant from Jeremiah 31 that were mentioned earlier in 8:10-12 — namely, empowerment and forgiveness.

Empowerment

As to empowerment, we read, "The Holy Spirit also testifies to us about this. First he says: 'This is the covenant I will make with them after that time, says the Lord. I will put my laws in their hearts, and I will write them on their minds'" (vv. 15, 16; cf. Jeremiah 31:33). Instead of putting his laws on stone tablets, they are placed in the very center of the believer's being, so that there is an inner impulse that both delights in knowing his law and doing his will.

Shortly after the armistice of World War I, Dr. Donald Grey Barnhouse visited the battlefields of Belgium. In the first year of the war the area around the city of Mons was the scene of the great British retreat. In the last year of the war it was the scene of the greater enemy retreat. For miles west of the city the roads were lined with artillery, tanks, trucks, and other materials of war that the enemy had abandoned in their hasty flight.

It was a lovely spring day. The sun was shining, and not a breath of wind was blowing. As he walked along, examining the war remains, he noticed leaves were falling from the great trees that arched along the road. He brushed at a leaf that had fallen against his chest. As he grasped at it, he pressed it in his fingers, and it disintegrated. He looked up curiously and saw several other leaves falling from the trees. Remember, it was spring, not autumn, nor was there enough wind to blow off the leaves. These leaves had outlived the winds of autumn and the frosts of winter. Yet they were falling that day, seemingly without cause.

Then Dr. Barnhouse realized why. The most potent force of all was causing them to fall. It was spring — the sap was beginning to run, and the buds were beginning to push from within. From down beneath the dark earth, roots were sending life along trunk, branch, and twig until it expelled every bit of deadness that remained from the previous year. It was, as a great Scottish preacher termed it, "the expulsive power of a new affection."[9]

This is what happens when God writes his will on our hearts. The new life within purges the deadness from our lives. Our renewed hearts pump fresh blood through us. The life of Christ in us — the same life that said "Here I am . . . I have come to do your will, O God" — animates us!

You may be saying to yourself, "I don't think I can ever live the Christian life" — and you are right! But a new heart, the expulsive inner power of new affection, will make it possible. The sense that you cannot do it is precisely why you should come to Christ. In fact, it is the qualification!

Forgiveness

The other perfection of the New Covenant mentioned here is forgiveness: "Then he adds: 'Their sins and lawless acts I will remember no more.' And where these have been forgiven, there is no longer any sacrifice for sin" (vv. 17, 18). Note the air of finality here — a completed sacrifice and complete forgiveness.

Amazingly, it is possible for people to think they believe what really in their heart they do not believe. It is possible to imagine they believe in the forgiveness of sins when they do not. Their belief is logical and theoretical but not actual. Then something happens, the truth appears clearer than ever before; they see it — and they believe with all their heart. Forgiveness follows belief.

It was said that Clara Barton, organizer of the American Red Cross, was never known to harbor resentment to anyone. On one occasion a friend recalled for her an incident that had taken place some years before, but Clara seemed not to remember. "Don't you remember the wrong that was done you?" asked her friend. Clara Barton answered calmly, "No, I distinctly remember forgetting that." Clara Barton willed to forgive and forget.

But God does even better. He really *does* forgive and forget — "Their sins and lawless acts I will remember no more." Do you believe you believe it? Or do you truly believe it? Believe it!

What folly to leave one's living spouse for her lifeless portrait. On the one hand, you "possess" a living person of so many inches, of a definite weight, with her own aroma, brimming with thought and action. But you leave her for her lifeless photograph with its fixed and sealed expression. What an absurd thought!

But there is an exercise of even greater absurdity, and that is to leave her for nothing. This is the folly of our age. Christ's joyous shout upon leaving Heaven was for you and me: "Then I said . . . 'I have come to do your will, O God.'" He died and rose to make you and me perfect, forgiving us completely and renewing our hearts. Heaven has been laid at our sinful feet. There can be no greater folly imaginable than to turn away from this to nothing. "Lord, to whom shall we go? You have the words of eternal life" (John 6:68).

Therefore, brothers, since we have confidence to enter the Most Holy Place by the blood of Jesus, by a new and living way opened for us through the curtain, that is, his body, and since we have a great priest over the house of God, let us draw near to God with a sincere heart in full assurance of faith, having our hearts sprinkled to cleanse us from a guilty conscience and having our bodies washed with pure water. Let us hold unswervingly to the hope we profess, for he who promised is faithful. And let us consider how we may spur one another on toward love and good deeds. Let us not give up meeting together, as some are in the habit of doing, but let us encourage one another — and all the more as you see the Day approaching. (10:19-25)

2

Full Access / Full Living

HEBREWS 10:19-25

Though we do not know who the author of Hebrews was, we do know he was a preacher with flaming pastoral instincts. He did not do theology for *theoretical* ends, but rather for down-to-earth, *practical* purposes. So we come here to the great turning-point in Hebrews where the writer turns from the *explanation* of the superiority of the person and work of Christ to the *application* of it in the lives of the storm-tossed church. The shift can be stated in various ways: from *doctrine* to *duty*, from *creed* to *conduct*, from *precept* to *practice*, from *instruction* to *exhortation*, all of which mean one thing — the writer becomes very explicit regarding how Christians ought to live.

In making transition from instruction to exhortation, the preacher assumes that the foregoing ten chapters, truly believed, ought to have produced a profound dual confidence: confidence in one's *access* to God, and confidence in one's *advocate* before God.

ACCESS (vv. 19, 20)

As he begins, he assumes matter-of-factly in the opening phrase that his hearers have a proper confidence in their divine *access*: "Therefore, brothers, since we have confidence to enter the Most Holy Place by the blood of Jesus, by a new and living way opened for us through the curtain, that is, his body . . ." (vv. 19, 20). Their confident access comes from the torn curtain of

29

Christ's crucified body. The rending of Jesus' flesh on the cross, which brought his death, perpetrated a simultaneous tearing from top to bottom of the curtain that had barred the way into the Holy of Holies (Matthew 27:51). They walked confidently through the torn curtain of Christ, so to speak, into the presence of the Father.

Whereas before they could only have surrogate access through the high priest, who slipped behind the curtain once a year for a heart-pounding few minutes, they now had permanent access through the blood and torn body of Christ. Their confidence was certainly not a swaggering thing, but it was a real confidence in permanent access. This nicely complemented the preacher's earlier encouragement: "Let us then approach the throne of grace with confidence, so that we may receive mercy and find grace to help us in our time of need" (4:16). They had deep confidence in their access to God.

ADVOCACY (v. 21)

This confidence in access is especially strong because it is coupled with a confidence in Christ's priestly advocacy: "since we have a great priest over the house of God" (v. 21). As we know, the appointments of the Tabernacle and the daily vestments of the Aaronic high priests were specifically spelled out to Moses by God, because they were shadows of Christ's ultimate heavenly advocacy. God's instructions demanded that the Old Testament high priest wear twelve stones on his breastplate — over his heart — to represent his people (Exodus 28:21), and representative stones on his shoulder as well, for "Aaron is to bear the names on his shoulders for a memorial before the Lord" (28:12). Now Jesus, our ultimate advocate, bears our names not just over his body and heart, but in the very center of his being, for we are *in* him, our advocate! Even more, he is our constant high priest. His intercession never ceases!

See this access and advocacy, the dual sources of our confidence, together. See what strength they bring. Jesus is both the curtain (our access) and the priest (our advocate). His torn body and shed blood provides our access to the presence of the Father. And in our access he is our perpetual priestly advocate.

This was meant to make the ancient Church (and us) confidently point our ship into the high seas with strength and power. We are not only to exist in a hostile culture but to buck its waves. While arrogance can never be the Christian's way, confidence must mark his life. Listen to Paul's bold confidence:

> If God is for us, who can be against us? He who did not spare his own Son, but gave him up for us all — how will he not also, along with him, graciously give us all things? Who will bring any charge

against those whom God has chosen? It is God who justifies. Who is he that condemns? Christ Jesus, who died — more than that, who was raised to life — is at the right hand of God and is also interceding for us. (Romans 8:31-34)

The logic here, seriously applied, pushes us to heights of confidence. It means more than God being graciously disposed toward us. It means we are victors. We may be defeated for a moment, but evil will never prevail. *Access* and *advocacy* — what confidence they bring!

When Chrysostom was brought before the Roman emperor, the emperor threatened him with banishment if he remained a Christian. Chrysostom replied:

> "You can not banish me for this world is my father's house." "But I will slay you," said the Emperor. "No, you can not," said the noble champion of the faith, "for my life is hid with Christ in God." "I will take away your treasures." "No, but you can not for my treasure is in heaven and my heart is there." "But I will drive you away from man and you shall have no friend left." "No, you can not, for I have a friend in heaven from whom you can not separate me. I defy you, for there is nothing you can do to hurt me."[1]

DRAW NEAR TO GOD (v. 22)

From the vantage-point of the remarkable confidence that ought to be every believer's, the preacher gives three sweeping exhortations, the first of which is to draw near to God. We can catch the force of the argument if we again consider verses 19-21, which lead up to it: "Therefore, brothers, since we have confidence to enter the Most Holy Place by the blood of Jesus, by a new and living way opened for us through the curtain, that is, his body, and since we have a great priest over the house of God . . ." That is, because of the *confidence* we have from our grand *access* and *advocacy*, "let us draw near to God with a sincere heart in full assurance of faith, having our hearts sprinkled to cleanse us from a guilty conscience and having our bodies washed with pure water" (v. 22).

Under the Old Covenant, when priests were consecrated they were sprinkled with blood (Exodus 29:21). Also, when the Old Covenant began, the people had been sprinkled with blood (Exodus 24:8). But with the New Covenant, when the people of this Hebrew church came to faith, their hearts were inwardly "sprinkled" with Christ's blood to cleanse them "from a guilty conscience" (cf. 9:14). For the first time in their lives the guilt was completely gone, and their conscience rested easy. Then they were baptized and their "bodies washed with pure water" — an outward, visible sign of the inner sprinkling or cleansing, they had experienced (cf. 1 Peter 3:21; Ephesians 5:25, 26).

To such lives the teacher's exhortation comes with great appeal and power: "Let us draw near to God with a sincere heart in full assurance of faith." The "heart" represents the whole inner life. There must be inner sincerity from one's whole being. One must be true, completely genuine, "wholehearted" (Moffatt). Commentators have noted that although the language is different, the sixth Beatitude carries the same idea, where we are called to be "pure in heart" (Matthew 5:8).[2] There are to be no mixed motives or divided loyalties. There must be pure and unmixed devotion, "sincere" love for God.

Negatively, we can picture this idea from everyday life as we reflect on those people who, after being introduced to us, keep talking and smiling but at the same time looking behind and around us at other people and things. They really are not interested in us. They only see us as objects or a means for something they want. In our relationship with the God-man, such behavior is anathema. Positively stated, a "sincere" heart is represented in the words *focus* or *wholeheartedness*.

Jesus makes essentially the same point in John 4:23 when he says God desires those who worship "in spirit" — that is, those whose entire human spirit is engaged in worship.

This is how we are to draw near to God in prayer — real, genuine, absorbed. The preacher sees this as being of key importance to those who are being distracted by the menacing waves. He knows that essential to their survival is the ability to perpetually come to God in prayer that is sincere and wholehearted, true and engaged. If they do this, they will emerge victorious. They must prayerfully "draw near to God with a sincere heart in full assurance of faith." The wisdom of this exhortation is as relevant and necessary today as it was in the first century.

HOLD TO THE HOPE (v. 23)

The next exhortation flows naturally from the preceding because if we draw near to God, we will be disposed to heed the command to persevere in hope: "Let us hold unswervingly to the hope we profess, for he who promised is faithful" (v. 23).

Hopelessness is the lot of the honest secularist. Bertrand Russell gave it famous expression in his book *A Free Man's Worship*:

> . . . the labours of the ages, all the devotion, all the inspiration, all the noonday brightness of human genius, are destined to extinction in the vast death of the solar system, and that the whole temple of Man's achievement must inevitably be buried beneath the debris of

a universe in ruins . . . only within the scaffolding of the truths, only on the firm foundation of unyielding despair, can the soul's habitation henceforth be safely built.[3]

The "firm foundation of unyielding despair"? It doesn't sound very firm to the ear, or to the logical mind.

Most people, however, are not as cerebral as philosopher Russell. They base their lives, rather, on a vague, shapeless, subjective hope. Professor William M. Marston of New York University asked three thousand people, "What have you to live for?" He was shocked to discover that 94 percent were simply enduring the present while they waited for the future . . . waited for "something to happen" . . . waited for "next year" . . . waited for a "better time" . . . waited for "someone to die" . . . waited "for tomorrow."[4]

> *Hope springs eternal in the human breast:*
> *Man never is, but always to be, blest.*
>
> (Alexander Pope, *An Essay on Man*)

So many people live on so little, surviving in this world, just putting one foot in front of the other as they depend on unsubstantiated, ungrounded "hope."

But the Christian's hope has substance! The hope that our text commends here in verse 23 is a conscious reference back to the writer's statement in 6:19, 20 — "We have this hope as an anchor for the soul, firm and secure. It enters the inner sanctuary behind the curtain, where Jesus, who went before us, has entered on our behalf." It is grounded in the life, death, resurrection, ascension, enthronement, and intercession of our Lord Jesus Christ. It is anchored at the right hand of God. It is so substantial and real that it is called "an anchor."

No ancient or modern sailor who knows what can happen during an ocean voyage would go to sea in a ship that carried no anchor, even today and even if the ship were the greatest and most modern vessel afloat. Every sailor knows that situations might arise when the hope of the ship and all her company will depend not on the captain, the crew, the engines, the compass, or the rudder, but on the anchor. When all else fails, there is hope in the anchor. It was so easy for Christians to appropriate this as their symbol because its very shape uses the form of the cross.

Literally, the author here commands, "And let us hold on *unbendingly* to the hope we confess, for he who promised is faithful." The anchor is not in the sea, but in Heaven, the celestial Holy of Holies. It is anchored in God's presence. As the winds pick up, as the ship bobs like a cork, as we sail through all life's troubles, we must hang on to the confession of our hope without wavering, for our hope is anchored in our access to and advocacy before God the Father. We must hang on with all we have. Such tenacity will endure any storm.

CONSIDER ONE ANOTHER (vv. 24, 25)

The final exhortation in this section is to mutually consider one another, and it extends through verse 25, which is actually a participial phrase carrying on the thought of verse 24: "And let us consider how we may spur one another on toward love and good deeds. Let us not give up meeting together, as some are in the habit of doing, but let us encourage one another — and all the more as you see the Day approaching" (vv. 24, 25).

A father was showing his young son through a church building when they came to a plaque on the wall. Curious, the little boy asked, "Daddy, what's that for?" His father replied, "Oh, that's a memorial to those who died in the service." The little boy said, "Which service, Daddy, the morning or the evening?"[5]

People have a thousand reasons to stay away from church. This is not a new problem. The early Jewish church had had a fall-off in attendance due to persecution, ostracism, apostasy, and arrogance. Today persecution and ostracism may not be our experience, but people find many other reasons to absent themselves from worship, not the least of which is laziness. But de-churched Christians have always been an aberration, as St. Cyprian, St. Augustine, Luther, Calvin, and the various classic confessions repeatedly affirm.[6] There are solid Biblical reasons why no one should forego church.

Ontology

The first is "ecclesial ontology," the special existence — the being or presence — of Christ in the gathered church. This is dramatically portrayed in the first chapter of Revelation as Christ, holding seven stars in his right hand, walks among the seven golden lampstands that are emblematic of the church (vv. 9-20). We meet Christ in a special way in corporate worship. It is true that a person does not have to go to church to be a Christian. He does not have to go home to be married either. But in both cases if he does not, he will have a very poor relationship.

Doxology

Next, if you absent yourself from church, you will encumber your ability to glorify God in worship. Congregational worship makes possible an intensity of adoration that does not as readily occur in solitude. On the tragic level, a mob tends to descend to a much deeper level of cruelty than individuals. It is also understood that the appreciation and enjoyment of an informed group of music lovers at a symphony is more intense than that of a single listener at home. This holds true for worship as well. Corporate worship provides a context where passion is joyously elevated and God's Word ministers with unique power.

Martin Luther spoke of this when he confided, "At home in my own house there is no warmth or vigor in me, but in the church when the multitude is gathered together, a fire is kindled in my heart and it breaks its way through."[7]

Theology

It is also true that giving up meeting with other believers hampers one's theology and doctrinal understanding. Paul, in Ephesians 3:18, prays that the church in Ephesus "may have power, together with all the saints, to grasp . . . and to know this love that surpasses knowledge." Great theological truths are best learned corporately — "with all the saints." Theology is to be done by the assembled church.

Psychology

Lastly, there is the matter of psychology—not in the sense of the study of the psyche, the soul — but rather its development. For example, the virtue of love enjoined by the second half of the Decalogue requires others for its development. One theoretically may be able to develop *faith* and *hope* while alone (though even this is questionable), but not *love*! Developing love is a communal activity of the church.

So for all these reasons — ontological, doxological, theological, psychological — it is impossible to be a good Christian while voluntarily absenting oneself from the assembled church. The author of Hebrews is pleading with his people not to make such a mistake, because he knows they would not survive. And neither would we. Laxity can destroy us, so we must beware.

What to do? The answer is in the exhortation that dominates this section: "And let us consider how we may spur one another on toward love and good deeds" (v. 24). This idea of spurring one another on is an exciting concept because the word translated "spur" is extremely strong. The RV translates it "provoke," the RSV "stir up," the NEB "arouse." It is the word *paroxysmos*, from which we get *paroxysm* — a sudden convulsion or a violent emotion. Normally, as in the rest of the New Testament, this is not a pleasant word (for example, "a sharp disagreement" — *paroxysmos* — came between Paul and Barnabas, Acts 15:39; cf. 1 Corinthians 13:5). But here it has a pleasant sense of prodding our brothers and sisters toward love and good deeds.

PROVOKE ONE ANOTHER

The author wants us to take knowledge of one another as to how we might provoke each other to blessed paroxysms of grace. Here we suggest several ways we can be positive irritants.

Prayer

If we specifically pray for each other by name and pray for the development of volitional, selfless love — *agape* — and for specific good deeds, it will happen! It is as simple as that. Do you think your pastor or spouse or boss or whoever is grouchy? Pray that he or she will have an attack of niceness!

Example

A second powerful way to spur one another on to "love and good deeds" is by example. Oswald Chambers said, "It is a most disturbing thing to be smitten in the ribs by some provoker from God, by someone who is full of spiritual activity."[8] I believe Jim Elliott was this way when he was writing things like the following and living them out: "Oh, the fullness, pleasure, sheer excitement of knowing God on earth. I care not if I never raise my voice again for Him, if only I may love Him, please Him."[9]

It is a fact that loving God and man and doing good deeds are more readily caught than taught. To provoke others upward by example is the high road, indeed.

God's Word

Of course, the Word of God is our basic primer for love and good deeds. When we internalize it, allowing God's Word to flow through us, we become conduits of its virtues and are gentle examples and provokers of grace.

Encouragement

Lastly, there is the responsibility to verbally spur others on through words of encouragement. Journalist Robert Maynard related the following story from his childhood in *The New York Daily News*: As a young boy Maynard was walking to school one day when he came upon an irresistible temptation. In front of him was a fresh piece of gray cement — a piece that had replaced a broken piece of sidewalk. He immediately stopped and began to scratch his name in it. Suddenly he became aware that standing over him with a garbage can lid was the biggest stone mason he had ever seen!

Maynard tried to run, but the big man grabbed him and shouted, "Why are you trying to spoil my work?" Maynard remembers babbling something about just wanting to put his name on the ground. A remarkable thing happened just then. The mason released the boy's arms, his voice softened, and his eyes lost their fire. Instead there was now a touch of warmth about the man. "What's your name, son?"

"Robert Maynard."

"Well, Robert Maynard, the sidewalk is no place for your name. If you want your name on something, you go into that school. You work hard and you become a lawyer and you hang your shingle out for all the world to see."

Tears came to Maynard's eyes, but the mason was not finished yet. "What do you want to be when you grow up?"

"A writer, I think."

Now the mason's voice burst forth in tones that could be heard all over the schoolyard. "A writer! A writer! Be a writer. Be a real writer! Have your name on books, not on this sidewalk."

Robert Maynard continued to cross the street, paused, and looked back. The mason was on his knees repairing the damage that Maynard's scratching had done. He looked up and saw the young boy watching and repeated, "Be a writer."[10]

There is amazing power in an encouraging word. You and I can change a life with a kind word. Encouragement is a Christian duty. Lives of provocation through prayer, example, Scripture and encouragement are gifts the church needs desperately.

Hebrews 10:19-25 is no insignificant text. Its role in moving from *instruction* to *application* gives it huge significance. It tells us that if we have the proper confidence that comes from our *access* and *advocacy* before God, there are three things we must do for the sake of the church and her survival.

- We must draw near in prayer to God with a wholehearted sincerity. Our entire human spirit must be engaged in prayer and worship.
- We must hold on to the anchor of hope we possess. Our hope is in Jesus and is anchored in Heaven, where he intercedes for us. This is no cock-eyed optimism but tremendous reality.
- We must devote ourselves to the corporate church and do everything we can to provoke each other to love and good deeds.

If we do this, the church will ride high on every storm that comes! And we must do this more and more as we "see the Day approaching."

If we deliberately keep on sinning after we have received the knowledge of the truth, no sacrifice for sins is left, but only a fearful expectation of judgment and of raging fire that will consume the enemies of God. Anyone who rejected the law of Moses died without mercy on the testimony of two or three witnesses. How much more severely do you think a man deserves to be punished who has trampled the Son of God under foot, who has treated as an unholy thing the blood of the covenant that sanctified him, and who has insulted the Spirit of grace? For we know him who said, "It is mine to avenge; I will repay," and again, "The Lord will judge his people." It is a dreadful thing to fall into the hands of the living God. (10:26-31)

3

The Perils of Apostasy

HEBREWS 10:26-31

Ⅰt is commonly thought by those who have only a passing recognition of Jonathan Edwards that his famous sermon "Sinners in the Hands of an Angry God" was preached with sadistic glee to his bewildered congregation. The supposition is that Edwards enjoyed afflicting his people and that the sermon was preached with pulpit-pounding vehemence.

Such thinking is wide of the mark. Shouting was not Edwards's style. It is a matter of historical fact that Edwards quietly read his sermons from tiny pieces of paper he held up in front of him. Neither did Edwards enjoy such preaching. Rather, it was necessitated by the famous "halfway" covenant, an earlier Puritan attempt to keep as many people as possible under the influence of the church, though they were not professed believers. The church in Enfield contained baptized unbelievers who were barred from the Lord's Table. Ultimately, Edwards was dismissed as pastor over the question of the admission of the unconverted to the Lord's Supper. Edwards was preaching for their souls, and also against the follies of the "halfway" covenant.

Therefore, we must understand that Jonathan Edwards's passionate love for God and his flock was the reason he employed every tool in his considerable stores of logic and metaphor to plead for his people's souls in "Sinners in the Hands of an Angry God." He was less concerned with God's wrath than with his grace, which was freely extended to sinners who repented.[1] Jonathan Edwards gave his people a whiff of the sulphurs of Hell that they might deeply inhale the fragrances of grace.

Edwards's intense concern joins him in heart with the preacher who wrote to the Hebrews some 1,700 years earlier. The stakes were identical — Heaven or Hell. And the symptoms, though not identical, were similar as well — a declining regard for the church's authority, a willfulness to define one's relationship to the church in one's own terms, and, in some cases, quitting the church altogether. To such are addressed the thunderous warnings in verses 26-31, in which the brilliant writer summons his own prodigious logic and literary talents. To glimpse his passion, we can imagine ourselves as parents raising our children along a boulevard on which huge trucks regularly pass at great speed. Our warnings are couched in the most dramatic terms and lurid illustrations — "Do you know what happens to little children if . . ." — in the hope that somehow what we say will penetrate the imagination and thinking process of our children, so they will stay out of the deadly street!

THE TERRORS OF APOSTASY (vv. 26, 27)

The writer begins his plea by graphically outlining the terrors of apostasy. The opening terror is that it obviates Christ's atoning sacrifice: "If we deliberately keep on sinning after we have received the knowledge of the truth, no sacrifice for sins is left" (v. 26). This is the terror of no sacrifice! Now, the preacher is *not* saying that if believers persist in sinning deliberately, there will come a point where the effect of Christ's sacrifice runs out, and Christ would say, "I have paid for your sins up to this point, but I'm not prepared to pay for them any further."[2] Rather, what the writer is describing is a graceless, reprobate state characterized by two things — *deliberateness* and *continuance*.

We only have to look at our own hearts, or the actions of our offspring, to know what deliberate sin is like. Case in point: our two-year-old grandson, Joshua Simpson, recently climbed up on the kitchen counter to get at a forbidden stick of gum. But, alas, his father appeared several inches from Joshua's face, saying, "Joshua, you may not have the gum. If you eat that gum, I will spank you!" Joshua looked at the gum, then at his father, and back at the gum. Then he took the gum, *slowly* unwrapped it as he watched his dad, and put it in his mouth. Joshua got his spanking! But there was more, because a few minutes later he returned and took another stick, climbed down, ducked behind a corner to unwrap it — and got another spanking. The boy is a sinner, and so are we all.

Our text is talking about deliberate, intentional sin. In fact, the word "deliberately" stands first in the Greek for emphasis. Moreover, this deliberate sin is continual. The person persists in open rebellion against God and his Word.

Here is the point: this individual has "received the knowledge of the truth" — the content of Christianity as truth. He knows what God has done in Christ, and he understands it.[3] But he intentionally — knowingly — rejects it and willfully continues on in an unremitting state of sin — as an apostate. Calvin explains:

> The apostle describes as sinners not those who fall in any kind of sin, but those who forsake the Church and separate themselves from Christict.... There is a great difference between individual lapses and universal desertion of the kind which makes for a total falling away from the grace of Christ.[4]

What is in view is what Jesus calls the sin against the Holy Spirit (Matthew 12:32; Mark 3:29). It is the same thing as was described in Hebrews 6:4-6:

> It is impossible for those who have once been enlightened, who have tasted the heavenly gift, who have shared in the Holy Spirit, who have tasted the goodness of the word of God and the powers of the coming age, if they fall away, to be brought back to repentance, because to their loss they are crucifying the Son of God all over again and subjecting him to public disgrace.

The ignorant cannot commit this sin. It cannot be committed inadvertently. It is a sin only "church people" can commit. To such, "no sacrifice for sins is left" because they have rejected the one and only valid sacrifice — Christ.

This terror is joined by a second great terror, because since there is no sacrifice, judgment follows: ". . . but only a fearful expectation of judgment and a raging fire that will consume the enemies of God" (v. 27). This is an echo of Isaiah 26:11 — "Let the fire reserved for your enemies consume them" — and is a gripping expression for judgment.

The point here is that those who have rejected Christ inherit a fearful expectation of judgment, whether or not they are aware of it. Some, of course, mask it, like Edward F. Prichard, a sometime politician and crook who used to say that when the last trumpet sounded, the Lord is not going to send people to Heaven or Hell. Rather, "He's going to take away their inhibitions, and everybody's going to go where he belongs."

Interesting thoughts, even amusing, when one is in good health. But it has proven far different with hardened apostates at the time of death when there comes "only a fearful expectation of judgment." Take Voltaire, for example. Of Christ, Voltaire said, "Curse the wretch!" He once boasted, "In twenty years Christianity will be no more. My single hand shall destroy the edifice it took twelve apostles to rear." Ironically, shortly after his death the very house in which he printed his literature became the depot of the Geneva Bible Society. The nurse who attended Voltaire said, "For all the wealth in Europe I would not see another infidel die." The physician Trochim, waiting with Voltaire at his death, said he cried out most desperately, "I am abandoned by God and man! I will give you half of what I am worth if you will give me six months' life. Then I shall go to hell and you will go with me."[5]

Or consider Thomas Paine, the renowned American author and enemy of Christianity who exerted considerable influence against belief in God and the Scriptures. He came to his last hour in 1809, a disillusioned and unhappy man. During his final moments on earth he said:

> I would give worlds, if I had them, that *Age of Reason* had not been published. O Lord, help me! Christ, help me! O God what have I done to suffer so much? But there is no God! But if there should be, what will become of me hereafter? Stay with me, for God's sake! Send even a child to stay with me, for it is hell to be alone. If ever the devil had an agent, I have been that one.[6]

Make no mistake about it — "If we deliberately keep on sinning after we have received the knowledge of the truth, no sacrifice for sins is left, but only a fearful expectation of judgment and of raging fire that will consume the enemies of God." What an awesome duo these terrors make — no sacrifice for sin, and inexorable judgment! Many church attenders would do well to quake in fear like those in Enfield and Northampton lest they become hardened in unbelief so that they consciously reject Christ's work and become terminally apostate.

THE LOGIC BEHIND THE TERRORS (vv. 28, 29)

Next the preacher/writer turns to an *a fortiori* argument as he lays out the relentless logic behind the terrors he has identified, arguing from the lesser case of rejecting the Law to the greater case of rejecting the grace of Christ.

Lesser

Of the lesser offense he says, "Anyone who rejected the law of Moses died without mercy on the testimony of two or three witnesses" (v. 28). For example, Deuteronomy 17:2-7 stipulates regarding anyone accused of idolatry:

> If a man or woman living among you in one of the towns the Lord gives you is found doing evil in the eyes of the Lord your God in violation of his covenant, and contrary to my command has worshiped other gods, bowing down to them or to the sun or the moon or the

stars of the sky, and this has been brought to your attention, then you must investigate it thoroughly. If it is true and it has been proved that this detestable thing has been done in Israel, take the man or woman who has done this evil deed to your city gate and stone that person to death. On the testimony of two or three witnesses a man shall be put to death, but no one shall be put to death on the testimony of only one witness. The hands of the witnesses must be the first in putting him to death, and then the hands of all the people. You must purge the evil from among you.

The accusation had to be proved beyond doubt. One witness was not enough. But when there were two or three witnesses who agreed, it was over. No mercy whatsoever. No appeal. Certain death!

Greater

If such pitiless judgment came from rejecting the lesser Old Covenant, imagine the case with rejecting the greater New Covenant: "How much more severely do you think a man deserves to be punished who has trampled the Son of God under foot, who has treated as an unholy thing the blood of the covenant that sanctified him, and who has insulted the Spirit of grace?" (v. 29). This greater judgment comes from three immense travesties that characterizes all apostasy. First, they "trampled the Son of God under foot." The January 1991 issue of *Harper's Magazine* carried a reproduction of an anti-Christian tract entitled *Dear Believer*, a "non-tract" published by the Freedom from Religion Foundation of Madison, Wisconsin. The tract variously attacked creation and miracles and then God himself, finally coming to Jesus and saying:

And Jesus is a chip off the old block. He said, "I and my father are one," and he upheld "every jot and tittle" of the Old Testament law. He preached the same old judgment: vengeance and death, wrath and distress, hell and torture for all nonconformists. He never denounced the subjugation of slaves or women. He irrationally cursed and withered a fig tree for being barren out of season. He mandated burning unbelievers. (The Church has complied with relish.) He stole a horse. You want me to accept Jesus, but I think I'll pick my own friends, thank you.

I also find Christianity to be morally repugnant. The concepts of original sin, depravity, substitutionary forgiveness, intolerance, eternal punishment, and humble worship are all beneath the dignity of intelligent human beings.

This tract captures the emotion of the word "trampled," which is a singularly powerful expression for disdain — as, for example, when the swine find your pearls and "trample them under their feet, and then turn and tear you to pieces" (Matthew 7:6; cf. Matthew 5:13; Luke 8:5). Figuratively, the metaphor portrays taking "the Son of God" — the highest accord given to Christ in Hebrews — and grinding him into the dirt.[7] Thus, turning away from Christ is an attack on his *person*.

Second, apostasy is an attack on Christ's *work*, for the one who has done this "has treated as an unholy thing the blood of the covenant that sanctified him" (v. 29). Hebrews 9 is especially a lyrical song about the superiority of Christ's blood. Because Christ's blood was nothing less than his divine life willingly offered, it could do what no animal's blood could do — namely, take away sin and bestow a clear conscience.

> *Oh, precious is the flow*
> *That makes me white as snow;*
> *No other fount I know,*
> *Nothing but the blood of Jesus.*

The sort of apostate pictured here had at one time *professed* faith in Christ, *listened* to the Word preached, and *celebrated* the Lord's Supper. Those initial acts "sanctified him." As elsewhere in Hebrews, the idea of being sanctified refers to the initial act of being set apart for God.[8] But his faith, such as it was, was not internal and was not genuine, and now he consciously rejects Christ's work. "Jesus' blood," he says, "is common, just like any other man's. There is nothing special about it."

Third, having rejected the *person* and *work* of Christ, he also rejects the *person and work* of the Holy Spirit, as verse 29 concludes: "who has insulted the Spirit of grace." This is the only place in the New Testament where the Holy Spirit is called "the Spirit of grace" (but cf. Zechariah 12:10), and what a beautiful and fitting title it is. He *enlightens* our minds, he *seals* our hearts in adoption, he *regenerates* us with spiritual life, and he *grafts* us into the Body of Christ — all effects of grace. We ought to make note of this lovely ascription and use it devotionally. The Spirit of grace — the Holy Spirit of grace — He gives and gives and gives!

To "insult the Spirit of grace" is an immense act of hubris and arrogance (the Greek verb for "insulted" comes from the noun *hybris*). What had happened is that the Holy Spirit had come to the apostate, witnessed to him about spiritual reality, and courted his soul, but the apostate rejected the Spirit's witness with outrageous arrogance. Such persons deliberately close their eyes to the light, just as the Pharisees had done when they attributed the Spirit's works of mercy and power to Beelzebub — and thus their condemnation is the same:

"And so I tell you, every sin and blasphemy will be forgiven men, but the blasphemy against the Spirit will not be forgiven. Anyone who speaks a word against the Son of Man will be forgiven, but anyone who speaks against the Holy Spirit will not be forgiven, either in this age or in the age to come." (Matthew 12:31, 32)

To reject the gracious work of the Spirit of grace renders one irremediably lost.

What frightening terrors lie behind apostasy: rejection of Christ's person, rejection of Christ's work, and rejection of the person and work of the Holy Spirit. Understanding this, the question of verse 29 explodes: "How much more severely do you think a man deserves to be punished . . . ?" One thing is sure — there will be no mercy shown for the hardened apostate, just as there was no mercy shown to those who willfully transgressed the Law. But the greater severity is that breaking the Old Covenant brought *physical* death, while rejecting Christ brings *spiritual* death.

Some today reject this idea by employing a one-sided view of Christ. They say that Jesus' emblem was a lamb, that Jesus took little children in his arms and blessed them, that he sighed over the deaf and dumb and wept over Jerusalem. But they forget that the Lamb of God will come with wrath — in judgment (Revelation 6:16), that he told all who cause any of his little ones to sin that it would be better for them to be thrown into the sea with a large millstone tied around their neck, and that the same Jesus who wept over Jerusalem judged it.

Listen to Jesus' words on a number of different occasions: "This is how it will be at the end of the age. The angels will come and separate the wicked from the righteous and throw them into the fiery furnace, where there will be weeping and gnashing of teeth" (Matthew 13:49, 50). "If your hand or your foot causes you to sin, cut it off and throw it away. It is better for you to enter life maimed or crippled than to have two hands or two feet and be thrown into eternal fire. And if your eye causes you to sin, gouge it out and throw it away. It is better for you to enter life with one eye than to have two eyes and be thrown into the fire of hell" (Matthew 18:8, 9). "Then the king told the attendants, 'Tie him hand and foot, and throw him outside, into the darkness, where there will be weeping and gnashing of teeth'" (Matthew 22:13). "Then he will say to those on his left, 'Depart from me, you who are cursed, into the eternal fire prepared for the devil and his angels'" (Matthew 25:41). "Then they will go away to eternal punishment, but the righteous to eternal life" (Matthew 25:46). "If your hand causes you to sin, cut it off. It is better for you to enter life maimed than with two hands to go into hell, where the fire never goes out" (Mark 9:43). "And if your eye causes you to sin, pluck it out. It is better for you to enter the kingdom of God with one eye than to have two eyes and be thrown into hell, where 'their worm does not die, and the fire is not quenched'" (Mark 9:47, 48). "Jesus looked directly at them and asked, 'Then what is the meaning of that which is written: "The stone the builders rejected has become the capstone"? Everyone who falls on that stone will be broken to pieces, but he on whom it falls will be crushed'" (Luke 20:17, 18).

You cannot have the Jesus of the Scriptures without the doctrines of judgment and Hell. "Think lightly of hell, and you will think lightly of the cross" (Spurgeon).

THE TERROR OF JUDGMENT (vv. 30, 31)

In verse 30, in order to drive home the terror of judgment, the author quotes loosely from the Song of Moses in Deuteronomy 32:35, 36 — "For we know him who said, 'It is mine to avenge; I will repay,' and again, 'The Lord will judge his people'" (cf. Romans 12:19). The phrases appear to be proverbial and were undoubtedly understood by everyone in the church.[9] Clearly, judgment is *inevitable*, and it is *impartial*. There will be equal justice for all.

In the gallery of Antoine Wiertz in Brussels, there is a collection of the most astounding and overpowering paintings — most of them exposing the brutality and horrors of war and the cruelty of conquerors, but some of them heralding the Empire of Peace and the triumph of Christ.

Walking down the hall where these awesome paintings hang, one is suddenly brought to a halt by a great painting entitled *A View of Hell*. With folded arms and familiar cocked hat on his head, there stands the figure of a man. There is no name given, but there is no need, for he is recognized as the Little Corporal from Corsica. On his shadowed face there is a look of astonishment, with just a trace of dread and fear, as he beholds what is all around him. By the light of the flames of Hell burning all about him, you can see behind him the ranks of the slain in battle. Little children stretch out clenched fists at the emperor. Mothers, with agony on their countenances, surround him, holding up the bleeding, amputated arms and legs of the slaughtered. On the faces of the children, the wives, and the mothers are depicted rage, horror, hate, and infinite pain and sorrow. The scene is macabre, terrible, horrible! Yes, and that is just what Wiertz meant it to be, for it is Napoleon in Hell! The artist's moral imagination has tried to picture Napoleon with his just deserts, an equitable punishment for a man who caused so much pain.[10]

God's judgment will be based on what each has been given. Those with greater knowledge, such as the apostates in the Hebrew church and in the New England church in Jonathan Edwards's day, will be judged with greater stringency. Judgment will have an equity impossible with men, however, because God knows the very thoughts and intents of the heart.

46

Finally, we come to the grand statement of terror, "It is a dreadful thing to fall into the hands of the living God" (v. 31). May we understand how dreadful and divine this is!

Divine Judgment

King David, after he had sinned against God by counting the number of fighting men in Israel and Judah, evidently viewed falling into God's hands as divine judgment, because when God commanded him to choose between three alternatives, his wise reply was, "Let us fall into the hands of the Lord, for his mercy is great" (2 Samuel 24:14). Very possibly this exact passage was on our author's mind and governed the form of the words he chose. However that may be, for the true believer there is nothing better than to fall repentantly into the hands of God. His hands are our hope!

> *The hands of Christ are very frail*
> *For they were broken with a nail.*
> *But only those reach Heaven at last*
> *Whom those frail, broken hands hold fast.*

Dreadful Judgment

But to fall into God's hands will be dreadful for those who have rejected him because, as we have mentioned, divine judgment will be *perfectly equitable*. The lurid picture of Napoleon does make the point. The horrible truth is that one will receive what is coming to him.

This will be dreadful because it involves *separation from God*. Union with God's nature is bliss, but separation from him is horror.[11]

It will be dreadful because it is *eternal*. If one could travel at the speed of light for one hundred years until he escaped this galaxy, and then travel for 3,000 years at the speed of light to reach the next galaxy, repeating the process one hundred thousand million times until he reached every galaxy — eternity would have just begun!

The dread of eternal separation and punishment is inconceivably painful. This is an excruciating doctrine. Jonathan Edwards's metaphors were not too strong, for the Bible is true! Our lives do hang by a mere thread. Eternity gapes before us.

Wonderful Salvation

But the dreadful is met by the wonderful arms of Jesus, which he extends to us. Those arms were stretched wide on the cross so that he might embrace us. He was not only our atoning sacrifice, but he propitiates our sins, turning aside the Father's righteous wrath. Jesus today still has those same human, atoning, propitiating arms — and all we have to do is fall into them.

Be blessed now through faith in Christ — and fall into the arms and hands of the living God!

Remember those earlier days after you had received the light, when you stood your ground in a great contest in the face of suffering. Sometimes you were publicly exposed to insult and persecution; at other times you stood side by side with those who were so treated. You sympathized with those in prison and joyfully accepted the confiscation of your property, because you knew that you yourselves had better and lasting possessions. So do not throw away your confidence; it will be richly rewarded. You need to persevere so that when you have done the will of God, you will receive what he has promised. For in just a very little while, "He who is coming will come and will not delay. But my righteous one will live by faith. And if he shrinks back, I will not be pleased with him." But we are not of those who shrink back and are destroyed, but of those who believe and are saved. (10:32-39)

4

Keep On!

HEBREWS 10:32-39

No good parent ever enjoys disciplining his children. It is no fun to sit a child down and give him a good talking-to and then perhaps a swat or two or three. No parent likes to see a little lip quiver or tears well in blinking eyes and roll down a sad face. It is really true — there are times you would rather take the talking-to and even the spanking yourself.

But there is also very often a special sweetness in discipline (though certainly not all the time!). It comes when you take a hot-teared little person in your arms, hold him close, then brush away the tears and gently encourage him and tell him that you love him and that he can, and will, do better. This is a unique, healing, domestic sweetness.

Fortunately, this is not limited to the home but is also the experience of the family of God. Hebrews 10 shows this. In verses 26-31, the pastor had delivered one of the most chastening warnings in all of Scripture, concluding with the terrifying words, "It is a dreadful thing to fall into the hands of the living God." There is no more aggressive, hard-hitting passage in God's Word. But now in verses 32-39 the writer figuratively takes his smarting, chastened listeners in his arms and bestows tender words of encouragement to keep on in the faith. St. Chrysostom saw the same thing here when he commented that the writer acts very much like a surgeon who comforts and encourages his patient after making a painful incision.[1]

The encouragement to continue on comes in two parts — first, to *remember* the past (vv. 32-34), and second, to *respond* in the present (vv. 35-39).

REMEMBERING THE PAST *(vv. 32-34)*

The writer begins with a call to remembrance, saying, "Remember those earlier days after you had received the light, when you stood your ground in a great contest in the face of suffering" (v. 32). This was a challenge to recall how they had marvelously stood unmoved some fifteen years earlier during the persecution under the Roman Emperor Claudius in A.D. 49. A famous quotation from the historian Suetonius indicates the character of the Claudian persecution: "There were riots in the Jewish quarter at the instigation of Chrestus. As a result, Claudius expelled the Jews from Rome" (*Life of the Deified Claudius*, 25.4). Historians believe "Chrestus" is a reference to Christ and that the riots and expulsion occurred when Jewish Christians were banished from the synagogue by the Jewish establishment. No one had been killed (cf. 12:4), but it was nevertheless a wrenching time of humiliation and abuse.

The word behind *contest* in our text's reference is the Greek word *athlesis*, from which we derive our English word *athletic*. The persecution was like a hard-fought athletic contest viewed by a partisan crowd. There was nothing passive in their display. In fact, they showed superb spiritual athleticism as they stood their ground!

Such athleticism is a beautiful thing in the eyes of God and the church — as it was, for example, in the life of Hugh Latimer, the great English Reformer. On one notable occasion Latimer preached before Henry VIII and offended Henry with his boldness. So Latimer was commanded to preach the following weekend and make an apology. On that following Sunday, after reading the text, he addressed himself as he began to preach:

> Hugh Latimer, dost thou know before whom thou art this day to speak? To the high and mighty monarch, the king's most excellent majesty, who can take away thy life if thou offendest; therefore, take heed that thou speakest not a word that may displease; but then consider well, Hugh, dost thou not know from whence thou comest; upon whose message thou art sent? Even by the great and mighty God! who is all-present, and who beholdeth all thy ways, and who is able to cast thy soul into hell! Therefore, take care that thou deliverest thy message faithfully.

He then gave Henry the *same* sermon he had preached the week before — only with more energy![2] Latimer was superb! And his memory is a great treasure of the Church.

Here our writer is calling for a similar remembrance of those storied days when the little church had been magnificent — "Remember those earlier days after you had received the light, when you stood your ground in a great contest in the face of suffering."

Since the preacher knew that such remembering would help them remain steadfast in the faith, he attempted to help them recall the sequence and character of their stand amidst persecution.

"Sometimes you were publicly exposed to insult and persecution" (v. 33a). The idea here is that they were made public theatre, because the word for "publicly exposed" (*theatrizo*) comes from *theatron*, "theatre." They were ridiculed and taunted as a theatre of the absurd. Along with that, the "persecution" they endured was of the nature of being squeezed and pressured. Persecution was one thing, but sardonic, smiling, rung-dropping insults made it even more devastating.

"At other times you stood side by side with those who were so treated" (v. 33b). Here their spiritual athleticism leaps forth, because they transcended the normal tendency to be passive and actively joined in suffering together. What gallantry and honor! "I stand with my brothers and sisters here. If you insult them, you insult me!" Side-by-side, with arms locked, they chose to face persecution together.

"You sympathized with those in prison" (v. 34a). That is, they literally had a "fellow-feeling" for or with those in prison. The same word is used in 4:15 of Christ's sympathy for us as our high priest! They lived out the later exhortation in Hebrews to "remember those in prison as if you were their fellow prisoners" (13:3). Even more, this was not *imagined* sympathy — it was *real*, because they visited their comrades in prison. In the first century prisoners had no means of survival apart from the visits of friends who brought food and water and clothing.[3] But such visiting placed one in grave danger. Yet, they did it willingly — and in doing so some visited Christ who said, "For I was hungry and you gave me something to eat, I was thirsty and you gave me something to drink . . . I needed clothes and you clothed me, I was sick and you looked after me, I was in prison and you came to visit me" (Matthew 25:35, 36).

The writer continues, ". . . and [you] joyfully accepted the confiscation of your property, because you knew that you yourselves had better and lasting possessions" (v. 34b). The human tendency is to hold on as hard as we can to what we have.

I once came across an ad that appealed to the desire of many to keep their household pets, which unfortunately do not have a lengthy life-expectancy. The advertisement was for freeze-drying! According to the ad, most people who have their pets freeze-dried do so because they want to "keep their pets around a little longer." The process takes several months, and the pet will remain natural-looking for up to twenty years after being freeze-dried. The price for this service ranges from $400 for a small pet up to $1400 for a pet the size of a golden retriever.[4] So, if your wish is to hang on to everything — even your dead dog — here's your chance!

But there is another way, the way of those in the early church who let go of their property — an amazing thing in itself, but even more amazing because they "joyfully accepted the confiscation of [their] property." They found themselves exhilarated by the loss! Why? Because they knew they "had better and lasting possessions." They believed Jesus' words, "Do not store up for yourselves treasures on earth, where moth and rust destroy, and where thieves break in and steal. But store up for yourselves treasures in heaven . . ." (Matthew 6:19, 20). They were "looking for the city that is to come" (13:14) — "the heavenly Jerusalem" (12:22).

What an astounding remembrance the church was called to. They had experienced amazing spiritual athleticism in the oppression that took place during the springtime of their spiritual lives during the Claudian persecution. Now they are called upon to remember it, to call to mind the sequence of events and ponder their significance.

The reason for this is twofold. First, they will be challenged by their own past character. Second, they will be faced afresh with the power of God to sustain and deliver them.

This works! We may have *begun* well and now want to *end* well. If so, part of the secret is to *remember* well. We'll say more about this later, but first we must focus on what the text says about our present response.

RESPONDING IN THE PRESENT (vv. 35-39)

Respond in Confidence

The author's advice for responding to the present is to remain confident: "So do not throw away your confidence; it will be richly rewarded" (v. 35).

We have all heard of the famous high-wire aerialists the Flying Wallendas, and about the tragic death of their leader, the great Karl Wallenda, in 1978. Shortly after the great Wallenda fell to his death (traversing a seventy-five-foot high-wire in downtown San Juan, Puerto Rico), his wife, also an aerialist, discussed that fateful San Juan walk. She recalled: "All Karl thought about for three straight months prior to it was falling. It was the first time he'd ever thought about that, and it seemed to me that he put all his energies into not falling rather than walking the tightrope." Mrs. Wallenda added that her husband even went so far as to personally supervise the installation of the tightrope, making certain the guy wires were secure, "something he had never even thought of doing before."[5] Wallenda's loss of confidence portended and even contributed to his death, though his past performances gave him every reason to be confident.

Spiritually, no true Christian has to surrender to the "Wallenda factor" because our confidence rests not on ourselves but on God. The writer's charge to "not throw away your confidence" means not to cast away confident confession of Christ in the midst of opposition.[6] The positive corollary is to proclaim confidence in the midst of opposition — like Peter and John before the Sanhedrin (Acts 4:13) and Latimer before King Henry.

Respond in Perseverance

Next, one's confident response is to be followed by perseverance: "You need to persevere so that when you have done the will of God, you will receive what he has promised" (v. 36).

I recall watching a high-school mile race in which one of the young runners took off like a shot out of a cannon and ran the first quarter in about fifty-four seconds, which positioned him about a hundred yards ahead of everyone else. He looked awesome. But predictably, he did not finish the race. What he needed was an *aggressive endurance*, a doggedness or steadfastness, as is recommended in our text. Such perseverance assures "what he has promised" — that is, full salvation in Christ.[7] Perseverance does not earn salvation, but rather is *prime facie* evidence of saving grace.

Respond in Persevering Faith

The key to successful perseverance is faith. It is significant that in verses 37, 38, as the preacher emphasizes the need of faith in order to persevere, he quotes from Habakkuk 2:3, 4 — "For in just a very little while, 'He who is coming will come and will not delay. But my righteous one will live by faith. And if he shrinks back, I will not be pleased with him.' But we are not of those who shrink back and are destroyed, but of those who believe and are saved."

Originally God gave this exhortation to the prophet Habakkuk as the prophet repeatedly complained about the advances of injustice and the suffering of the righteous, God's bottom-line advice being that "the righteous will live by his faith" (Habakkuk 2:4). "Live by faith, Habakkuk!" Later on in Habakkuk's writing, when the prophet had allowed this truth to sink in, he rose above his depression and complaint and sang this great song of faith: "Though the fig tree does not bud and there are no grapes on the vines, though the olive crop fails and the fields produce no food, though there are no sheep in the pen and no cattle in the stalls, yet I will rejoice in the Lord, I will be joyful in God my Savior" (Habakkuk 3:17, 18).

Here in Hebrews, though the quotation from Habakkuk is taken from the Septuagint's rearranged Messianic rendering of the Hebrew text, the application is still the same — *the righteous will live by faith*. The meaning here in Hebrews is this: 1) Jesus is returning soon — "He who is coming will come and will not delay" (v. 37); 2) the saved will persevere by faith — "But my righteous one will live by faith" (v. 38a); 3) the lost will shrink back — "And if he shrinks back, I will not be pleased with him" (vv. 38b).

Therefore, on the basis of this argument, we understand that the grand key for perseverance is *faith*. Knowing this, we are set up for the greatest exposition of the subject of faith found anywhere in Scripture — in chapter 11. But here we must also understand that Habakkuk's great song of faith is precisely what the young Hebrew church had experienced during the Claudian persecution when they "joyfully accepted the confiscation of [their] property" (v. 34) — an experience very parallel to Habakkuk when he said that if there were no fruit or crops or flocks, "yet I will rejoice in the Lord, I will be joyful in God my Savior. The Sovereign Lord is my strength; he makes my feet like the feet of a deer, he enables me to go on the heights" (Habakkuk 3:18, 19).

Faith is everything. Paul quotes Habakkuk 2:4 in Romans 1:17 to explain that salvation is totally by faith: "For in the gospel a righteousness from God is revealed, a righteousness that is by faith from first to last, just as it is written: 'The righteous will live by faith.'" Here in Hebrews the writer quotes Habakkuk 2:4 to stress that the whole Christian life is to be lived by faith. It is *sola fide*, both for salvation and Christian living.

Think about that tiny storm-tossed church that had earlier triumphed in the Claudian persecution in A.D. 49 and is presently on the eve of the terrible Neronian persecution of A.D. 64. The writer has chastened them with a fiery warning (vv. 25-31) and now has sweetly encouraged them to do two things: 1) remember the past; 2) respond in the present with confidence and persevering faith.

The principles for enduring in triumph are universal and eternal. *Remembering* is the place to begin, as was shown to Israel after they crossed the Jordan. As all Israel stood gazing, the twelve select men solemnly descended the river's banks and approached the Ark of the Covenant in the middle of the empty riverbed. Then, kneeling at the priests' feet, each pried a large stone from the river bottom and began a reverent procession up the west bank and across the plain to Gilgal. To the symbol-oriented Israelites, the significance of the twelve stones was easily understood. They represented the twelve tribes of Israel and their deliverance from the river.

Arriving in Gilgal, the twelve men stacked the rocks into a small mound — a very unimpressive one, especially in comparison to the momentous event they commemorated. Having completed this, the twelve then each selected a stone from dry land and walked back to the Ark, where they formed a duplicate mound on the riverbed. Then, for the first time in hours, the Ark began to move as the weary priests who bore it slowly moved up the bank. When the last priest's foot crossed the edge, back roared the fabled Jordan, and a tumultuous cheer rolled across the great host of Israel.

The celebration in Gilgal must have been something to behold. The people rejoiced that the reproach of forty years of wandering was over. We can be sure that most of them danced and sang around their fires far into the night. Perhaps Joshua himself joined the dancing around the campfires, or perhaps he was too tired, but we can be sure of this — he returned to observe in the flickering light that mound of crude, unworked stones from the bottom of the Jordan.

God had done it! Again and again Joshua re-ran the mental tapes of that day through his mind. God was with him! God's power could do anything! Joshua's leadership was verified! He was God's man!

Joshua had much to think about as he viewed those stones, and he thought a lot about them over the years. Gilgal became the command head-quarters for conquering the Promised Land. It was the place to which he frequently returned after victories, in the midst of battles, and after defeats such as that at Ai. Here he gathered wisdom and strength to go on, for here lay the stones of remembrance. It was much the same for the early church, and now for us.

We need to remember how God has helped us in the past. The writer to the Hebrews held up the church's stones of remembrance one by one. Each stone told them of two things — God's faithfulness, and the strength that had been theirs when they trusted him. All of us have such memories. We need to replay the tapes. It is a divine duty.

Finally, we need to respond in the present. Be confident! Do not succumb to the "Wallenda factor." Persevere in faith. Look back in faith. Look up in faith. "My righteous one," says God, "will live by faith."

Now faith is being sure of what we hope for and certain of what we do not see. This is what the ancients were commended for. By faith we understand that the universe was formed at God's command, so that what is seen was not made out of what was visible. (11:1-3)

5

Faith Is . . .

HEBREWS 11:1-3

As the story goes, a man despairing of life had climbed the railing of the Brooklyn Bridge and was about to leap into the river when a policeman caught him by the collar and pulled him back. The would-be suicide protested, "You don't understand how miserable I am and how hopeless my life is. Please let me jump."

The kind-hearted officer reasoned with him and said, "I'll make this proposition to you. Take five minutes and give your reasons why life is hopeless and not worth living, and then I'll take five minutes and give my reasons why I think life is worth living, both for you and for me. If at the end of ten minutes you still feel like jumping from the bridge, I won't stop you."

The man took his five minutes, and the officer took his five minutes. Then they stood up, joined hands, and jumped off the bridge!

Gallows humor to be sure, but it is painfully parabolic of today's culture, which has abandoned its Christian roots for vacuous secularism. Indeed, if one factors God out of life's equation and adopts the view that we are little more than cosmic accidents, life, with its inevitable hardships and suffering, becomes hard to defend. In fact, suicide has been considered intellectually consistent, even stylish, by some existential intellectuals in recent years.

But for the Christian there is substantial reason for hope in this life and the life to come because of the promises of God's Word. In fact, 1 Peter 1:3 tells that we have been "born again to a living hope" (NASB). The degree of our experience of hope is proportionate to the degree of our faith. The more profound our faith, the more profound our hope. A deeply intense faith spawns a deeply intense hope.

This was important to the writer of Hebrews because of the rising storm of persecution that was about to fall on the church. He knew that the key to survival was a solid faith and an attendant hope. That is why in Hebrews 10:38 he quoted Habakkuk 2:4, "But my righteous one will live by faith." There is a spiritual axiom implicit here: *faith* produces *hope*, and hope produces *perseverance*. Without faith one will inevitably shrink back.

This understood, the preacher launches into an eloquent song of faith that occupies the whole of Chapter 11, beginning with a brief description of faith in verses 1-3 that is followed by a lyrical catalogue of grand examples in verses 4-40. As we take up verses 1-3 and the theme of what "faith is," we must keep in mind that this is not an exhaustive definition, but rather a description of a faith that perseveres. We will consider faith under three headings: *Faith's Character*, v. 1; *Faith's Activism*, v. 2; and *Faith's Understanding*, v. 3.

FAITH'S CHARACTER (v. 1)

The character of faith is spelled out with great care in the famous lines of verse 1: "Now faith is being sure of what we hope for and certain of what we do not see." Faith's character is, in a word, *certitude* — a dynamic certainty about what God has promised. It is *not* a feeling, like the line from *Oklahoma*:

> *O what a beautiful morning,*
> *O what a beautiful day.*
> *I've got a wonderful feeling,*
> *Everything's going my way!*

It is not optimism or bootstrap positive thinking either. It is not a hunch. It is not sentimentality. An old song says, "You gotta have faith" — the sentiment being that if you somehow have faith in faith, you will be okay. And faith is not brainless. The cynical Ambrose Bierce wrongly described faith in his *Devil's Dictionary* as "belief without evidence in what is told by one who speaks without knowledge of things without parallel."

True faith is neither brainless nor a sentimental feeling. It is a solid conviction resting on God's words that makes the future present and the invisible seen. Faith has at its core a massive sense of certainty. The great Bishop Westcott says of verse 1, "The general scope of the statement is to indicate that the future and the unseen can be made real by faith."[1] What is the huge certainty of faith like?

Future Certitude

The first half of the verse expresses the future certitude that faith brings: "Now faith is being sure of what we hope for." The words "being sure" are a translation of a single Greek noun — *hupostasis*, which literally means, "That which stands under" or "foundation" and hence "*substance*." This word has appeared twice earlier in Hebrews where it was translated objectively ("being") in 1:3 and subjectively ("confidence") in 3:14.[2]

The KJV here uses the objective translation: "Now faith is the substance of things hoped for." Likewise, the NEB says, "Faith gives substance to our hopes" — the idea being that faith grabs hold of what is hoped for, as something real and substantial. Most other translations render the word subjectively — "the assurance" (RSV, ASV, NASB, NAB) or "the guarantee" (JB) or "being sure" (NIV). Actually, the objective and subjective tenses of the word are not at odds because genuine faith does bring an assurance of what we hope for that is solid and substantive. The subjective certainty in our hearts has an objective solidity to it — *real certitude*! "Now faith is a solid sureness, a substantial certitude of what we hope for" (author's interpretive paraphrase).

The solid certainty is about the future — "what we hope for." What are the things we hope for?

We hope for *Christ's return* — "for the blessed hope — the glorious appearing of our great God and Savior, Jesus Christ" (Titus 2:13).

We hope for the *resurrection* because "in his great mercy he has given us new birth into a living hope through the resurrection of Jesus Christ from the dead" (1 Peter 1:3).

We hope for *glorification* — "But we know that when he appears, we shall be like him, for we shall see him as he is. Everyone who has this hope in him purifies himself, just as he is pure" (1 John 3:2, 3).

We hope to *reign* with him, for "if we endure we will also reign with him" (2 Timothy 2:12). "There will be no more night. They will not need the light of a lamp or the light of the sun, for the Lord God will give them light. And they will reign for ever and ever" (Revelation 22:5).

The believer's faith gives him such an inner certitude that the return of Christ, the resurrection, the glorification, a place in Heaven, and a coming reign all become present to him! As William Lane explains:

Faith celebrates now the reality of the future blessings which make up the objective content of Christian hope. Faith gives to the objects of hope the force of present realities, and it enables the person of faith to enjoy the full certainty that in the future these realities will be experienced.[3]

Think of the staying power that comes to a life where, through faith, all the above are present realities! Church history illustrates this as it records that in the early days of persecution, a humble Christian was brought before the judges. He told them that nothing they could do could shake him because he believed that if he were true to God, God would be true to him. "Do you really think," asked the judge, "that the like of you will go to God and His glory?" "I do not think," said the man. "I *know*."[4]

Visual Certitude

The second half of verse 1 joins faith's future certitude to the parallel visual certitude that comes through faith, because faith means being "certain of what we do not see." The KJV translates this, "the evidence of things not seen," and the RSV says, "the conviction of things not seen." These translations augment each other because the evidence by which a thing is proved brings conviction and certainty to the mind.

Our faith is the organ by which we are enabled to see the invisible order — and to see it with certainty, just as our eyes behold the physical world around us. What do we see? As we have mentioned, we see the future because it is made present to us through faith. But we also see more — namely, the invisible spiritual kingdom around us.

Genesis 28 records how Jacob, on that miserable night he fled from Esau into the wilderness, forlorn and alone, laid his weary head on a rock to sleep and "had a dream in which he saw a stairway resting on the earth, with its top reaching to heaven, and the angels of God were ascending and descending on it" (28:12). In a flash he saw what had been around him all the time — angelic commerce between Heaven and earth on his behalf! The account records that "When Jacob awoke from his sleep, he thought, 'Surely the Lord is in this place, and I was not aware of it.' He was afraid and said, 'How awesome is this place! This is none other than the house of God; this is the gate of heaven'" (vv. 16, 17). Jacob saw the unseen spiritual order, and that is what we see by faith.

> So to faith's enlightened sight
> All the mountain flamed with light.

There truly is an active spiritual order around us. If we could see it, it would change our lives! But we can see it, and we do see it! Faith brings visual certitude so that we are "certain of what we do not see." I have never seen a flaming seraph or cherub or one of the lesser angels with my physical eyes. But I do see them every day through my eyes of faith. They are everywhere around me ministering to me and my family and my church — in fact, to all those who are God's elect children.

Faith brings a dynamic dual certitude to everyday life. First, there is

62

future certitude as that which is to come becomes present to us. Second, there is a *visual certitude* as we see the invisible.

So here is the possibility we must consider if we are serious about following Christ: it is possible by faith to live in *future certitude* — to be present at Christ's return, to be present at our resurrection and glorification, to be present in Heaven, and to reign with him. It is also possible by faith to live in *visual certitude* — in the supernatural — to see all the mountain flaming with light — to see the traffic between Heaven and earth in our behalf. This is what our passage is calling us to, just as Abraham by faith put his stock in the future heavenly country, and just as Moses saw him who is invisible.

FAITH'S ACTIVISM (v. 2)

Having given us *faith's character* in verse 1, the writer now calls to mind *faith's activism* in verse 2: "This is what the ancients were commended for." All the ancients in Israel who received divine commendation received it because of the character of their faith — their faith's *future certitude* as they were sure of what they hoped for — and their faith's *visual certitude* as they were certain of the invisible. This certitude produced a dynamic activism. Think of Shadrach, Meshach and Abednego (alluded to in 11:34). They had nothing but God's word to rest on. They had no visible evidence that they would be delivered in this life. But they knew they would ultimately be delivered — they knew it so well that it was a present reality.

> Shadrach, Meshach and Abednego replied to the king, "O Nebuchadnezzar, we do not need to defend ourselves before you in this matter. If we are thrown into the blazing furnace, the God we serve is able to save us from it, and he will rescue us from your hand, O king. But even if he does not, we want you to know, O king, that we will not serve your gods or worship the image of gold you have set up." (Daniel 3:16-18)

There is no evidence that any of them had ever seen the invisible world at work around them, but they did see it by faith and were certain of it. Graciously, God did let them see it with their physical eyes when he delivered them. Remember Nebuchadnezzar's astonished words as he watched the trio in the flaming furnace:

> Then King Nebuchadnezzar leaped to his feet in amazement and asked his advisers, "Wasn't it three men that we tied up and threw into the fire?" They replied, "Certainly, O king." He said, "Look! I see four men walking around in the fire, unbound and unharmed, and the fourth looks like a son of the gods." (Daniel 3:24, 25)

The faith of the trio consisted simply in taking God at his word and living their lives accordingly. Things yet future, as far as their experience went, were *present* to their faith. Things unseen were *visible* to their individual eyes of faith.

And so it goes for every example in the great Hall of Faith of Hebrews 11 — from Abel to Samuel to the unnamed heroes of the faith. And so it goes for us. By certain faith we will endure in blessed activism. And by certain faith we will receive God's commendation.

FAITH'S UNDERSTANDING (v. 3)

Faith not only makes the future promises present and unveils the unseen — it also enlightens our understanding of the cosmos. "By faith," says the writer, "we understand that the universe was formed at God's command" (v. 3). As we have noted earlier in our studies of Hebrews, the universe is staggering in its size and glories. The nearest star in our very average galaxy, Alpha Centauri, is 25,000,000 miles away. Our glorious sun that fills our sky and lights our days is but a mere speck in our galaxy. The huge star Betelgeuse is 27,000,000 times larger than our sun. It would take fourteen 25,000,000-mile trips (the distance to Alpha Centauri) to travel the diameter of Betelgeuse. All that, and yet our galaxy is only one of a hundred thousand million other galaxies. The universe ought to cause us to praise God, as did the great astronomer Kepler, who constantly did so — especially when he discovered the third law of planetary motion and said, "I yield freely to the sacred frenzy; I dare frankly to confess that I have stolen the golden vessels of the Egyptians to build a tabernacle for my God far from the bounds of Egypt. If you pardon me, I shall rejoice; if you reproach me, I shall endure."[5]

But not all praise God. Many, in fact, employing the same scientific method, manage to deny the Creator. They are like the piano mice who lived all their lives in a large piano. The music of the instrument came to them in their "piano world," filling all the dark spaces with sound and harmony. At first the mice were impressed by it. They drew comfort and wonder from the thought that there was someone who made the music — though invisible to them — someone above, yet close to them. They loved to think of the Great Player whom they could not see.

Then one day a daring mouse climbed up part of the piano and returned very thoughtful. He had found out how the music was made. Wires were the secret — tightly stretched wires of graduated lengths that trembled and vibrated. They must revise all their old beliefs. None but the most conservative could any longer believe in the Unseen Player. Later another explorer carried the explanation further. Hammers were now the secret — great numbers of hammers dancing and leaping on the wires. This was a more complicated theory, but it all went to show that they lived in a purely mechanical and mathematical world. The Unseen Player came to be thought of as a myth, though the pianist continued to play.[6]

For the believer, those who know the Pianist, it is all so clear: "By faith we understand that the universe was formed at God's command, so that what is seen was not made out of what was visible." We do not hold our breath to see if Stephen Hawking re-embraces the Big Bang theory. That theory is somewhat congenial to the Biblical account, but we do not need it. We know that God simply spoke the universe into existence: "By the word of the Lord were the heavens made, their starry host by the breath of his mouth. . . . For he spoke, and it came to be; he commanded, and it stood firm" (Psalm 33:6, 9). Moreover, he did it *ex nihilo* — out of nothing. He did not have a rabbit, and he did not have a hat! By faith in God's Word we know for a certainty that every star was created by God — all 10,000,000,000,000,000,000, 000,000,000! (i.e., ten octillion).

We smile, bemused at the story of the befuddled policeman joining hands with his depressed friend and jumping off the bridge. "Sure thing," we think, assuming such things do not happen. But that is exactly what so many ostensible believers do today as they uncritically imbibe the world's despair.

What is needed is a rebirth, or perhaps birth, of Hebrews 11 faith — the kind that is characterized by a dynamic twofold certainty: a *future certainty* that is so "sure of what we hope for" that it considers God's promises to be present — and a *visual certainty* that renders us "certain of what we do not see." This is *certitude* — full belief in what we believe — bounding hope! Such a faith produces a dynamic activism such as that which "the ancients were commended for" — and a place in God's Hall of Faith. Finally, the certainty and activism of faith is crowned with a dynamic understanding of God's creatorship.

What is the benefit of all this? Certainly, the will to persevere. But also something else very important — the ability by God's grace to take the hand of the despairing and lead them away from the bridge to a life of certitude and love and life and understanding and action.

By faith Abel offered God a better sacrifice than Cain did. By faith he was commended as a righteous man, when God spoke well of his offerings. And by faith he still speaks, even though he is dead. (11:4)

6

Abel's Faith

HEBREWS 11:4

Irst read, without prior explanation, the story of Cain and Abel is mysterious and enigmatic. Adam and Eve had two sons — Cain, who went into agriculture — and Abel, who took up shepherding or animal husbandry. Both were religious men, and when it came time to worship each brought an offering appropriate to his profession — Abel from his flock, and Cain from his fields. But curiously, God favored Abel's sacrifice and rejected Cain's.

Cain, in turn, became angry. God warned him, "If you do what is right, will you not be accepted? But if you do not do what is right, sin is crouching at your door; it desires to have you, but you must master it" (Genesis 4:7). But Cain nursed his rage and murdered Abel, whose blood cried out to God from the ground. The story ends in tragic closure: "So Cain went out from the Lord's presence and lived in the land of Nod, east of Eden" (Genesis 4:16). What a strange story, one thinks. What is the reasoning behind this primitive drama?

St. Augustine understood it and penetrated to its very core in his famous *City of God* when he explained: "Cain was the first-born, and he belonged to the city of men; after him was born Abel, who belonged to the city of God."[1] Augustine correctly saw that each was representative of radically different approaches to religion and to God. There was the way of Cain — a way of *unbelief* and of self-righteous, man-made religion. Jude 11 warns, "Woe to them! They have taken the way of Cain." In contrast was the way of

Abel — a way of *faith* described in the present text: "By faith Abel offered God a better sacrifice than Cain did. By faith he was commended as a righteous man, when God spoke well of his offerings. And by faith he still speaks, even though he is dead" (11:4).

So the theme of this first example of faith in Hebrews 11 is a contrast of two cities, two streams — the two ways of faith and unbelief. As such, it provides unique insight into the anatomy of an authentic faith — a faith that endures. Abel's faith produced and was characterized by three things that are consecutively mentioned in verse 4: 1) authentic worship, 2) authentic righteousness, and 3) authentic witness.

BY FAITH: AUTHENTIC WORSHIP

The authentic nature of Abel's worship is explicitly attributed to his faith in the opening sentence of our verse: "By faith Abel offered God a better sacrifice [i.e., better worship] than Cain did."

Approved Through Obedience

To do a thing "by faith," you must do it in response to and according to a word from God. You hear God's word indicating his will, and "by faith" you respond in obedience. "Faith comes from hearing, and hearing by the word of Christ" (Romans 10:17, NASB).

From this we must understand that God evidently had given explicit instructions to Cain and Abel indicating that only animal sacrifices were acceptable. Very likely they learned this through their parents, Adam and Eve, because Genesis 3:21 indicates that after that couple's sin and fall, God provided garments of animals slain to clothe their nakedness — an implicit inference that animal blood was spilled in direct response to their sin. While it is true that the categories of ritual animal sacrifices were not established until Moses' time, the earliest believers nevertheless met at the altar on the basis of blood sacrifice (Genesis 8:20-22; 15:1-11).

Not only had God communicated his will regarding the necessity of animal sacrifices, but if, as we think, he communicated this first to Adam and Eve, then Cain and Abel had been conforming to the practice for some 100 years, because Cain was 129 years old at this time![2] Moreover, Genesis 4:3 says, "In the course of time Cain brought . . . an offering," and "course of time" is literally "at the end of days" (Young's translation), indicating the end of a specific period of time — very possibly a time God had designated for regular sacrifice. Therefore, we surmise that both Cain and Abel had known God's word regarding the necessity of animal sacrifice ever since they were children and had obeyed it for years.

To this may be added the thought that Cain and Abel both understood the substitutionary atoning nature of the blood sacrifice because when God provided the skins to clothe their parents, he established the principle of covering sin through the shedding of blood. Abel's faith was an expression of his conscious need for atonement.[3]

But not so with Cain! He came his own way — "the way of Cain." By refusing to bring the prescribed offering, and instead presenting his garden produce, he was saying that one's own good works and character is enough. Cain may have reasoned, "What I am presenting is far more beautiful than a bloody animal. I myself would prefer the lovely fruits of a harvest any day. And I worked far harder than Abel to raise my offering. It took real toil and sweat. And it is even of greater market value! Enough of this animal sacrifice business, God. My way is far better!"

Cain's offering was a monument to pride and self-righteousness — "the way of Cain." Abel, on the other hand, believed and obeyed God: "By faith Abel offered God a better sacrifice than Cain did." He brought God what God wanted. This was acceptable worship.

Approved Through Attitude

The other reason Abel's offering was accepted was his heart attitude. Cain's attitude puts it all in stark perspective. The Scriptures indicate that when God rejected Cain's offering, Cain became "very angry, and his face was downcast" (Genesis 4:5), thus revealing just how shallow his devotion was. And when God pleaded with Cain to desist and do what was right, warning him with powerful metaphorical language that sin was crouching like a monster at his door and desiring to have him (Genesis 4:6, 7), God's plea was met by ominous silence. Whereas Cain's mother had been talked into sin, Cain would not be talked out of it.

It seems that Cain was determined to stay angry. He liked being mad. And so it has been with Cain's children — like the famous author Henrik Ibsen, who was a specialist in anger, a man to whom anger was a kind of art form in itself. For example, when he wrote the ferocious play *Brand*, he recorded: "I had on my table a scorpion in an empty beer glass. From time to time the brute would ail. Then I would throw a piece of ripe fruit into it, on which it would cast itself in a rage and inject its poison into it. Then it was well again."[4] Cain too drew strength from his rage. The release of venom was his elixir. He would rather kill than turn to God's gentle pleadings and repent. So he directed his hatred for God at his brother Abel and killed him.

But Abel had come to God with a completely different spirit — a submissive, devoted heart. Abel brought "portions from some of the firstborn of his flock" (Genesis 4:4) — his best. This was in accord with the later directives of God's Word — for example, "Honor the Lord from your wealth, and from the first of all your produce" (Proverbs 3:9, NASB). God saw Abel's heart and was pleased with his motives, for "God loves a cheerful giver" (2 Corinthians 9:7).

How God desires devoted hearts in his worshipers! Jesus said that the time "has now come when the true worshipers will worship the Father in spirit and truth, for they are the kind of worshipers the Father seeks. God is spirit, and his worshipers must worship in spirit and in truth" (John 4:23, 24). God longs for those who worship him with the complete devotion of their human spirits. In fact, nowhere in the entire corpus of Holy Scripture do we read of God's seeking anything else from a child of God. God desires sincere heart worship above all else! The Psalmist recognized this and sang, "My heart is steadfast, O God; I will sing and make music with all my soul" (Psalm 108:1) — saying in effect, "Everything in my human spirit shall be engaged in worshiping and praising you, O God." When the disciples harshly rebuked Mary for anointing Jesus' head and feet, he in turn rebuked them: "Leave her alone. . . . She has done a beautiful thing to me" (Mark 14:6).

It is very significant that this great chapter on faith begins with a worshiper — because worship is fundamental to everything else we do in life. As we shall see when we come to Abraham, everywhere he went, he built an altar. He knew that faith and service grow out of authentic worship.

So there we have it. The opening sentence of our text tells us that faith is essential to acceptable worship: "By faith Abel offered God a better sacrifice than Cain did." Why? First, because Abel's faith produced faithful *obedience* to God's expressed will and word. Cain did it his way, but Abel did it God's way. Abel brought God exactly what he asked for. Today, if we would come to God we must come not with our own works, but rather with and through the sacrifice of Christ — the way of Christ, not "the way of Cain."

Second, we must come with the heart *attitude* with which Abel brought his "better sacrifice" — joyously giving his very best from his very first. This is what the Lord is looking for — followers who bring what he asks for with a joyous heart. This is approved, authentic worship, and it can only happen through faith!

BY FAITH: AUTHENTIC RIGHTEOUSNESS

Having taught us that authentic *worship* comes through faith, the preacher in the next sentence shows that authentic *righteousness* also results from faith: "By faith he was commended as a righteous man, when God spoke well of his offerings."

Just how God spoke well of (or attested) Abel's offerings is not indicated. Jewish tradition and then Christian tradition have it that fire came down from Heaven and consumed Abel's offering but not Cain's. And Scriptures do record fire descending on acceptable offerings in at least five other instances (cf. Leviticus 9:23, 24; Judges 6:21; 13:19, 20; 1 Kings 18:30-39; 2 Chronicles 7:1). Such greats as St. Chrysostom, Thomas

Aquinas, Martin Luther, John Owen, and Franz Delitzsch believe that fire did, indeed, descend on Abel's offering.[5]

And it is very likely — especially at this primal event. Perhaps it was memorably spectacular, like the experience of Manoah and his wife when fire fell from Heaven incinerating the sacrifice, and the angel of the Lord ascended in the flame! However it was, we do know that God "spoke well" of Abel's offerings and that on account of his faithful offerings he was "commended as a righteous man" — a right-living man. In fact, Jesus called him "righteous Abel" (Matthew 23:35). And St. John emphasized a life of love by contrasting Cain's evil actions with Abel's righteous actions (1 John 3:12). So Abel rightly has a huge reputation for righteous living.

Here's the connection: When there is authentic faith, which in turn authentically worships (obediently bringing to God what he asks for in joyful attitude), that faith will produce practical, living, authentic righteousness. James says essentially the same thing when he argues that faith and works are inseparable (cf. James 2:17, 18). True, living faith produces fruit — living action.

Faith and righteous works are like the wings of a bird. There can be no real life, no flight, with a single wing, whether works or faith. But when the two are pumping in concert, their owner soars through the heavens. Authentic faith produces an authentic life that flies high, like Abel of old.

BY FAITH: AUTHENTIC WITNESS

Now comes the final logic of Abel's faith: authentic faith produces an authentic witness — "And by faith he still speaks, even though he is dead" (v. 4).

Among William Blake's most famous paintings is one depicting the murder of Abel. In the background lies Abel's muscular body, pale grey in death. In the foreground flees Cain. His body is moving away as he sprints by, but his torso is twisted back so that he faces the observer. His eyes are wide in terror, his mouth gaping in wrenching agony. And his hands are stopping up his ears in an attempt to shut out the wail of his brother's blood screaming from the ground. In Genesis we see Abel's blood crying for retribution! But here in the present text, it is Abel's illustrious example of faith that sweetly calls to us in profound witness — "And by faith he still speaks, even though he is dead."

There is great power in example. St. Francis once called to one of his young monks, "Let's go down to the town to preach." The novice, delighted at being singled out to be the companion of Francis, quickly obeyed. They passed through the principal streets, turned down many of the byways and alleys, made their way out to some of the suburbs, and at length returned by a winding route to the monastery gate. As they approached it, the younger man reminded Francis of his original intention. "You have forgotten, Father," he said, "that we went down to the town to preach!" "My son," Francis replied, "we *have* preached. We were preaching while we were walking. We have been seen by many; our behaviour has been closely watched; it was thus that we preached our morning sermon. It is of no use, my son, to walk anywhere to preach unless we preach everywhere as we walk!"[6]

This could be genuinely said of Abel. Though none of his words have been preserved, he has been eloquently preaching for thousands and thousands of years about authentic faith.

And what does he say to us? First, that true faith spawns *authentic worship* — "By faith Abel offered God a better sacrifice than Cain did." It was "better" because it was *obedient* to God, giving him what he asked for. This tells us that we dare not bring anything to God until we bring the blood of Christ.

> *Nothing in my hand*
> *I bring.*
> *Simply to the cross*
> *I cling.*

It was "better" because it was presented with a *joyful attitude* of the heart — "But Abel brought fat portions from some of the firstborn of his flock" (Genesis 4:4). Faith produces authentic worship, which gives God what he wants with all one's heart. This is what God is looking for today.

Second, Abel's life witnesses to us that authentic faith produces a life of *authentic righteousness* — "By faith he was commended as a righteous man, when God spoke well of his offerings." Abel walked his talk. His authentic faith produced authentic worship, which in turn produced authentic righteousness.

Third, Abel's life testifies that true faith's *worship* and *righteousness* produce an eternal *authentic witness* — "and by faith he still speaks, even though he is dead."

This is what the world has always needed!

By faith Enoch was taken from this life, so that he did not experience death; he could not be found, because God had taken him away. For before he was taken, he was commended as one who pleased God. And without faith it is impossible to please God, because anyone who comes to him must believe that he exists and that he rewards those who earnestly seek him. (11:5, 6)

7

Enoch's Faith

HEBREWS 11:5, 6

Enoch is one of the truly mysterious figures in Scriptural history.

ABOUT ENOCH

Enoch's Longevity

He was one of those long-lived ante-diluvians. That is, he lived before the Deluge (Noah's great flood) and was early in the line of primal fathers who lived to incredible ages. Genesis 5:21-24 devotes only fifty-one words (in English) to describing Enoch:

> When Enoch had lived 65 years, he became the father of Methuselah. And after he became the father of Methuselah, Enoch walked with God 300 years and had other sons and daughters. Altogether, Enoch lived 365 years. Enoch walked with God; then he was no more, because God took him away.

So we know that Enoch lived over three and a half centuries on this earth. This means that if Enoch's 365-year life span had ended in 1992, he would have been born in 1627 — the year before Salem was founded by our Pilgrim fathers on Massachusetts Bay. That same year Francis Bacon published *New Atlantis* in London. On Enoch's hundredth birthday in 1727, young Jonathan Edwards would have been installed as assistant pastor to his grandfather, Solomon Stoddard, in Northampton, and the Danish explorer Vitus Bering would have discovered the strait between Asia and North America.

When Enoch celebrated his second century in 1827, Jedediah Smith blazed the first trail from Southern California to Fort Vancouver. And at the other end of the country, New Orleans would celebrate its first Mardi Gras when students from Paris introduced the Shrove Tuesday event.

In 1927, on his 300th birthday (the cake would have melted from the heat of the candles!), Charles Lindbergh would pilot the *Spirit of St. Louis* across the Atlantic to Paris, Babe Ruth would hit sixty home runs, and the first "talkie" (*The Jazz Singer* with Al Jolson) would be produced.[1]

And finally, in 1992, the whole world would know of his departure in one instant through satellite cable communication. Not only that, but Enoch's son, Methuselah, born when Enoch was sixty-five in 1692, would not die until the twenty-seventh century, A.D. 2,661 — at the ripe old age of 969 years (cf. Genesis 5:27).

The point of all this is that though Enoch's tenure was brief in comparison with that of his father and son, it is nonetheless an amazing stint of time — and those 300-plus years were given to righteous living in the midst of a terribly evil ante-diluvian world that was destroyed precisely because of its depravity (cf. Genesis 6:11-13).

Not only that, but Enoch served as a prophet for over three centuries, preaching the unwelcome message of coming judgment. Jude 14, 15 records this, saying:

> Enoch, the seventh from Adam, prophesied . . . "See, the Lord is coming with thousands upon thousands of his holy ones to judge everyone, and to convict all the ungodly of all the ungodly acts they have done in the ungodly way, and of all the harsh words ungodly sinners have spoken against him."

Enoch was no wilting flower! His prophetic bloom remained fresh and full for 300 years!

Enoch's Translation

Enoch was a man of immense age and character, but he is most famous for the incredible thing that happened to him, as described in the Genesis account: "Enoch walked with God; then he was no more, because God took him away" (5:24). God translated him to be with himself without going through death. We know this because of the way Genesis 5 reads, with every one of the ante-diluvians' lives ending with the words, "and then he died" — except for Enoch where it says, "then he was no more, because God took him." This understanding is confirmed by Hebrews 11:5, which says, "By faith Enoch was taken from this life, so that he did not experience death; he could not be found, because God had taken him away."

The Scriptures do not say exactly how this happened. Possibly God took Enoch up in a whirlwind as he did Elijah, the only other person in history who did not see death (cf. 2 Kings 2:1ff.). What a way to go! — like moving right up the whirling spiral of a Kansas tornado. Some ride! "Yeowww! Here I come Lord!" Maybe he was just walking along, and *poof*! — he was no more. It is fun to speculate, but it is not speculation to say that "in a flash, in the twinkling of an eye" his perishable body put on an imperishable body (1 Corinthians 15:52, 53), because it is written that "flesh and blood cannot inherit the kingdom of God, nor does the perishable inherit the imperishable" (v. 50).

We have already made some mention as to why Enoch was taken away — namely, the character of his life. Helpfully, Hebrews 11:5 is very explicit in exploring this, giving us two specific reasons he was taken. First, because of *his faith* — "by faith Enoch was taken from this life" (v. 5a). And second, because *he pleased God* — "For before he was taken, he was commended as one who pleased God" (v. 5b).

Faith and pleasing God are but opposite sides of the same coin, and it is profitable to examine each side.

Enoch's Walk

The fact that Enoch was taken because he "pleased God" refers to Enoch's walk with God, because 11:5 is based on the Septuagint for Genesis 5:24: "Enoch walked with God." "Walked with God" and "pleased God" mean the same thing.[2]

But the metaphor of walking more exactly reveals how Enoch pleased God. Walking with another person suggests a mutual agreement of soul, as the prophet Amos understood when he asked, "Do two walk together unless they have agreed to do so?" (Amos 3:3). It is impossible to walk together unless there are several mutual agreements. To begin with, you must agree on the destination. Husbands and wives know that the paths to Bloomingdale's and Eddie Bauer are not the same! You cannot walk together and go to separate destinations. Enoch was heading in God's direction.

Of course, it is quite possible to be headed to the same destination but by separate paths. But again, two cannot walk together unless they have the same destination and follow the same path. This Enoch did with God!

There is one other requirement in walking together. Two must not only be traveling to the same *place* on the same *path*, but they must also go at the same *pace*. Enoch was in step with God. We too must "keep in step with the Spirit" (Galatians 5:25).

Enoch's great walk produced two wonderful things — fellowship and righteousness. When two walk toward the same *place* on the same *path* at the same *pace* for 300 years, they are in fellowship! And this is the primary meaning of *walk*: fellowship, sacred communion.

Matching God stride for stride along the path of life while headed for the city of God also produced in Enoch a righteous walk. Malachi 2:6 describes such a walk: "True instruction was in his [Levi's] mouth, and unrighteousness was not found on his lips; he walked with Me in peace and uprightness, and he turned many back from iniquity" (NASB). Enoch walked in profound fellowship with God and had a profound righteousness. Thus, Enoch pleased God.

Warren Wiersbe writes,

> Enoch had been walking with God for so many years that his transfer to heaven was not even an interruption. Enoch had been practicing Colossians [chapter] three centuries before Paul wrote the words: ". . . keep seeking the things above. . . . Set your mind on the things above, not on the things that are on earth" (vv. 1, 2).[3]

It was little wonder that God took him!

Enoch's Faith

The other side of this coin, the primary side that so pleased God that he decided to take Enoch to Heaven, was *Enoch's faith* — "By faith Enoch was taken from this life, so that he did not experience death; he could not be found, because God had taken him away" (11:5a). Though the Old Testament does not say Enoch had faith, the inspired author of Hebrews says that was his primary characteristic. Faith and a righteous walk with God are inseparably joined in the author's mind — just as he had observed about Abel in the previous verse: "By faith he was commended as a righteous man" (v. 4). The preacher is saying that *faith* precedes and produces the *walk* with God that so pleases him.

This understood, the way is now prepared for the great statement that the preacher has been leading up to: "Without faith it is impossible to please God" (v. 6a). Notice that he does not say that "without faith it is *difficult* to please God," or "without faith you will have to work *extra-hard* to please God." He says categorically that it is *impossible!* This resonates with Paul's insistence that God cannot and will not be pleased apart from the righteousness that comes from God through faith (cf. Romans 3:21, 22; Philippians 3:9). Indeed, without this faith all are under the wrath of God (cf. Romans 1:17, 18; 2:5-8). Christians understand that "it is by grace you have been saved, through faith — and this not from yourselves, it is the gift of God — not by works, so that no one can boast" (Ephesians 2:8, 9).

But the great emphasis here in Hebrews 11:6 is on day-to-day practical faith, which is necessary for anyone, especially believers, in order to please God. In other words, if we are not living a life of faith, we cannot be pleasing to God. We *cannot* have God's smile on our lives without faith.

So the question we must pose, and which the text answers, is: What is the faith that pleases God like? The answer is twofold. It is a faith that believes, first, that *God exists*, and second, that he *rewards* those who diligently seek Him.

THAT HE EXISTS (v. 6a)

"And without faith it is impossible to please God, because anyone who comes to him must believe that he exists" (v. 6a). God's smile is only upon those who believe he exists! This involves three levels of belief.

The first level is simply that "he is" — as the Greek literally says. This is by no means a given in the twentieth century. The human race has descended from being pagan theists like the ancients to being modern pagan atheists. As Annie Dillard says, "We have drained the light from the boughs in the sacred grove and snuffed it in the high places and along the banks of sacred streams. We as a people have moved from pantheism to pan-atheism."[4]

In this, our modern culture does not even do as well as the demons, for there is not a demon in the universe who is an atheist (cf. James 2:19)! There are, no doubt, evil spirits of atheism, demons who have influenced and danced on the graves of atheists. But all demons are thoroughgoing monotheists, and Trinitarians to boot! So, believing "God is" is only the beginning.

But there is a second level of belief required to believe that "God is" (which comes from the fact that chapter 11 is a panoramic survey of the Old Testament) — and that is a belief in the great God of the Old Testament as the God who exists. We must believe in the Creator God of Genesis 1, who spoke creation into existence in symphonic sequence one note at a time until all creation stood in marvelous harmony — "while the morning stars sang together and all the angels shouted for joy" (Job 38:7).

We must believe in the personal Creator of Psalm 139 who knit us together in our mother's wombs (v. 13). As Job so beautifully celebrated, "Did you not pour me out like milk and curdle me like cheese, clothe me with skin and flesh and knit me together with bones and sinews? You gave me life and showed me kindness, and in your providence watched over my spirit" (Job 10:10-12). We must believe that this personal God is!

Likewise, we must believe in the miracle-working God of the Old Testament. We must believe in the God who saved his people by rolling back the Red Sea as with a squeegee over a wet floor — who sent coveys of quail into Israel's camp so thick one could grab them from the air, and in the morning spread sweet manna like cake frosting on the ground — who parted the

Jordan so that its bed ran dry down to the Dead Sea and who then brought down the walls of Jericho — and who surrounded his besieged servants with incendiary chariots chuck-full of flaming angels. This kind of belief begins to activate the pleasure lines on the face of God.

But for us who live in the glow of the cross, there is a third level of belief incumbent upon us, and that is a belief in the massive God of the New Testament as revealed in Christ the Son. It is not a revelation of a greater God, but a greater revelation of God. "In the past God spoke to our forefathers through the prophets at many times and in various ways, but in these last days he has spoken to us by his Son" (1:1, 2). Jesus is God's final Word — his ultimate revelation.

Nowhere is this revelation made more clear than in Colossians 1:15-20, a great hymn to Christ.

Creator

The hymn celebrates Christ's being the Creator of everything: "For by him all things were created: things in heaven and on earth, visible and invisible, whether thrones or powers or rulers or authorities; all things were created by him and for him" (v. 16). In thinking about our solar system, we can glimpse the scale of things if we think of our sun as the size of an orange, which would make the earth the size of a grain of sand circling around the orange at thirty feet out. But within our galaxy would be one hundred thousand million oranges, each separated from its neighbor by a distance of a thousand miles. And there would be one hundred thousand million more galaxies like our own galaxy, each having one hundred thousand million oranges — and some of the oranges would be more than twenty-seven million times bigger than our orange.

Jesus made everything — "all things were created by him" (v. 16). Every crevice on every celestial "orange," every texture, every aroma, every shape, every size, every trajectory, every mite that crawls on or in each one — all were made by him.

Sustainer

Even more, he is not only Creator but Sustainer: "He is before all things, and in him all things hold together" (v. 17). If one could travel at the speed of light for seventy-eight years to the Big Dipper's handle and the star Mizar, and then another 120 light-years along its handle to Alcaid, the handle's end, and then out past the Milky Way beyond the rim of our galaxy, our island universe, and then make a left turn and head off for a million light-years toward some black hole, and then come across a floating grain of stellar dust — it would all be held together by Christ, for "in him all things hold together." Similarly, if he spoke the word, everything would come apart in ultimate nihilism!

The Goal

And there is more, because Christ is also the goal of the universe: "All things were created by him, and for him" (v. 16b). This is an astonishing statement. There is nothing like it anywhere else in Biblical literature. What is particularly dramatic is that "for him" has the sense of "toward him" — "all things have been created by him and *toward* him."[5] All creation is moving toward its goal in him. He is the Alpha and Omega, the beginning and the end, the first and the last. Everything in creation, history, and spiritual reality is moving toward him and for him.

The Lover of Our Souls

Lastly, he is the *lover of our souls* — "For God was pleased to have all his fullness dwell in him, and through him to reconcile to himself all things, whether things on earth or things in heaven, by making peace through his blood, shed on the cross" (vv. 19, 20).

Our great God, Jesus Christ, reconciled us by his own blood on the cross! How could the Creator, Sustainer, and goal of the universe do this? Why did he do this? Our minds become exhausted in contemplation of this, and we are driven to this explanation, for there can be no other: "For God so loved the world that he gave his one and only Son, that whoever believes in him shall not perish but have eternal life" (John 3:16). Christ loves us — and the cross is the measure of his love.

Now, if you truly believe that God is the Creator, Sustainer, goal, and lover of your soul, then you believe in the God who is — "who exists" — and you are under his smile. He is grinning widely over you as you please him. Enoch believed that "God is." To be sure, he didn't have the elegant charts of modern physics and astronomy at his disposal. But he believed in the awesome Creator and personal God of the Bible — he rested in that — and it changed his life.

We do not need any greater revelations or more grand and subtly nuanced doctrines. We simply need to believe what we believe. If we will *subjectively* begin to believe what we know to be *objectively* true — that he is the *Creator* of all creation — the *Sustainer* of all — the *goal* of all, so that everything will be summed up in him — and that he is the *lover of our souls* — if we subjectively (on the inside) believe it, it will change our life. Do we truly believe?

THAT HE REWARDS (v. 6b)

Enoch's great faith, which led him to walk with God and please him, lies behind the final component of a faith that pleases God. Once we believe God exists, we must also believe "that he is a rewarder of them that diligently seek him" (KJV). Enoch was sure of this. It was implicit in his message of judgment:

> See, the Lord is coming with thousands upon thousands of his holy ones to judge everyone, and to convict all the ungodly of all the ungodly acts they have done in the ungodly way, and of all the harsh words ungodly sinners have spoken against him. (Jude 14, 15)

This same God would also reward the godly. Enoch knew that God would be equitable to him.

Here is the great and grand point: Enoch lived in dark, hostile days that were uncongenial to his faith. Life was so inhospitable that finally, in the time of Noah:

> Now the earth was corrupt in God's sight and was full of violence. God saw how corrupt the earth had become, for all the people on earth had corrupted their ways. So God said to Noah, "I am going to put an end to all people, for the earth is filled with violence because of them. I am surely going to destroy both them and the earth." (Genesis 6:11-13)

However, Enoch resisted the sinful gravity of his culture and walked with God for over 300 years! He set his goal on the city of God — God's *place*; so he walked the same *path* — striding in step with God's *pace*. Three hundred years of faithfulness!

Why was he able to do it? First, because he believed that God is, that "he exists" in all his creative and personal power. Second, because he believed that God "rewards those who earnestly seek him." Enoch was sure God would be equitable to him. As a result, there was great pleasure in Heaven — and God took him. Perhaps the stars echoed with God's joyous laughter.

The lesson was there for the early church, riding on the restless seas and moving toward persecution, and it is here for us: We can walk with God if we believe 1) that he exists, and 2) that he rewards those who earnestly seek him.

The question is, do we truly believe?

By faith Noah, when warned about things not yet seen, in holy fear built an ark to save his family. By his faith he condemned the world and became heir of the righteousness that comes by faith. (11:7)

8

Noah's Faith

HEBREWS 11:7

Recently *Time* Magazine editor Lance Morrow penned some grim humor in expressing his despair at the world's ever deeper plunge into evil. Playing off the well-known persona of Willard Scott, the bright, cheerful weatherman of NBC's *Today Show*, he says:

I think there should be a Dark Willard.

In the network's studio in New York City, Dark Willard would recite the morning's evil report. The map of the world behind him would be a multicolored Mercator projection. Some parts of the earth, where the overnight good prevailed, would glow with a bright transparency. But much of the map would be speckled and blotched. Over Third World and First World, over cities and plains and miserable islands would be smudges of evil, ragged blights, storm systems of massacre or famine, murders, black snows. Here and there, a genocide, a true abyss.

"*Homo homini lupus*," Dark Willard would remark. "That's Latin, guys. Man is a wolf to man."

Dark Willard would . . . add up the moral evils — the horrors accomplished overnight by man and woman. Anything new among the suffering Kurds? Among the Central American death squads? New hackings in South Africa? Updating on the father who set fire to his eight-year-old son? Or on those boys accused of shotgunning their parents in Beverly Hills to speed their inheritance of a $14 million estate? An anniversary: two years already since Tiananmen Square.

The only depravity uncharted might be cannibalism, a last frontier that fastidious man has mostly declined to explore. Evil is a different sort of gourmet.[1]

Here's the weather in your part of the country: acid rain is falling on Chicago today . . . tornado funnels expected over the western suburbs.

Dark Willard is right. The world is in bad shape. Most of it is dark, with a few mottled areas and some bright spots. Of course, this is because of what humans are — sinners who are tainted in every part of their persons with sin. Most are not as bad as they can be. But apart from God's grace, many have descended deep into darkness, though through God's grace there are yet bright spots in this world.

What a depressing job poor Willard has, we think. But it could be worse. Think how it would have been for a pre-diluvian Dark Willard! Except for one tiny point of light, the entire forecast would have been darkness. Remember God's assessment of Noah's days in Genesis 6 — "The Lord saw how great man's wickedness on the earth had become, and that every inclination of the thoughts of his heart was only evil all the time" (v. 5). As bad as our world is today, this cannot yet be said of it. True, all humans are depraved and are naturally given to evil thoughts. But it is not true that "every inclination" of the thoughts of every man and woman's heart are "only evil all the time."

But this, indeed, was the pre-diluvian assessment and forecast. Every forming, every purposing of their thoughts (as the Hebrew suggests) was evil.[2] Moreover, the debasement was universal, as the account further describes: "Now the earth was corrupt in God's sight and was full of violence. God saw how corrupt the earth had become, for all the people on earth had corrupted their ways" (Genesis 6:11, 12).

Dark Willard's pre-diluvian forecast would have been monotonously routine:

> *Darkness,*
> *Darkness everywhere*
> *And not*
> *A light to spare.*

Except for one minuscule pinpoint emanating from the wilds of Palestine.

Thus we read, "So the Lord said, 'I will wipe mankind, whom I have created, from the face of the earth — men and animals, and creatures that move along the ground, and birds of the air — for I am grieved that I have made them.' But Noah found favor in the eyes of the Lord" (Genesis 6:7, 8). Noah was the sole ray of light in a world gone dark! It is this singular man, and his great faith amidst the darkness of an unbelieving world, that we will now consider.

FAITH'S CERTAINTY

Faith must have something to believe — and in this case it was a warning from God because our text tells us Noah was "warned about things not yet seen." The primary unseen thing he was warned about was, of course, that the earth's population was going to be destroyed by a monstrous cataclysmic flood — judgment by water (cf. Genesis 6:17). Implicit in this was a second thing not seen and certainly never dreamed of — that God was going to deliver Noah and his family through a great ark which Noah himself was going to build. In fact, the Genesis account records God's explicit instructions: "This is how you are to build it: The ark is to be 450 feet long, 75 feet wide and 45 feet high" (Genesis 6:15). In terms we can visualize, it would be one and a half football fields long, about as wide as a football field, and about four stories high.

Now imagine how this all came down on this pre-diluvian farmer. The only floods he had ever seen, if indeed he had seen any,[3] were the wadi washers which came from an occasional thunderstorm. And he had certainly never set his eyes on anything as big as the ark, much less a ship! But he heard God's Word, and he considered it (some respected scholars, such as the famous Bishop Westcott think God's words were also heard by others)[4] — and after thinking for a moment *he alone believed* God!

As to what took place inside him, we are given clear instruction because here the phase "warned about things not yet seen" is meant to direct us back to the opening verse of the chapter: "Now faith is being sure of what we hope for and certain of what we do not see." Inwardly, Noah came to possess *visual certitude*. He saw a terrible mountain of water come and cover the entire earth, destroying "every creature that has the breath of life in it" (Genesis 6:17). And he saw an immense ark of cypress wood, the work of his hands, riding high on the tempest.

This visual certitude was combined with a *future certitude*, for he was "sure of what he hoped for" — namely, the promise of salvation for him and his family. Thus, a dynamic certainty swept over his soul. *He believed God.* He saw the unseen flood. For him the future promise of salvation was so real, it was present. And this great belief was combined with trust in God, so that he became a man of towering faith. Faith is always more than certainty of belief. Faith is belief plus trust. In an instant Noah entrusted everything to God.

Long ago, before the Flood, the standard for faith was set in the midst of a midnight of unbelief. Faith hears God's word and believes with a profound certainty that makes the promise present so that the believer actually sees it and rests everything on God. Faith still requires that we believe God's word and rest our lives on it.

FAITH'S OBEDIENCE

The next great thing we see about Noah's faith is that it brought obedience — the obedience of faith — as evidenced when Noah began to build the ark: "By faith Noah, when warned about things not yet seen, in holy fear built an ark to save his family." There on a broad expanse of dry land, presumably far from the ocean, somewhere in the Fertile Crescent, Noah began to lay the ship's great keel. Here the words of our text provide two beautiful insights into the nature of Noah's obedience.

Reverent Obedience

First, he obeys in "holy fear," which I believe is better translated as "holy reverence," because fear does not fit Noah or the context in Genesis.[5] Noah obeys, not because he dreads the consequences of disobedience, but because of the sweet reverence he has for God. If there is any "fear" here, it is that of holy regard and devotional awe. Noah's obedience is built on a warm heart for God — not a servile fear, but a loving fear like that of a child who does not want to displease his father.

Noah's reverent obedience tells us that at the very heart of a life of obedience, there must be, and there always is, a holy reverence for God. We need to beware of obedience that is unemotional, that leaves our hearts beating at the same rate as before we believed. A reverent heart is a holy point of light in a dark world, for it is an obedient heart.

Practical Obedience

Understanding that faith's obedience is fueled by a reverent heart, we must next understand that obedience must always be practical. Noah got right down to doing what God had told him and "built an ark to save his family." The Genesis account adds, "Noah did everything just as God commanded him" (6:22; cf. 7:5). He followed the blueprints implicitly.

As Noah finished the incredible 450-foot keel and began to install some of the ark's ribs, we can imagine the abuse he took! How many "Noah jokes" and clever jibes do you think people could come up with in 120 years? Imagine the insults and taunts and amusement that came at the expense of

Noah and his own. "How many of Noah's children does it take to . . . ?" But Noah maintained his practical obedience, doing exactly what God said, for twenty-five . . . fifty . . . seventy-five . . . 100 . . . 120 years — until the ark lay like a huge coffin on the land.

Faith always obeys! It obeys with a *reverential* heart in ways eminently *practical*. And true faith always acts! Bringing this down to where we live, we understand that there was no way Noah could truly believe that the Flood was coming without doing what God told him to do to save his family. And, therefore, we must ask ourselves if *we* truly believe God's word — that he is coming in judgment — if we do nothing to bring salvation to those around us.

FAITH'S WITNESS

There is a beautiful sequence that emanates from true faith: faith involves certitude of *belief*, which produces *obedience*, which in turn produces *witness*. And this is precisely what Noah's faith did because his witness condemned the world — "By his faith he condemned the world," or as the NEB has it, "through his faith he put the whole world in the wrong." This he did by the witness of his *word* and *life*.

Word Witness

The Apostle Peter tells us that Noah was a "preacher of righteousness" (2 Peter 2:5). This means that for 120 years while he labored on the ark, he preached to all who would listen. Perhaps sometimes he preached from the construction scaffolding to the curious "tire kickers" who came out to gawk. Other times, no doubt, he went on preaching missions throughout the countryside. His message was a call to faith in God, repentance, and righteous living. The ancient *Sibylline Oracles* imagined this passionate address from his lips:

> Faithless men, maddened by passion, do not forget the great things God has done; for the immortal all-provident Saviour knows all things, and he has commanded me to be a messenger to you, lest you be destroyed by your madness. Sober yourselves, cease from your evil practices and from murderous violence against each other, soaking the earth with human blood. Reverence, my fellow mortals, the supreme and unassailable Creator in heaven, the imperishable God who dwells on high. Call upon him, all of you (for he is good) to be merciful to you all. For this whole vast world of men will be destroyed with water and you will then utter cries of terror. Suddenly the elements will turn against you and the wrath of Almighty God will come upon you from heaven.[6]

Life Witness

So Noah faithfully preached righteousness for twelve decades — one long pastorate! But along with this was the witness of his life. His continual preparation of the ark was a constant visual witness that judgment was coming. But there was also the powerful witness of the way he lived his life, because Noah was a profoundly righteous man.

Francois Mauriac, in his novel *Viper's Tangle*, has his lead character, an alienated non-Christian named Louis, write to his religious self-righteous wife about how the witness of a righteous, pure boy awakened a sense of evil in his own heart:

> Your paraded principles, your assumptions, your airs of disgust, your pursed mouth would never have given me any consciousness of evil, such as was conveyed to me by that boy, all unknown to myself. It was not until long afterwards that I realised this.[7]

Such was the effect of Noah's life.

What a powerful witness Noah was in the *word* and the *life* he preached. Both eloquently condemned the world and put it in the wrong.

Some people were probably reproved by Noah's word and walk. Some may have even begun to long for righteousness. But, sadly, not one person responded in a century-plus of such consistent witness. In fact, the world became progressively darker.

The abiding lesson? True faith witnesses both by *word* and by *life*. But the results must be left to God.

FAITH'S INHERITANCE

Next, a faith like Noah's makes one heir to a grand inheritance, as our text indicates in its closing line: "By his faith he condemned the world and became heir of the righteousness that comes by faith."

Objective Righteousness

This is the author of Hebrews' one and only use of "righteousness" in the objective, Pauline sense of righteousness that comes from God through faith. I like to call it an *alien* righteousness because "alien" stresses the fact that it does not come from man, but is an objective gift from God. The great Pauline texts often repeat the phrase "righteousness from God." For example:

> I am not ashamed of the gospel, because it is the power of God for the salvation of everyone who believes: first for the Jew, then for the Gentile. For in the gospel a *righteousness from God* is revealed, a

righteousness that is by faith from first to last, just as it is written: "The righteous will live by faith." (Romans 1:16, 17, italics added)

But now a *righteousness from God*, apart from law, has been made known, to which the Law and the Prophets testify. This *righteousness from God* comes through faith in Jesus Christ to all who believe. (Romans 3:21, 22, italics added)

Similarly, in Philippians 3:9 Paul expresses a desire that he might "be found in him, not having a righteousness of my own that comes from the law, but that which is through faith in Christ — the *righteousness that comes from God* and is by faith" (italics added).

The sublime result of receiving this "alien" righteousness is that we become *the righteousness of God*, as it says in 2 Corinthians 5:21 — "God made him who had no sin to be sin for us, so that in him we might become the righteousness of God."

The point we must see here is that this righteousness from God is necessary for salvation. Self-generated righteousness is never enough. Moreover, we can never earn salvation, for it comes by faith, as the verses cited above emphasize. Romans 1:17 — "a righteousness that is by faith from first to last." Romans 3:22 — "This righteousness from God comes through faith in Christ." Philippians 3:9 — "the righteousness that comes from God and is by faith."

The only way we can obtain this righteousness is by faith in Christ (*belief* that he died for our sins, plus *trust* in him alone for our salvation}.

Subjective Righteousness

When we have true faith and receive the *objective* gift of righteousness and salvation from God, it enacts in us a growing *subjective* righteousness (a righteousness that grows from within). And this is precisely what happened to Noah, as Genesis 6:9 beautifully testifies: "Noah was a righteous man, blameless among the people of his time, and he walked with God." He was "righteous" within. He was "blameless." He "walked with God" toward the same *place* on the same *path* at the same *pace*. He lived a beautiful life that pleased God.

FAITH'S SALVATION

Noah was saved by faith — his faith led to his salvation. There came the day when the rain began — it continued for forty days without stopping — and the pre-diluvians began to think perhaps Noah was not so crazy. Noah got into the ark, and the jokes stopped for good as the water rose to their knees and over their still lips.

Just as God came to the pre-diluvians through Noah, he comes today to us post-diluvians through the words of his Son who says:

> As it was in the days of Noah, so it will be at the coming of the Son of Man. For in the days before the flood, people were eating and drinking, marrying and giving in marriage, up to the day Noah entered the ark; and they knew nothing about what would happen until the flood came and took them all away. That is how it will be at the coming of the Son of Man. (Matthew 24:37-39)

Dark Willard's forecasts are not promising. The world is still very much as it was in the early 1960s when the Kingston Trio used to sing:

> *They're rioting in Africa*
> *They're starving in Spain.*
> *There are hurricanes in Florida*
> *And Texas needs rain.*
>
> *The whole world is seething*
> *With unhappy souls.*
> *The French hate the Germans.*
> *The Germans hate the Poles.*
>
> *The Poles hate the Yugoslavs,*
> *South Africans hate the Dutch,*
> *And I don't like anybody very much.*[8]

But in this dark world there is light wherever there is faith. The light comes from those who believe God's Word with such faith that they are sure of what they hope for (*future certitude*) and certain of what they do not see (*visual certitude*) — which together produce a *dynamic certitude* of faith.

Those who are granted this sure faith are also graced with the *objective* righteousness that comes from God and thus are granted a perfect standing before him. Objective righteousness, in turn, makes it possible to live in *subjective* righteousness — manifested in Noah-like obedience and witness.

This faith, of course, is a saving faith that will deliver the faithful from the judgment to come.

The truth has always been, and ever shall be, "the righteous will live by faith" (10:38; cf. Habakkuk 2:4).

How about you? How about me? Are we walking by faith?

By faith Abraham, when called to go to a place he would later receive as his inheritance, obeyed and went, even though he did not know where he was going. By faith he made his home in the promised land like a stranger in a foreign country; he lived in tents, as did Isaac and Jacob, who were heirs with him of the same promise. For he was looking forward to the city with foundations, whose architect and builder is God. By faith Abraham, even though he was past age — and Sarah herself was barren — was enabled to become a father because he considered him faithful who had made the promise. And so from this one man, and he as good as dead, came descendants as numerous as the stars in the sky and as countless as the sand on the seashore. All these people were still living by faith when they died. They did not receive the things promised; they only saw them and welcomed them from a distance. And they admitted that they were aliens and strangers on earth. People who say such things show that they are looking for a country of their own. If they had been thinking of the country they had left, they would have had opportunity to return. Instead, they were longing for a better country — a heavenly one. Therefore God is not ashamed to be called their God, for he has prepared a city for them. (11:8-16)

9

Abraham's Faith

HEBREWS 11:8-16

Without any doubt Abraham is the greatest example of faith in the Bible. Of course, others such as Enoch and Noah lived extraordinary lives of faith, but none are so closely chronicled as that of Abraham. And we do not find such detail about the inception, progress, and ultimate display of faith as is given regarding Abraham in his epic life as recorded in Genesis 12 – 25. His faith was so celebrated in Old Testament times that the Levitical prayer of confession extolled God and lauded Abraham's faith: "You are the Lord God, who chose Abram and brought him out of Ur of the Chaldeans and named him Abraham. You found his heart faithful to you . . ." (Nehemiah 9:7, 8).

The New Testament likewise holds him up as the great example of faith and the father of all who truly believe: "Consider Abraham: 'He believed God, and it was credited to him as righteousness.' Understand, then, that those who believe are children of Abraham" (Galatians 3:6, 7; cf. Hebrews 2:16). James adds that because of Abraham's faith, Abraham was called "God's friend" (2:23). Abraham is thus the undisputed paragon of faith. And so, because of the greatness of Abraham's faith, we have much to gain from his example, which is given extended coverage in Hebrews' great Hall of Faith.

Our knowledge of Abraham extends back to the nineteenth century B.C. Scripture indicates he was a citizen of the city of Ur, located on the Euphrates River in what is today southern Iraq. Ur was already an ancient city in

Abraham's time and boasted an elaborate system of writing, sophisticated mathematical calculations, educational facilities, and extensive business and religious records. The city was dominated by a massive three-staged Ziggurat built by Ur-Nammu during the beginning of the second millennium B.C. Each stage was colored distinctively, with the top level bearing the silver one-roomed shrine of Nammu, the moon-god. The royal cemetery reveals that ritual burials were sealed with the horrors of human sacrifice.[1] So Ur, advanced as it was, was nevertheless in the bonds of darkest paganism. And Abraham, as an idolater (Joshua 24:2), was a part of its conventional social and religious structure.

We also know from Stephen's speech before the Sanhedrin that there in Ur of the Chaldeans, "The God of glory appeared" to Abraham, and that the Lord delivered this singular message: "Leave your country and your people . . . and go to the land I will show you" (Acts 7:2, 3). We know, too, what happened inside Abraham, because the universal pattern of faith, which introduces the discussion of faith in the opening verse of chapter 11, was activated in his heart. He believed God's word with a certainty so powerful that he regarded the future promise as virtually present. "Now faith is being sure of what we hope for." He became so certain that God had called him and would lead him to a land where he would establish a great people that the future promise was transposed to the present. Philo of Alexandria said Abraham considered "things not present as beyond question already present by reason of the sure steadfastness of him that promised them."[2]

This *future certitude* was coupled with Abraham's *visual certitude* as he became "certain of what [he did] not see" — that is, he saw God's promise fulfilled in his mind's eye. Thus Abraham experienced the characteristic *dynamic certitude* of real faith: "Now faith is being sure of what we hope for and certain of what we do not see." Certainty welled in Abraham's heart right there in the pagan city of Ur. Abraham believed God!

FAITH AND THE PROMISED LAND (vv. 8-10)

Having seen what happened *inside* Abraham when he heard God's promise about the land, we now note what happened on the *outside* — namely, he obeyed God. "By faith," reads verse 8, "Abraham, when called to go to a place he would later receive as his inheritance, obeyed and went, even though he did not know where he was going."

Faith Obeys

It is important to note that Abraham's believing life began with an immediate act of obedience. Faith and obedience being inseparable in man's relation to God, Abraham would never have obeyed God's call if he had not truly taken God at his word. Abraham's obedience was thus an *outward* evidence of his *inward* faith. His obedience was so prompt that the Greek text presents Abraham as setting out on his journey while the word of God was still ringing in his ears.[3] What is more, the text adds that he "obeyed and went, even though he did not know where he was going." It was not until later that his destination was revealed to be the land of Canaan.[4] There was a glorious element of abandon in Abraham's faith! And it cost. Martin Luther remarked:

> It was hard to leave his native land, which it is natural for us to love. Indeed, love for the fatherland is numbered among the greatest virtues of the heathen. Furthermore, it is hard to leave friends and their companionship, but most of all to leave relatives. . . . And then it is clear that with his obedience of faith Abraham gave a supreme example of an evangelical life, because he left everything and followed the Lord. Preferring the Word of God to everything and loving it above everything.[5]

Faith spawns reflexive steps of obedience. It steps out. We must not imagine that we have faith if we do not obey. Are we truly obeying God's word to us? Has he been calling us to a specific task or action, but we have passively ignored it? Where is our faith?

Faith Sojourns

Having shown that it was by faith that Abraham obeyed, setting out for the Promised Land, the writer adds that it was also by faith that he was able to be a sojourner in the Promised Land: "By faith he made his home in the promised land like a stranger in a foreign country; he lived in tents, as did Isaac and Jacob, who were heirs with him of the same promise" (v. 9). God had promised the land of Canaan to Abraham, but during his life (and the lives of his sons, Isaac and Jacob) God "gave him no inheritance . . . not even a foot of ground" (Acts 7:5). The only land Abraham ever owned was Sarah's tomb, a cave in a field in Machpelah near Hebron, which he bought from Ephron the Hittite (Genesis 23).

To get a feel for what this was like, imagine God promising you and your descendants the land of Guatemala, and then in obedience traveling there and living the rest of your life in your camper, along with your sons' families in their campers, moving from place to place. You remain an alien for the remainder of your sojourn, without full citizenship rights, a perpetual outsider.

The word for Abraham's existence was *dissonance* — he never fit in. His religion was different and far above that of the land. He was a monotheist, and his neighbors were polytheistic pagans. His standards of morality were rooted in the character of God, while theirs came from the gods they themselves had created. His worldview invited repeated collisions with that of the inhabitants. He was always living in conscious dissonance.

What a lesson for us! The life of faith demands that we live in dissonance with the unbelieving world. A life of faith is not anti-cultural, but countercultural. Thus, a vibrant faith is always matched with a sense of dis-ease, a pervasive in-betweenness, a sense of being a camper. This does not mean, of course, that Abraham was separate from culture. To the contrary, the Genesis records reveals he was deeply involved in the politics of the land. But there was always that dissonance. He was never at home!

The parallels between Abraham's experience and that of the Christian are easy to see, because the Christian has the promise of an ultimate land. In fact, every believer is called to step out in faithful obedience and to follow Christ as he leads on to that land. All of us are, by faith, to obey and go as God directs, though we do not know where the path will take us. All of us are, by faith, to become willing sojourners, living in constant dissonance with the world as we await our final inheritance. It is a dangerous thing when a Christian begins to feel permanently settled in this world.

Have we stepped out in obedience to our individual call? Are we living in such a way in this world that there is the discomfort of dissonance?

Abraham *went out*, and Abraham *camped out*. But in his obedience and sojourn he was overall (with some famous exceptions) a patient "happy camper." Why? Because of his ultimate faith-perspective — "For he was looking forward to the city with foundations, whose architect and builder is God" (v. 10). Literally the Greek reads, "For he was looking for the city which had the foundations" — the idea being that he was looking for the *only* city with enduring foundations.[6] There was simply no other!

This city was, and is, totally designed by God. "Builder," *demiourgos*, signifies the one who does the actual work. The city was designed in God's mind and built with his hands. The city "owes nothing to any inferior being" (Morris).[7] Significantly, it was a *city*, a place that is intrinsically social. As Bishop Westcott observed, "The object of his desire was social and not personal only."[8] There he would not only see God, but he would dwell with believers in harmony rather than dissonance (cf. 12:22-24). No more camping! No more dis-ease. No more alienation. No more pilgrim life.

How much more our faith would be strengthened to step out and sojourn if we, like Abraham, would continue "looking forward to the city with foundations, whose architect and builder is God." Soon the writer to the Hebrews will greatly expand this thought — much to our souls' benefit.

FAITH AND THE PROMISED SON *(vv. 11, 12)*

Having explained how Abraham's faith worked in relation to the promise of the land, the writer now begins to explain Abraham's faith and the obtaining of a promised son:

> By faith Abraham, even though he was past age — and Sarah herself was barren — was enabled to become a father because he considered him faithful who had made the promise. And so from this one man, and he as good as dead, came descendants as numerous as the stars in the sky and as countless as the sand on the seashore. (vv. 11, 12)

Some translations other than the NIV make Sarah and her faith the subject of verse 11 — for example, the RSV: "By faith Sarah herself received power to conceive. . . ." But this is impossible because the phrase "received power to conceive" literally is "power for the deposition of seed/sperm" (*dynamin eis katabolen spermatos*), a patently male function. Thus Abraham has to be the subject of the sentence.

This is the view of nearly all contemporary New Testament scholars including F. F. Bruce, Leon Morris, and Simon Kistemaker. Most believe the misunderstanding is due to a wrong accent mark in the Greek that incorrectly renders "Sarah herself" as a nominative and not as dative. The corrective dative translation gives the right sense: "By faith he [Abraham] also, together with Sarah, received power to beget a child when he was past age, since he counted him faithful who had promised."[9] The parenthetical way the NIV mentions Sarah, though not technically accurate, does preserve the proper emphasis on Abraham.

The point is, it was biologically impossible for Abraham, as well as Sarah, to have children at the time the promise of a son was reaffirmed to them with the giving of the covenant of circumcision (Genesis 17). Abraham was ninety-nine years old, and his bride was ninety (cf. Genesis 17:1, 24)! Sarah's personal assessment was, "I am worn out and my master is old" (Genesis 18:12). The assertion that he was "as good as dead" (perfect passive participle) in verse 12 is exactly the same in the Greek as in Romans 4:19, where Paul said that Abraham "faced the fact that his body was as good as dead — since he was about a hundred years old — and that Sarah's womb was also dead."

Faith's Conception

Abraham knew the situation and that it was humanly impossible, but he came to faith. Some people are under the impression that when a person has faith, he inwardly agrees to ignore the facts. They see faith and facts as mutually exclusive. But faith without reason is *fideism*, and reason without faith is *rationalism*. In practice, there must be no reduction of faith to reason. And likewise, there must be no reduction of reason to faith. Biblical faith is a composite of the two. Abraham did not take an unreasonable leap of faith.

How did Abraham come to such a massive exercise of faith? He weighed the human impossibility of becoming a father against the divine impossibility of God being able to break his word and decided that since God is God, nothing is impossible. In other words, he believed that "[God] is, and that he is a rewarder of them that diligently seek him" (11:6, KJV). Thus he became certain that God would do what he said — dynamic certitude! He had *visual certitude* as he saw that promised baby boy in his mind's eye and *future certitude* as he saw it as present.

Faith's Optimism

George Sweeting, a past president of Moody Bible Institute, once gave this memorable definition of optimism: "Optimism is when an 85 year-old man marries a 35 year-old woman and moves into a 12 room house next to an elementary school!" But I have a better definition for him: Optimism is when a ninety-nine-year-old man and his ninety year-old bride hear God say they are going to be parents and believe their offspring will fill, not a schoolhouse, but the whole earth — that they will be "as numerous as the stars in the sky and as countless as the sand on the seashore" (v. 12)!

We are not to indulge in *fideism* — faith without reason — or *rationalism* — reason without faith. We are to rationally assess all of life. We are to live reasonably. When we are aware that God's Word says thus-and-so, we are to rationally assess it. Does God's Word actually say that, or is it man's fallible interpretation? And if God's Word does indeed say it, we must then be supremely rational, weighing the human impossibility against the divine impossibility of God being able to break his word. And we must believe.

FAITH TO THE END (vv. 13-16)

Finishing by Faith

The next section is introduced by the author's statement that Abraham, Sarah, and Isaac finished well. "All these people," he says, "were still living by faith when they died. They did not receive the things promised; they only saw them and welcomed them from a distance" (v. 13a). Death is the final test of faith, and they all passed with flying colors, living by faith right up to the last breath. The beauty of their dying was that they died in faith though never receiving the fullness of the universal blessing that had been promised. The reason they could do this was, they saw the unseen — they were certain of what they did not see. The patriarchs could see through the eye of faith the ultimate fulfillment of the promises, like sailors who become content they can see their final destination on the horizon. Land ahoy!

Along with this they recognized and accepted the dissonance of being a camper in this world — "And they admitted that they were aliens and strangers on earth" (v. 13b). They embraced the life of a pilgrim as the only proper way for them to live.

> *This world is not my home*
> *I'm just a passing through*
> *My treasures are laid up*
> *Somewhere beyond the blue*
> *The angels beckon me*
> *From heaven's open door*
> *And I can't feel at home*
> *In this world anymore.*

They died well because by faith they embraced the dissonance and saw the far-off fulfillment of the promise. This is how we, too, can die well.

Living by Faith

The subject of finishing by faith is rounded off by advice for living by faith — specifically by setting one's eyes on a heavenly country. "People who say such things," writes the author, "show that they are looking for a country of their own. If they had been thinking of the country they had left, they would have had opportunity to return. Instead, they were longing for a better country — a heavenly one" (vv. 14-16a).

When Abraham and his family admitted they were aliens, they were making it clear they were not in their home country. And so it might be supposed that they longed to go back. And if in fact their hearts were still in the old country, they could have returned. But they did not! The reason is, they were "longing for a better country — a heavenly one." And it is this spiritual longing which enabled them to persevere in faith.

May this example not be wasted on us! Paul tells us in Philippians that "our citizenship (*politeuma*) is in heaven" (3:20). In Ephesians he says, "You are no longer foreigners and aliens, but fellow citizens (*sumpolitai*) with God's people and members of God's household" (2:19). We are supernaturalized citizens, and our citizenship is not only with one another, but is rooted in Heaven! Paul again alludes to this reality when he says:

> Since, then, you have been raised with Christ, set your hearts on things above, where Christ is seated at the right hand of God. Set your minds on things above, not on earthly things. For you died, and your life is now hidden with Christ in God. When Christ, who is your life, appears, then you also will appear with him in glory. (Colossians 3:1-4)

Being willing to do this greatly enables a life of faith!

And what will be the result? Our text beautifully answers, "Therefore God is not ashamed to be called their God, for he has prepared a city for them" (v. 16b). Because the patriarchs believed God's word with dynamic certitude — because when God called Abraham to leave Ur, he believed and obeyed — because aged Abraham believed God when he said he would be a father, "God is not ashamed to be called their God." In fact, God later proclaimed to Moses, "I am [present tense] . . . the God of Abraham, the God of Isaac and the God of Jacob" (Exodus 3:6).

No higher tribute could be paid to any mortal. But God proudly claims whoever trusts and obeys him, and they can humbly insert their name in the divine proclamation, "I am the God of _____!"

Just after the turn of the century, pioneer missionary Henry C. Morrison was returning to New York after forty years in Africa. That same boat also bore home the wildly popular President Theodore Roosevelt. As they entered New York harbor, the President was greeted with a huge fanfare. Morrison felt rather dejected. After all, he had spent four decades in the Lord's service. But then a small voice came to Morrison, saying, "Henry . . . you're not home yet."

And was the voice ever right, for God had "prepared a city" far greater than the Big Apple for Henry Morrison. God says, "I am the God of Henry C. Morrison. And here, Henry, are the keys to the city!"

With faith, it *is* possible to please God!

By faith Abraham, when God tested him, offered Isaac as a sacrifice. He who had received the promises was about to sacrifice his one and only son, even though God had said to him, "It is through Isaac that your offspring will be reckoned." Abraham reasoned that God could raise the dead, and figuratively speaking, he did receive Isaac back from death. By faith Isaac blessed Jacob and Esau in regard to their future. By faith Jacob, when he was dying, blessed each of Joseph's sons, and worshiped as he leaned on the top of his staff. By faith Joseph, when his end was near, spoke about the exodus of the Israelites from Egypt and gave instructions about his bones. (11:17-22)

10

Abraham's and the Patriarchs' Faith

Hebrews 11:17-22

When aged Abraham, just one year short of a century, was told by God that he must change Sarai's name to Sarah ("princess") because she was going to have a son and thus would become the mother of many nations, "Abraham fell facedown; he laughed and said to himself, 'Will a son be born to a man a hundred years old? Will Sarah bear a child at the age of ninety?'" (Genesis 17:17). Abraham, of course, had earlier come to believe he would have an heir and innumerable offspring (cf. Genesis 15:4-6). But the assertion that two old nonagenarians (ninety-year-olds) would have a baby struck his funny-bone, and, though properly prostrate before God, he could not help laughing. However, his incredulous laughter was only momentary, for when God explained that the birth would take place the following year, Abraham believed with all his heart, as Hebrews 11:11 has made so clear: "By faith Abraham, even though he was past age — and Sarah herself was barren — was enabled to become a father because he considered him faithful who had made the promise."

A short time later when Sarah, listening at the door of their tent, overheard three mysterious guest-angels tell Abraham that about the same time next year they would be parents, the old princess inwardly chuckled.

So Sarah laughed to herself as she thought, "After I am worn out and my master is old, will I now have this pleasure?" Then the Lord said to Abraham, "Why did Sarah laugh and say, 'Will I really have a child, now that I am old?' Is anything too hard for the Lord? I will return to you at the appointed time next year and Sarah will have a son." Sarah was afraid, so she lied and said, "I did not laugh." But he said, "Yes, you did laugh." (Genesis 18:12-15)

So the great prince and princess, the father and mother of all who believe, fell to incredulous laughter as a prelude to profound faith.

There is divine poetry here, because God had the last laugh (and a very gentle and joyous laugh it was!), for God specified that the baby boy be called "Isaac," which means "he laughs" (cf. Genesis 17:19). And when Isaac was born, "Sarah said, 'God has brought me laughter, and everyone who hears about this will laugh with me'" (Genesis 21:6). Sarah was ninety-one years old, and she had given birth to her *first* child! She laughed, Abraham laughed, laughter filled all the tents — and Heaven smiled!

Isaac's name was a sure prophecy of what he brought to life. The old couple would take baby Isaac in their age-spotted hands and hold him close before their wrinkled visages, and their eyes would light as the smile lines drew taut — they would chuckle — and baby Isaac would laugh. If there ever were doting parents, Abraham and Sarah were surely prime examples. The boy was everything to them — the amalgam of their bodies and souls, the miraculous fulfillment of prophecy, the hope of the world. Isaac's every move was lovingly chronicled — his first word, the first step, his likes and dislikes, his tendencies. And as he grew to boyhood and on toward manhood, Abraham and Sarah would see aspects of their younger selves in their son — perhaps Abraham's height and carriage and Sarah's stride and grace.

There can be no doubt that either parent would have died in an instant for Isaac. They were so utterly proud of their son — "laughter."

ABRAHAM'S OBEDIENCE (GENESIS 22:1-18)

A Call to Obedience

Over the years Abraham had learned to respond to God's voice. So, Abraham's quick and courteous reflex to God's address in Genesis 22:1 is most natural: "Some time later God tested Abraham. He said to him, 'Abraham!' 'Here I am,' he replied" — the sense being, "at your service" or "ready."[1]

But the brightness in the old patriarch's response faded when he heard God's charge: "Take your son, your only son, Isaac, whom you love, and go to the region of Moriah. Sacrifice him there as a burnt offering on one of the mountains I will tell you about" (v. 2). Immediate horror fell on Abraham's soul, and revulsion repeatedly welled up in dark waves of emotional nausea. God was calling him to put Isaac to death with his own hand, and to then incinerate the remains as a burnt offering to God. This divine command was contrary to everything in Abraham — his common sense, his natural affections, his lifelong dream. He had no natural interest and no natural sympathy for this word from God. The only thing natural was his utter revulsion!

A Journey of Obedience

But Abraham knew God had spoken. So at the first gleam of dawn, without a word to poor old Sarah, Abraham saddled his donkey, quietly summoned two trusted servants, split wood for the sacrificial pyre, roused Isaac, and began the three-day journey to Moriah. Finally seeing the mountain in the distance, he bid his servants to stay with the donkey (he knew they would surely oppose him if they saw the plan unfold) and informed them that he and Isaac would "worship" and return (cf. Genesis 22:3-5).

Then Abraham and Isaac began their ascent of Mt. Moriah. Abraham placed the wood on his strapping young son and slipped the dagger into his belt. Thus lovable, talkative Isaac, happy to be alone with his father, and Abraham, preoccupied and wearier than he had ever felt, began the climb. "As the two of them went on together, Isaac spoke up and said to his father Abraham, 'Father?'" (v. 7). Isaac used the patronymic "*Abi (Abba)*," which could well be translated, "Daddy" or "Dearest Father." "*Abi?*" "'Yes, my son?' Abraham replied. 'The fire and wood are here,' Isaac said, 'but where is the lamb for the burnt offering?' Abraham answered, 'God himself will provide the lamb for the burnt offering, my son.' And the two of them went on together" (vv. 6b-8). Abraham felt older than any man who had ever lived. How he managed the ascent, only God knows!

A Sacrifice of Obedience

With leaden hands Abraham gathered stones and piled them into a rough altar and arranged the wood atop it. Then Abraham's whole existence began to play to the cadence of a heartbeat — the slow pumping music of his son's brief life. No one really knows how old Isaac was (tradition generally has regarded him as a grown man, though there is no proof). He could have been a teenager or an adult. I personally think he was young, which accounts for his apparent naiveté during the journey. However that may be, one thing is sure — Isaac must have cooperated with his ancient father because he could have certainly outrun Abraham or overpowered him if necessary.

When Abraham made his terrible intention known, Isaac began to shudder. Both wept aloud as Isaac submitted himself to be bound for slaughter upon the altar. Abraham's heart pounded, and he gasped for air. His wet eyes closed in darkness as he raised the blade to its apex and his fingers tightened for the plunge. But then Heaven spoke:

> But the angel of the Lord called out to him from heaven, "Abraham! Abraham!" "Here I am," he replied. "Do not lay a hand on the boy," he said. "Do not do anything to him. Now I know that you fear God, because you have not withheld from me your son, your only son." Abraham looked up and there in a thicket he saw a ram caught by its horns. He went over and took the ram and sacrificed it as a burnt offering instead of his son. So Abraham called that place "The Lord will provide." And to this day it is said, "On the mountain of the Lord it will be provided." (vv. 11-14)

And then there was light and fire . . . And laughter rolled from the top of Moriah across the Promised Land!

ABRAHAM'S FAITH (vv. 17-19)

Faith's "Sacrifice"

The story of Abraham's offering of Isaac is, of course, a story of towering faith. And the writer of Hebrews takes great pains to display the anatomy of such faithful obedience. "By faith," he says, "Abraham, when God tested him, offered Isaac as a sacrifice. He who had received the promises was about to sacrifice his one and only son, even though God had said to him, 'It is through Isaac that your offspring will be reckoned'" (vv. 17, 18).

The author states implicitly that Abraham's faith produced *immediate obedience* because the phrase, "when God tested him [he] offered" indicates that his obedience came at the same instant he heard the call to offer Isaac.[2] The Genesis account corroborates this when it says, "Early the next morning Abraham got up and saddled his donkey" (22:3). He did not stall, and he did not procrastinate. There was no arguing with God, no bargaining, no equivocating. Abraham had learned well from the lessons of life — for example, his own wasted sojourn in Haran, or the unforgettable tragedy of Lot's wife. Therefore, his obedience was immediate and explicit. Though every fiber of his natural being rebelled against what God was calling him to do, though his feet felt like lead, he did not turn aside. What amazing faith!

Not only that, but he really did "sacrifice" Isaac. The Greek perfect tense is used when the text says that he "offered Isaac as a sacrifice" — and the perfect tense refers to a completed action in past time. This means that the *sacrifice actually took place* as far as Abraham's resolve and obedience were concerned. From the divine perspective, as well as from Abraham's perspective, Abraham did it! But immediately the *same* verb is used in the imperfect tense in the following statement — he "was about to sacrifice his one and only son" — indicating that it did not physically happen.[3] The point is, in terms of obedience to God, Abraham did it. He completely offered his beloved Isaac, the laughter and joy of his life.

Faith's Reasoning

How was Abraham able to do this? Our text gives the memorable answer, "Abraham reasoned that God could raise the dead, and figuratively speaking, he did receive Isaac back from death" (v. 19). The word for "reasoned" is *logisamenos*, from which we get the word *logarithm*. It means "to calculate or compute." The idea is that Abraham used his stores of logic to reason the situation out. He didn't indulge in *fideism* — faith without reason, blind faith. He was eminently logical — almost mathematical — in his reasoning.[4]

And his logic was audacious. God had said that Abraham would have children as numerous as the stars and the sand — and Abraham believed God (Genesis 15:5, 6). God had said that through Isaac the great covenant and blessing would come — and Abraham believed God even though his body was "as good as dead" (11:12; cf. 11:1; Genesis 17:15-22; Romans 4:18-21). Abraham knew Isaac had come through a miraculous prophetic fulfillment of God's word. He also knew Isaac had no children and, in fact, was not even married. Yet God had clearly told him to sacrifice Isaac. There was no mistake or misunderstanding. Therefore, Isaac was as good as dead! And from Abraham's perspective it was now God's problem, for God's word through Isaac had to be fulfilled. Abraham's breath-taking logic was: God could and would raise the dead. There had never been a resurrection, but he knew God *had* to bring Isaac back to life. There was no other way. God would keep his word! "Stay here with the donkey," he told his servants, "while I and the boy go over there. We will worship and then *we* will come back to you" (Genesis 22:5, italics added).

Think of this in the context of the categories Hebrews 11 supplies. Abraham's faith rested upon *the greatness of God*. He believed that God "exists and that he rewards those who earnestly seek him" (v. 6). Abraham's faith also was grounded on *the creative power of God*. By faith he understood "that the universe was formed at God's command, so that what is seen was not made out of what was visible" (v. 3). He knew that God could bring forth the living out of nothing. In fact, his body had been "as good as dead" when he fathered Isaac (v. 12). Abraham's faith was characterized with the *dynamic certitude* of verse 1: "Now faith is being sure of what we hope for and certain of what we do not see." So certain was he of God's promise through Isaac that he saw it as present!

What astounding faith! No wonder he is the father of all who believe. No wonder he is called the friend of God.

Some of us may be thinking, "But this is so far beyond me. How could

I ever rise to such great heights of faith? Abraham is one-of-a-kind — *sui generis*. Men like him only come along every one or two millennia!" But we must understand that Abraham's great faith did not begin with the offering of Isaac. Certainly, he did begin in faith (as all spiritual life must) when he stepped out from Ur and began his sojourn. And it was a great act of faith to believe God's promise that he and Sarah would be parents when they were both "as good as dead."

But we must also remember the down times in Abraham's life, his lapses of faith — for example, the occasions on which he lied to save his own skin, saying Sarah was his sister (Genesis 12:13; 20:11-13) or when, impatient for an heir, he and Sarah took matters into their own hands and engaged Hagar to become the mother of Ishmael (Genesis 16:1-15).

We must understand that it was through ups and downs that Abraham grew in faith — until he became capable of the ultimate display. The Spanish philosopher Miguel de Unamuno wrote these perceptive words: "Those who believe that they believe in God, but without passion in their hearts, without anguish in mind, without uncertainty, without doubt, without an element of despair even in their consolation, believe only in the God idea, not God Himself."[5] We must understand, then, that "faith" that never doubts is a dead faith because it is never exercised. As believers, we are sinners who have trusted in God, notwithstanding our sin and weakness, and we are called to ascend to a dynamic certitude that profoundly believes and obeys God's word, as did Abraham. But the road to strong faith is never smooth. Faith will be tested. Inevitably there will be times of uncertainty and doubt and even despair. But the soul that clings to God will experience growth and notable triumphs of faith.

ABRAHAM'S LEGACY (vv. 20-22)

When Abraham died, he was succeeded by patriarchs who were nevertheless similarly imperfect men — Isaac, Jacob, and Joseph. But what impresses the writer of Hebrews is that when they came to what they considered to be their final hour, they had a faith that looked beyond death — they were sure of what they hoped for and certain of what they did not see (v. 1). They all were convinced that death would not frustrate God's purposes — that his word would be fulfilled.

Isaac's Faith

"By faith," says the preacher, "Isaac blessed Jacob and Esau in regard to their future" (v. 20). Actually, when he pronounced the blessing, Isaac meant to give the blessing of the firstborn to Esau, but he was deceived (Genesis 27). Nevertheless, after the blessing was given to Jacob, Isaac knew that it was binding and would not fail. In fact, he later blessed Jacob with full knowledge of what he was doing (cf. Genesis 27:33; 28:1-4). The main thing is that by faith Isaac knew his blessing would be perfectly fulfilled in the future.

Jacob's Faith

Next the author says, "By faith Jacob, when he was dying, blessed each of Joseph's sons, and worshiped as he leaned on the top of his staff" (v. 21). Aged Jacob, leaning on his staff, had Joseph bring his sons to be blessed. The older Manasseh was placed by his right hand in order to receive the greater blessing, and the younger Ephraim on his left. But Jacob, responding to the direction of God, crossed his hands, reversing the blessings (Genesis 48:17-20). Thus, by faith in God's word he was sure about the future even though it was contrary to human convention. Nothing, he was convinced, would thwart God's purposes. And, indeed, in the course of time the tribe of Ephraim became a leader in Israel.

Joseph's Faith

The last patriarch mentioned here, Joseph, was sure nothing would annul God's promise that Israel would one day possess the land. "By faith Joseph, when his end was near, spoke about the exodus of the Israelites from Egypt and gave instructions about his bones" (v. 22). This is remarkable because he had left Canaan when he was seventeen (Genesis 37:2) and lived in Egypt until his death at the age of 110 (Genesis 50:26). But in fulfillment of his faith's directive, Joseph's mummy was carried out of Egypt by Moses (Exodus 13:19) and later was buried in Shechem by Joshua when he conquered the land (Joshua 24:32). The overall point is that all these patriarchs ended well, for they had learned to trust God's bare word. They were sure regarding what would happen after their deaths.

But Abraham is the transcending example. When he raised his trembling hand above the shuddering body of his son, it was because he had learned the logic of faith: first, that God's word never fails, and second, that it must be obeyed at all costs. So the questions for us are:

Does God's Word Say It?

Not does the pastor say it, or does the committee say it? Rather, is it the clear teaching of God's Word — the Scriptures? And, as a point of fact, most of God's Word is very clear as to what it means. As Mark Twain said, it is not what we do not understand about God's Word that troubles us; it is what we do understand! While there are some inscrutable passages in the Bible, most of it is perfectly clear. The perspicacity of Scripture was one of the great principles of the Reformation. So we can, and must, ascertain what God's Word says.

Do We Believe It?

Do we believe what God's Word says about Jesus? "In the beginning was the Word, and the Word was with God, and the Word was God. He was with God in the beginning. Through him all things were made; without him nothing was made that has been made" (John 1:1-3).

Do I believe what it says about salvation? "Jesus answered, 'I am the way and the truth and the life. No one comes to the Father except through me'" (John 14:6).

Do I believe what it says about judgment? "Then I saw a great white throne and him who was seated on it. Earth and sky fled from his presence, and there was no place for them. And I saw the dead, great and small, standing before the throne, and books were opened. Another book was opened, which is the book of life. The dead were judged according to what they had done as recorded in the books. The sea gave up the dead that were in it, and death and Hades gave up the dead that were in them, and each person was judged according to what he had done. Then death and Hades were thrown into the lake of fire. The lake of fire is the second death. If anyone's name was not found written in the book of life, he was thrown into the lake of fire" (Revelation 20:11-15).

Do I believe what it says about riches? Jesus said, "Do not store up for yourselves treasures on earth, where moth and rust destroy, and where thieves break in and steal. But store up for yourselves treasures in heaven, where moth and rust do not destroy, and where thieves do not break in and steal. For where your treasure is, there your heart will be also" (Matthew 6:19-21).

Do I believe what it says about purity? "It is God's will that you should be holy; that you should avoid sexual immorality; that each of you should learn to control his own body in a way that is holy and honorable, not in passionate lust like the heathen, who do not know God; and that in this matter no one should wrong his brother or take advantage of him. The Lord will punish men for all such sins, as we have already told you and warned you" (1 Thessalonians 4:3-6).

And finally, *do we obey God's Word?*

By faith Moses' parents hid him for three months after he was born, because they saw he was no ordinary child, and they were not afraid of the king's edict. By faith Moses, when he had grown up, refused to be known as the son of Pharaoh's daughter. He chose to be mistreated along with the people of God rather than to enjoy the pleasures of sin for a short time. He regarded disgrace for the sake of Christ as of greater value than the treasures of Egypt, because he was looking ahead to his reward. By faith he left Egypt, not fearing the king's anger; he persevered because he saw him who is invisible. By faith he kept the Passover and the sprinkling of blood, so that the destroyer of the firstborn would not touch the firstborn of Israel. By faith the people passed through the Red Sea as on dry land; but when the Egyptians tried to do so, they were drowned. (11:23-29)

11

Moses' Faith

HEBREWS 11:23-29

The book of Deuteronomy ends with Moses' unparalleled epitaph:

Since then no prophet has risen in Israel like Moses, whom the Lord knew face to face, who did all those miraculous signs and wonders the Lord sent him to do in Egypt — to Pharaoh and to all his officials and to his whole land. For no one has ever shown the mighty power or performed the awesome deeds that Moses did in the sight of all Israel. (34:10-12)

To all Jews, Moses was the greatest of all men. According to one early tradition, Moses had higher rank and privilege than the ministering angels.[1]

He was Israel's greatest *prophet*. God communicated directly to him and testified regarding their relationship:

When a prophet of the Lord is among you,
I reveal myself to him in visions,
I speak to him in dreams.
But this is not true of my servant Moses;
he is faithful in all my house.
With him I speak face to face,

clearly and not in riddles;
he sees the form of the Lord.
(Numbers 12:6-8)

This is why his face was luminous when he descended Mt. Sinai with the Ten Commandments.

He was Israel's greatest *lawgiver*. Virtually everything in their religion recalled his name.

He was Israel's great *historian*. Moses authored everything from Genesis to Deuteronomy.

He was considered Israel's greatest *saint*, for Scripture says he was "more humble than any one else on the face of the earth" (Numbers 12:3). This is perhaps most amazing of all because often those who have accomplished great things are anything but humble. But Moses was the humblest of the entire human race!

He was Israel's greatest *deliverer*. His feats are wonderfully chronicled throughout the book of Exodus.

Significantly, in regard to Moses' deliverance of Israel from Egypt, his liberating work was a huge act of faith from beginning to end. And this is what the author of Hebrews focuses on in verses 23-29 in the great Hall of Faith. Here we have the anatomy of a faith that delivers others and sets them free. This insightful teaching had special relevance to the ancient church suffering in its own inhospitable "exile" in the Roman Empire. Certainly, this section has direct relevance for every believing soul who senses any dissonance with the unbelieving world.

Moses' faith is conveniently explained under five brief sections, each successively introduced with "By faith."

BY FAITH: MOSES' PRESERVATION (v. 23)

The initial faith we are shown is not Moses' faith, but the heroic faith of his parents: "By faith Moses' parents hid him for three months after he was born, because they saw he was no ordinary child, and they were not afraid of the king's edict" (v. 23). Both parents were from the tribe of Levi (cf. Exodus 2:1), and Exodus 6:20 tells us that their names were Amram and Jochebed and that they also had another son — Aaron, who would be high priest. They also had a daughter — Miriam, the prophetess.

The couple's marriage came at a dark time for Israel — when the oppression of the Egyptians had become utterly diabolical. First, Pharaoh had commanded the Hebrew midwives to murder all males immediately upon birth. When that plan failed, his command became more crude and effective — all newborn baby boys were to be tossed into the Nile as food for the crocodiles (cf. Exodus 1:15-22).

Nevertheless, Jochebed conceived. Interestingly, Josephus says the pregnancy was accomplished by Amram's obedience to a vision in which God told him he would have a son who would deliver his people. Says Josephus:

> These things revealed to him in vision, Amram on awaking disclosed to Jochabel(e), his wife; and their fears were only the more intensified by the prediction in the dream. For it was not merely for a child that they were anxious, but for that high felicity for which he was destined.[2]

Josephus' account is not inspired revelation, though some respected commentators believe something like this may have led to their faith.[3]

However that may be, when baby Moses came, his parents' faith was in full force: "By faith Moses' parents hid him for three months after he was born, because they saw he was no ordinary child" — literally, they saw that he was a "beautiful child" (RSV, NASB, NKJV). This seems an odd reason, especially in the light of universal parental experience. All my children were "beautiful" and extraordinary — and so were all yours! Right? Amram and Jochebed had nothing on us!

Obviously, there was something about him that was more than beautiful. Possibly there was something unique about his presence that confirmed God's word. John Calvin wisely remarked:

> It seems contrary to the nature of faith that he says that they were induced to do this by the beauty of his form. We know that Jesse was rebuked when he brought his sons to Samuel in the order of their physical excellence, and certainly God does not hold us to external appearances. I reply that the parents of Moses were not induced by his beauty to be touched with pity and save him as men are commonly affected, but there was some sort of mark of excellence to come, engraved on the boy which gave promise of something out of the ordinary for him.[4]

The point is, the parents were so encouraged in their faith by the extraordinary nature of their child that they hid him for three months. And then, when it became impossible to conceal his presence, they came up with a creative plan that floated him right into Pharaoh's palace! Jochebed took a papyrus basket, coated it with pitch, put her beautiful baby in it, placed it in the reeds where Pharaoh's daughter bathed, and set big sister Miriam there to watch.

Baby Moses, of course, melted the heart of Pharaoh's daughter. And as she cooed over him, up popped big sister with the brilliant suggestion of a surrogate nurse. Result: Jochebed got paid to nurse her own baby and to raise him during his early years!

So Moses was preserved by his parents' heroic faith. But there is more, for he was also nurtured by their faith. There in the slave hut of his parents Moses was surrounded by the pure atmosphere of faith. There he became aware of his own origins. There he was taught to fear God. And there he was made conscious of his call to deliver his people. Stephen informs us in his great sermon (Acts 7:25) that when Moses made his first attempt to defend his people, "Moses thought that his own people would realize that God was using him to rescue them."

What encouragement there is here for any who are attempting to try to raise a godly family in today's secular desert. Moses was preserved by his parents' faith. Their faith, their prayers, their bravery, and their creativity saved him. And more, he became a great man of faith through their faith. His experience was exactly that of the preacher who gave his mother the tribute, "My mother practices what I preach!" Moses preached and practiced the faith he saw at home as a child. Those of us who are parents and grandparents and aunts and uncles and teachers not only have great power, but also immense responsibility to the children in our lives. Israel's deliverance began with an obscure couple believing God in the midst of darkness. Think what a faith like that could accomplish today!

BY FAITH: MOSES' IDENTIFICATION (vv. 24-26)

There is a time lapse of some forty years between verse 23 and the second "by faith," which covers verses 24-26. Here we see how Moses identified with his people by faith.

His identification began with a *negative choice*: "By faith Moses, when he had grown up, refused to be known as the son of Pharaoh's daughter" (v. 24). Moses was known by the royal designation "son of Pharaoh's daughter" — a title of self-conscious dignity that is emphasized here in the Greek by the absence of definite articles.[5] A modern equivalent might be Duke of York.

To be such during Egypt's Nineteenth Dynasty would have meant immense prestige and wealth. Any pleasure that the oriental or occidental mind could conceive of was his for the asking. Such privilege could be personally deluding, as Boris Pasternak observed of the Russian aristocracy in *Dr. Zhivago* when the doctor remarked that wealth "could itself create an illusion of genuine character and originality."[6] But Moses suffered no such delusions. He was a mature man — an adult. And as such, he publicly refused the title — thus committing a grievous and dangerous insult to Pharaoh. Faith is courageous!

True faith will announce its discord whenever God and conscience call for it. Believers can love their culture, and there is much to love in most cultures, but they will refuse to be identified with the godless *zeitgeist* or spirit of the age.

Moses' negation was, of course, also motivated by a *positive act of his will*: "He chose to be mistreated along with the people of God rather than to enjoy the pleasures of sin for a short time" (v. 25). Moses' sin, had he remained part of the Egyptian system, would have been apostasy — for he would have had to abandon the truth. There is no doubt that the pleasures of sin in Egypt were substantial. But like all physical pleasures, they were only pleasurable for a moment. The pleasures of sin are like a Chinese dinner. No matter how much you eat, you are hungry again in a couple of hours!

So, rather than embracing Egypt's evanescent pleasures, Moses consciously "chose to be mistreated along with the people of God." Moses believed that Israel stood in unique relationship with the living God and had a unique role to play in world history. Moses chose the most exciting path he could possibly take. To him, life in the brilliance of the Egyptian court was a dull, ignoble thing when compared with the society of mistreated Israel.

Christians, likewise, must absorb Moses' wisdom because the Church is the only thing that will outlive this world. The elements will melt with a fervent heat, and everything will become ashes — but the Church will go on and on. When the 10,000,000,000,000,000,000,000,000,000 stars of the universe are only burned-down, flickering candles, it will still be springtime for the Church!

How could Moses turn his back on Egyptian delights and embrace the affections of his stigmatized people? The answer reveals his faith: "He regarded disgrace for the sake of Christ as of greater value than the treasures of Egypt, because he was looking ahead to his reward" (v. 26). When Moses identified with Israel, he was aligning himself with the people with whom Jesus Christ had been identified from their inception. He had always been one with his people. "In all their distress he too was distressed" (Isaiah 63:9). Thus, Moses' identification with the disgrace of the Messianic people was an identification with Christ[7] — he endured disgrace "for the sake of Christ."

The great truth for us is that Moses could do this "because he was looking ahead to his reward." Here the author again takes us back to the foundational truth of verse 1: "Now faith is being sure of what we hope for." Moses was, quite simply, sure of his reward. He was so certain that it was what we have called *future certitude*.

This is what will enable us to refuse to be called the sons and daughters of Pharaoh and to forego the fleeting pleasures of sin and to identify with God's people and their struggles. If we truly believe in the reward, as did Moses and the saints, we will do just fine. Paul said, "I consider that our present sufferings are not worth comparing with the glory that will be revealed in us" (Romans 8:18). A couple of paragraphs later he said:

And we know that in all things God works for the good of those who love him, who have been called according to his purpose. For those God foreknew he also predestined to be conformed to the likeness of his Son, that he might be the firstborn among many brothers. And those he predestined, he also called; those he called, he also justified; those he justified, he also glorified. (Romans 8:28-30)

Similarly, he encouraged the Corinthians:

Therefore we do not lose heart. Though outwardly we are wasting away, yet inwardly we are being renewed day by day. For our light and momentary troubles are achieving for us an eternal glory that far outweighs them all. So we fix our eyes not on what is seen, but on what is unseen. For what is seen is temporary, but what is unseen is eternal. (2 Corinthians 4:16-18)

These are the things we must believe!

I know what would produce such faith in each one of us. Sixty seconds in Heaven. Fifteen seconds to view the face of Christ (though it would be impossible to move our gaze after such a short time). Fifteen seconds to survey the angelic host. Fifteen seconds to glimpse Heaven's architecture. And fifteen seconds to behold the face of a loved one now glorified. That is all it would take. But God is not going to do that for any of us. I could pray until I was blue in the face, and I wouldn't get a second in Heaven until eternity.

I know what else would do it, and that is simply what Moses did: *believing God's word*. And we can all do that now. If we are having trouble believing, we ought to read these passages carefully, then ask God for the capability to believe, and then *believe*!

BY FAITH: MOSES' SEPARATION (v. 27)

Next, the author explains that Moses' forty-year separation from Egypt in the land of Midian[8] was also a result of faith: "By faith he left Egypt, not fearing the king's anger; he persevered because he saw him who is invisible" (v. 27). Here again, the author references the second half of his essential definition of faith in verse 1: "Faith is being ... certain of what we do not see" — *visual certitude*.

The paradoxical phrase "he saw him who is invisible" does not mean he saw God with the naked eye. Faith's eye saw what the physical eye is incapable of seeing. But there did also come a time when God was so pleased with Moses' spiritual vision that he graced him with physical vision of a part of God's glory (cf. Exodus 33:18-23) and spoke to him face to face (cf. Exodus 33:9-11; Numbers 12:7, 8).

I personally believe that seeing "him who is invisible" is *not* extraordinary. Rather, it is ordinary, normal Christianity. In fact, if you do not see the unseen, you are abnormal and below the divinely ordained norm.

Christianity is supernatural, and it is to be lived supernaturally. Elisha's prayer is just as relevant today for the church as it was when he prayed it over his anxious servant: "And Elisha prayed, 'O Lord, open his eyes so he may see.' Then the Lord opened the servant's eyes, and he looked and saw the hills full of horses and chariots of fire all around Elisha" (2 Kings 6:17).

BY FAITH: MOSES' SALVATION (v. 28)

The last of the ten plagues that secured Israel's exodus from Egypt was the destruction of all the male firstborn of both man and beast (cf. Exodus 12:12). But God provided a way of salvation for his people. They were directed through Moses to slaughter a lamb, take some hyssop and dip it in the lamb's blood, and daub the blood on the top and sides of the doorways of their homes. Homes so anointed would be under God's protection, and the destroyer would not be permitted to enter (cf. Exodus 12:21-23). So our text reads, "By faith he kept the Passover and the sprinkling of blood, so that the destroyer of the firstborn would not touch the firstborn of Israel" (11:28).

The point is that Moses and Israel so believed God that they obeyed God to the letter. As Raymond Brown notes:

> The instructions were strange, the demands costly (a lamb without blemish) and the ritual unprecedented, but they did precisely as they were told. In simple faith they *kept the Passover.* They relied on the God who had spoken to them through his servant: "Then the people of Israel went and did so; as the Lord had commanded Moses and Aaron, so they did" (Exodus 12:1-3, 28).[9]

But what is even more remarkable is that the phrase "by faith he kept the Passover" actually means that he *instituted* the Passover (perfect tense). Moses actually instituted the Passover as a "lasting ordinance" to be done year after year (Exodus 12:14) — which means that Moses never doubted in the least that the people would be delivered from Egypt! He had nothing to go on but God's word, but he believed it implicitly. Moses' massive faith saved Israel!

BY FAITH: MOSES' (AND ISRAEL'S) DELIVERANCE (v. 29)

The final "by faith" in our section is charitable to a fault if it is read without reference to Moses: "By faith the people passed through the Red Sea as on dry land; but when the Egyptians tried to do so, they were drowned" (v. 29).

121

The reason this is overly charitable is that Israel did not show faith but held back in craven fear, decrying Moses:

> They said to Moses, "Was it because there were no graves in Egypt that you brought us to the desert to die? What have you done to us by bringing us out of Egypt? Didn't we say to you in Egypt, 'Leave us alone; let us serve the Egyptians'? It would have been better for us to serve the Egyptians than to die in the desert!" (Exodus 14:11, 12)

Their faithlessness is corroborated by the fact that all of them later died in the desert because of their lack of faith, with the exception of Joshua and Caleb.

Actually, it was Moses' faith that rallied them and secured their deliverance: "Moses answered the people, 'Do not be afraid. Stand firm and you will see the deliverance the Lord will bring you today. The Egyptians you see today you will never see again. The Lord will fight for you; you need only to be still'" (Exodus 14:13, 14). This eventuated in Moses' preeminent display of faith when he stretched his hand out over the Red Sea, and the Lord drove back the waters with a strong east wind, and Israel passed through as on dry land (cf. Exodus 14:21, 22).

What a sublime fact we have here! One man's faith can be so authentic and effectual that it can elevate a whole people and secure their deliverance! In lesser ways we have seen this in the lives of such people as Martin Luther and John Wesley and Jonathan Edwards. This truth holds great promise for us. Vibrant, authentic faith can elevate our families, churches, and communities. It is not too much to say that it can even be the vehicle for corporate deliverance! Never underestimate the power of real faith!

Moses' peerless life shouts faith from beginning to end.

- By faith — the faith of Amram and Jochebed — Moses was *preserved* and nurtured.
- By faith Moses *identified* with his oppressed people as he turned his back on Egypt and took on the stigmata of Israel.
- By faith Moses *separated* from Egypt for forty years so God could prepare him to be a deliverer.
- By faith Moses obtained the *salvation* of his people by instituting the Passover.
- By faith Moses effected the *deliverance* of Israel through the Red Sea.

What does this all mean to us? We understand what it meant to the early Jewish church, which saw itself in a kind of "exile" set amidst the mounting hostility of Roman culture. What was going to get them through their "Egypt" was faith — believing God's word about the promise of future reward and seeing the unseen. This is what is necessary to survive.

Our culture is becoming increasingly Philistine — so much so that I am convinced that early in the next millennium simple Biblical faith will become so abhorrent to popular culture that faithful Christians will be persecuted.

I am further convinced that some, by God's grace, will draw upon Moses' example and will thereby gain strength to live for God. Moses prevailed because:

- He believed in God's promise of reward.
- He lived a normal Christian life — he saw the unseen.
  He who has ears to hear, let him hear!

By faith the walls of Jericho fell, after the people had marched around them for seven days. (11:30)

12

Joshua's and His People's Faith

HEBREWS 11:30

Israel had crossed the Jordan. Virtually nothing remained before the campaign for possession of the land of Canaan would begin. War loomed only hours away. Behind the masses of God's people, the flooding Jordan blocked all retreat. Before them rose the ominous ramparts of Jericho, her gates sealed tight, her men of war on the walls. Most of the Israelites had never seen a fortified city, and with what we know of the recurrent pessimism of this people, we can be sure that fear ran high in the camp — despite the great things God had done for them.

Humanly speaking, Joshua bore all the lonely responsibility of the leadership of his fickle, frightened people. How he would have liked to have Moses there to talk to. But there was no Moses. Joshua had sole authority. He needed to get away to pray, to meditate, to plan the conquest.

A DIVINE ENCOUNTER

So Joshua stole out of the camp in the darkness to view Jericho for himself and to seek God's guidance. The Hebrew word that tells us Joshua was "near Jericho" (Joshua 5:13) expresses the idea of immediate proximity.[1] He was very close, perhaps close enough to feel the oppression of the city described as "walled up to heaven" (cf. Deuteronomy 1:28, KJV).

There he remained in the night — brooding, meditating, patroling, his eyes wide to the darkness — when he detected some movement on which he fixed his eyes. What he saw set his heart racing and adrenaline pumping — for there stood a warrior in full battle-dress, his sword bare and gleaming blue in the moon's light.

A less courageous man would have bolted — but not Joshua. His hand was very likely upon his own sword as he strode forward, calling out to the menacing figure, "Are you for us or for our enemies?" (Joshua 5:13). In other words, "Which side are you on — ours or the enemy's? Because if you are from Jericho, it will be steel against steel!" Joshua was no armchair general!

There was no way Joshua could have anticipated the sublimity which lay ahead. He certainly did not know that the next few minutes would become a spiritual milestone in his life.

Joshua's ringing challenge, "Are you for us or for our enemies?" was met by an answer that put him flat on his face: "Neither, but as commander of the army of the Lord I have now come" (v. 14). I believe (along with Calvin and Keil and Delitzsch) that this "commander of the army of the Lord" was a theophany, an appearance of Jehovah in the form of an angelic messenger.

I am convinced of this for several reasons. First, Joshua was told to take off his sandals. This very same command had been given to Moses *by God* from the burning bush:

> "Take off your sandals, for the place where you are standing is holy ground." Then he said, "I am the God of your father, the God of Abraham, the God of Isaac and the God of Jacob." At this, Moses hid his face, because he was afraid to look at God. (Exodus 3:5, 6)

Joshua realized, through the command to take off his sandals, that this "commander" was the same God who had spoken to Moses. Second, the "commander" who spoke to Joshua is identified as "the Lord" in Joshua 6:2-5: "Then the Lord said to Joshua . . ." Third, as Origen said in his Sixth Homily on Joshua, "Joshua knew not only that he was of God, but that he was God. For he would not have worshipped him, had he not recognized him to be God."[2] These three reasons convince me that the "commander of the army of the Lord" was God in angelic form — "the angel of the Lord."

This encounter with God served to steel Joshua and arm him for the conquering of Jericho, for very specific reasons. He saw not only that God was with him, but God's mystic appearance — with his sword pulled from his scabbard and held ready for battle — was indelibly printed on Joshua's consciousness. God would fight for him! He knew that whatever the enemy mobilized, it would be matched and exceeded by heavenly mobilization. It was this same awareness that galvanized Philipp Melanchthon, the primary theologian of the Reformation, for the immense battles he fought, for his favorite verse was Romans 8:31: "If God is for us, who can be against us?" Melanchthon is said to have referenced this verse many times in his writings — and on his death bed. It was his repeated (victorious!) refrain.

Also, Joshua's encounter with God left him steeled by fully informing him regarding what God wanted him to do in taking Jericho:

> Then the Lord said to Joshua, "See, I have delivered Jericho into your hands, along with its king and its fighting men. March around the city once with all the armed men. Do this for six days. Have seven priests carry trumpets of rams' horns in front of the ark. On the seventh day, march around the city seven times, with the priests blowing the trumpets. When you hear them sound a long blast on the trumpets, have all the people give a loud shout; then the wall of the city will collapse and the people will go up, every man straight in." (Joshua 6:2-5)

What was the effect of all this upon Joshua? In a word, it produced the bedrock faith that introduces Hebrews 11 — "Now faith is being sure of what we hope for and certain of what we do not see" — faith's *dynamic dual certitude*. He had incredible *visual certitude*, for he had seen the unseen. His conviction regarding the invisible would gird him in every battle. He had awesome *future certitude* regarding what he hoped for — namely, the fall of Jericho and the taking of the Promised Land. He was sure those walls would fall! And this dual certitude made him the great General Joshua, the son of Nun — or to give it a more martial ring, Field Marshal Joshua Von Nun!

Joshua's dynamic sureness enabled him to lead Israel to victory. And here we must emphasize again that, as with Moses' believing parents and Moses himself, one person's faith can make all the difference for God's people. As we shall see, Joshua's faith was communicated to and elevated the whole nation's faith — and so can yours and mine. No matter where we are planted — whether it is behind a machine or a desk or in a house — if we live a life of dynamic certainty regarding God's Word, we will elevate and energize others to live as they ought. One person's faith can raise the level of their whole church.

That morning, as the bright rays of the early sun illuminated the thousands of orderly arranged tents of his people, Joshua knew what he had to do — and in the storied days that followed, he did it. The writer of Hebrews tells us, in a simple sentence, that "By faith the walls of Jericho fell, after the people had marched around them for seven days" (11:30). This is the key to the spiritual understanding of the fall of Jericho: *the walls of Jericho fell because of the faith of Joshua and his people*. It was the greatest corporate act of faith

127

in Israel's history, one never to be exceeded. And as such, it forms an extended object lesson for us. Let us consider faith's factors.

THE OBEDIENCE OF FAITH

The Lord himself had given *explicit* instructions to Joshua that demanded *implicit* obedience (cf. Joshua 6:2-5 and 6-10). They detailed the order and conduct of the famous procession around Jericho. The precise order was: soldiers, then seven priests carrying seven rams' horns called shofars, then (significantly in the middle) the Ark of the Covenant on the shoulders of more priests, then the people, and finally the rearguard of soldiers.

The conduct of this unusual procession was likewise carefully specified. During the first six days they were to march once around the walls each day, maintaining absolute silence while the priests blared intermittently on their shofars. On the seventh day they were to maintain silence as they circled the walls *seven* times — until Joshua gave the command to "shout" (v. 10).

Absurdity

By any outside estimation these instructions were ridiculous! The uniform witness of military history is that the foe is conquered by force. City walls are cleared by bombardment. Then they are scaled by ladders and ropes. Gates are smashed by battering rams, troops taken by sword. Cities do not fall by mystics making bad music on rams' horns! When the Canaanites got a good look at the procession, they undoubtedly exploded in incredulous laughter and then hoots and catcalls. They could not believe their eyes. What fools these Israelites were — clowns! And secretly some of the Hebrews agreed.

Belief

But though the instructions looked foolishly contrary to human logic, Israel, as a corporate body, believed. Why their uncharacteristic faith? Obviously because of their recent experience in watching the Jordan dry up when the Ark penetrated its boundary. The freshness of that recent miracle made them receptive to faith. The other reason, already touched upon, was the faith and character of Joshua. The iron certitude of Field Marshall Joshua Von Nun energized them all!

Thus, Israel really did believe God was going to give them Jericho. When the writer of Hebrews, under the inspiration of the Holy Spirit, says, "By faith the walls of Jericho fell," he means that the Israelites actually did have faith. They were not pretending to believe. Theirs was not a bogus faith. As they marched silently around the wall, they did believe the walls would come tumbling down! Their faith pleased God because they were believing that "he exists and that he rewards those who earnestly seek him" (11:6).

Obedience

The evidence that they believed God's Word is that they *obeyed* it. It was a little after dawn. The sun had lifted just above the horizon. Joshua had assembled his elders and had given them the instructions of the divine "commander." Now they were moving quickly throughout the camp, calling the people together. Soon a long procession began to wind from the camp. Though it was vast in number, it did not include all the people, but involved a representative delegation from each tribe.

The ordered procession made its way toward the walled city in silence, broken only by the discordant, elephantine blasts of the shofars. The trip from Gilgal to Jericho took about two hours, although Jericho was encircled in about twenty-five to thirty minutes.

Joshua kept the Israelites well beyond the range of Jericho's archers, but of course not beyond the taunts of the increasing number of her inhabitants who lined her walls. Yet Israel never broke silence. The strange parade continued its absurd procession for six consecutive days. The Amorites shouted on, but the grim silence of the circling fools began to wear on them.

The enduring object lesson here is that a life of faith is evidenced by a life of obedience to God's word, even when it seems absurd. Paul's comments in his second letter to the Corinthians (10:3, 4) are appropriate here: "For though we live in the world, we do not wage war as the world does. The weapons we fight with are not the weapons of the world." To the unbelieving mind, the Christian's weapons appear not only impotent but ridiculous. Who ever stormed a walled city wearing truth for his war belt, righteousness for a breastplate, the good news for shoes, faith for a shield, salvation for a helmet, the Bible for a sword? Come on! This is the armament of clowns — fools' armor.

But God gives us directions in his Word on how to meet our Jerichos, instructions that are folly to human logic.

- A man is filling out his income tax form and realizes that if he lists his extra hidden income, it will put him in a higher tax bracket and he will not have money to pay his taxes. He is up against a dark wall indeed. He has a choice to make — do what is logical (just like everyone else does) or be absurdly truthful, trusting God to take care of him.
- A student is doing poorly in class. He needs a B to get into grad school, and as he works on his final exam he realizes it is not going to happen. But he notices that his neighboring A student

is working in such a way that he can read all his answers without being seen. What to do? Rationalize and say "God provides!" or be a fool, fixing his eyes on his own miserable dunce paper, trusting God to work things out as he sees fit?

- You have been wronged by an enemy. Now you have the chance to do him ill, and he will never know who did it. Everyone would applaud you for it if they knew you did it. And you know that you can get away with it. But you remember the words of Jesus, "You have heard that it was said, 'Love your neighbor and hate your enemy.' But I tell you: Love your enemies and pray for those who persecute you" (Matthew 5:43, 44). Will you join the fools' parade and actually pray for blessing on the one who has wronged you?

The Scriptures reveal a spiritual law: disobedience reveals our unbelief, but obedience to God evidences our faith. When difficult circumstances assail us, unbelief draws from the arsenals of the world, whereas faith causes us to take up the armor of God and join the absurd march around Jericho. Any Jerichos facing you? Are you wavering between God's way and the world's way of meeting it? Do you believe God's Word? The authenticity of your belief will be determined by the weapon you choose.

THE FOCUS OF FAITH

The first great dimension of Israel's victorious faith is *obedience*. The second factor is the *focus* of Israel's faith.

The centerpiece of the narrative here is the golden Ark of the Covenant — *God's presence*. The account mentions the Ark no less than eleven times! The Ark was borne, as we have noted, in the exact middle of the procession, with the priests' horns blasting constantly as heralds of God's presence. This is what shofars were used for — just as they had earlier been sounded at Mt. Sinai to announce the presence of God (cf. Exodus 19:16). It was God's presence that circled Jericho those seven days, and it was his presence that would bring its fall.

Central to Israel's great exercise of faith was the awareness that God was with them, leading them. We must emphasize that they were *not* imagining this. God was truly present. But he manifested himself specially through the Ark. And the realization that he was physically in their midst had a massive impact on the Israelites' exercise of faith.

In John Bunyan's church in Bedford, England, there is a poem framed in the wall of the anteroom from which the preacher exits to walk to the pulpit. It reads:

Enter this door
As if the floor
Within were gold,
And every wall
Of jewels, all
Of wealth untold,
As if a choir,
In robes of fire
Were singing here;
Nor shout, nor rush,
But hush,
For God is near.

And so he is! This is what we need. This is what will enable us to conquer the evil opposition that confronts us — a sense that God is specially with us. If on a given Sunday morning we suddenly had the ability to see the unseen, we would see angels among us — maybe sitting next to us in human form. Perhaps if the preaching were good, we might see angels with their Bibles out listening intently, for Peter tells us that "even angels long to look into these things" (1 Peter 1:12). The Greek gives the idea of them bending over or stooping to search the mysteries of God's Word. And the writer of Hebrews says, "Are not all angels ministering spirits sent to serve those who will inherit salvation?" (1:14).

As the Israelites encircled Jericho, the Canaanites saw nothing more than a ragtag people carrying a golden box, but the Israelites saw the unseen. Their focus was on God, and they knew God's special presence went with them. This is faith's focus. This is the focus that brings down enemy walls!

A DECLARATION OF FAITH

It must have been very difficult for the Israelites to keep silent during those first six days. Their enemies practiced no restraint — we can be sure of that. Moreover, not one stone in the walls had loosened, there were no cracks in the city "wall up to heaven," and the citizenry was far from saying "uncle."

It must, then, have been a great relief on the seventh day when Joshua ordered them to rise early and circle Jericho seven times, finishing with a great shout at his cue. Verses 15-17, 20 describe the climactic event:

On the seventh day they got up at daybreak and marched around the city seven times in the same manner, except that on that day they circled the city seven times. The seventh time around, when the priests sounded the trumpet blast, Joshua commanded the people, "Shout! For the Lord has given you the city! The city and all that is in it are

131

to be devoted to the Lord. Only Rahab the prostitute and all who are with her in her house shall be spared, because she hid the spies we sent."

When the trumpets sounded, the people shouted. And at the sound of the trumpet, when the people gave a loud shout, the wall collapsed, every man charged in, and they took the city.

That was the voice of faith. It was the outward expression of the Israelites' inward confidence in the power of God. Conquering faith declares itself. Faith that does not do so is not faith at all. "For it is with your heart that you believe and are justified, and it is with your mouth that you confess and are saved" (Romans 10:10). Ancient Job announced, "I know that my Redeemer lives, and that in the end he will stand upon the earth. And after my skin has been destroyed, yet in my flesh I will see God; I myself will see him" (Job 19:25-27). The lips declare what is within. What do our lips say about our faith?

Surely that was some shout there at Jericho! All their repressed human emotions came forth in a cry heard all the way to Gilgal, and the walls came tumbling down. Literally, "the wall fell in its place."

- True faith *obeys* God and his Word, even when it seems absurd. It rejects the world's armament and dons the ridiculous armor of God. It marches confidently in a fools' army — to victory.
- True faith *focuses* upon God and sees the unseen. It cultivates a special sense of his presence — that he is with his people — and refuses to divert its focus.
- True faith *declares* itself to a fallen world.

How is our faith? These things happened as an example for us who still fight the battles of faith. By learning from them, we too can achieve victory in the Lord, and he will cause impossible walls to tumble before us.

By faith the prostitute Rahab, because she welcomed the spies, was not killed with those who were disobedient. (11:31)

13

Rahab's Faith

HEBREWS 11:31

We have considered the amazing faith of Joshua and the people of Israel as they followed God's seemingly absurd instructions — and saw the great city of Jericho fall flat on its face! But not all the faith was outside the city.

FAITH INSIDE JERICHO

The collapse was complete, except for one small section from which a scarlet cord tossed in the wake of the concussion. It was the cord of faith. Hebrews 11:30, 31 tells us, "By faith the walls of Jericho fell, after the people had marched around them for seven days. By faith the prostitute Rahab, because she welcomed the spies, was not killed with those who were disobedient."

During those last seven days, all faith's factors —which we examined in the previous chapter — had developed and swelled through Rahab's growing soul.

Obedience

She gave implicit *obedience* to the explicit directions given her by God through the spies. She kept all her family in her home, just as she had been told. Though some of them very likely questioned her wisdom, she did not capitulate, but rather insisted that they remain. Her obedience bears testimony to an amazing faith. Rahab's obedience matched that of the encircling Israelites.

Focus

Day after day Rahab rose to the trumpeting of the shofars as they announced the approach of God and the Ark, then peered out over her scarlet cord. The Israelites silently and knowingly stared back, and she rested her faith in the fact that God really was with them. Hers was a focused faith. Perhaps she recited to her family something of the testimony she had given to the spies:

> I know that the Lord has given this land to you. . . . We have heard how the Lord dried up the water of the Red Sea for you when you came out of Egypt, and what you did to Sihon and Og, the two kings of the Amorites east of the Jordan, whom you completely destroyed. When we heard of it, our hearts melted and everyone's courage failed because of you, for the Lord your God is God in heaven above and on the earth below. (Joshua 2:9-11)

By faith, like Noah and Moses before her, Rahab saw the unseen, and that changed her whole life.

Declaration

Finally, there was the *declaration*, the shout of faith. Earlier she had declared her faith to Israel's spies. And because of this she probably shouted out in concert with her new people, for faith declares itself.

The story of Rahab will bring us immeasurable encouragement and fuel for faith.

THE FAITH OF RAHAB

First we will consider some background to the story of Rahab. The older faithless generation of Israelites had perished in the wilderness. God had buried Moses in a secret place in one of the valleys of Moab and made Joshua the leader of his people. Now Israel had to spy out the land and consecrate itself to the great work before her. Joshua 2:1-3 describes the spies' mission:

> Then Joshua son of Nun secretly sent two spies from Shittim. "Go, look over the land," he said, "especially Jericho." So they went and entered the house of a prostitute named Rahab and stayed there. The king of Jericho was told, "Look! Some of the Israelites have come here tonight to spy out the land." So the king of Jericho sent this mes-

sage to Rahab, "Bring out the men who came to you and entered your house, because they have come to spy out the whole land."

This reconnaissance was extra-perilous because Jericho was a walled city situated in an open valley, and its inhabitants, the Amorites, were on special alert. The ominous massed presence of Israel at the Jordan had made them suspicious of everyone and everything.

Accordingly, the spies took every precaution, carefully disguising themselves, discarding anything characteristically Hebrew, and doing their best to appear Canaanite-Amorite in clothing and speech. They approached the city with great caution. The Jordan was flooding, so they probably traveled to the north where the fords were easier, then turned southwest to enter Jericho from the west side — the side away from the Israeli presence. This was advantageous because they would have the cover of the caves in the mountains west of Jericho, and the king would be less likely to detect infiltration from that side.[1]

Apparently unnoticed, they slipped through Jericho's gates, and, in a premeditated, studied attempt to "get lost" in the city, sought hiding in the house of a prostitute named Rahab. Lodging in such a place was characteristic of traveling merchants, and the spies felt their chances of escaping notice were best served there.

But the strategy failed in two respects. First, someone saw them enter Jericho and followed them to Rahab's establishment. Second, the prostitute immediately discerned their identity.

From all appearances everything had fallen apart, and they were doomed. The king was searching for them. They could not retreat back into the city. And if they jumped through the window, horsemen would easily run them down on the plain. It looked like their time had come, except for one totally unexpected thing — *the faith and good works of a prostitute.* God's agents were saved by a madame, the proprietress of a bordello, a woman who sold her body for money, who submitted to any man who crossed her doorway if he had the cash. Some try to tone down the facts, but the New Testament is clear — she was a *pornee*, a prostitute (see James 2:25; Hebrews 11:31). So unanticipated, and so extraordinary, was this madame's courageous faith that she is included in the Hall of Faith in Hebrews 11, along with the likes of Enoch, Noah, Abraham and Moses: "By faith the prostitute Rahab, because she welcomed the spies, was not killed with those who were disobedient" (v. 31).

It is most significant that the final person to receive individual commentary in the list of champions of faith is a woman and a Gentile and a prostitute.[2] Rahab's faith, a *prostitute's faith*, is given as an example for all who desire to have true faith — especially those who know they are sinners and who deep down want to be pleasing to God.

We are going to look at this from three revealing angles: 1) *Faith's work* — its demonstration, 2) *Faith's formation* — its nature and development, and 3) *Faith's reward* — its astounding benefits.

FAITH'S WORK

Faith's Lie

Verses 4 and 5 of Joshua 2 present a very awkward truth — Rahab's first work of faith was a lie!

> But the woman had taken the two men and hidden them. She said, "Yes, the men came to me, but I did not know where they had come from. At dusk, when it was time to close the city gate, the men left. I don't know which way they went. Go after them quickly. You may catch up with them."

Actually Rahab told three lies in one. First, she said she did not know where they came from. Secondly, she said they had gone. And finally, she said she did not know where they were. So here we have it — a lie was the first work of Rahab's faith!

Does this mean it is okay to lie in certain situations? I personally do not think so, though some highly respected theologians do.[3] I agree with Calvin, who comments on Rahab's deception:

> As to the falsehood, we must admit that though it was done for a good purpose, it was not free from fault. For those who hold what is called a "dutiful lie" to be altogether excusable, do not sufficiently consider how precious truth is in the sight of God. Therefore, although our purpose be to assist our brethren, to consult for their safety and relieve them, it never can be lawful to lie, because that cannot be right which is contrary to the nature of God. And God is truth. . . . On the whole, it was the will of God that the spies should be delivered, but He did not approve of saving their lives by falsehood.[4]

The Scripture does, of course, record the lies of saints such as Abraham (Genesis 12:10-20), but it never approves such deception. Rather, God's Word uniformly condemns falsehood and calls us to be men and women of truth. Moreover, the life of Christ, our model *par excellence*, provides us with the supreme example of truthfulness. Our Lord never lied or deceived anyone. And as members of his Body, we are obligated to do our best to live according to his example.

Nevertheless, Rahab's calculated lie was a stupendous act of true faith, for her subsequent actions — when she assisted the spies in their escape through the window and cleverly advised them to hide three days in the hill country — put her life in deadly peril (cf. vv. 15, 16). In fact, if the king had gotten wind of her doings, her death would have been immediate and terrible. Rahab's faith was great and deserves the status it has been given.

We must consider Rahab's lie against the backdrop of her pagan culture and lowly profession. She had no knowledge of the revelation given to Israel at Sinai. We can be sure that godly morality and its radical truth ethic had not penetrated her pagan mind. True, she possessed a moral conscience, but it was not informed by God's Word. Hence it very likely did not occur to her that she was doing wrong. I am not saying that her lie was OK or that people are better off not knowing what is right and what is not. But I am saying that God recognized the motive behind the act — and that motive was faith!

The lessons Rahab leaves us are many, and one we should particularly keep in mind is that we must be sympathetic and patient with the character of recent converts. It is a matter of historical fact that John Newton, the author of "Amazing Grace," composer of the famous Olney hymns, and one of the early fathers of the evangelical movement in the Church of England, continued to participate in the slave trade for over a year after his dramatic conversion.[5] Faith and sin mingled without conscious contradiction in his new life.

This is often characteristic today of those coming out of our Biblically ignorant post-Christian culture. One of my long-time missionary friends tells how he came to Christ in the midst of a hard-drinking business environment — and how he fortified himself with six martinis to get the courage to share Christ the first time! An inebriated evangelist? Rahab would have understood this completely.

Often real faith is salted with sin, and God finds faith where we do not (and often cannot) see it. We should be slow to judge sin and quick to perceive faith.

Faith's Trust

The classic symbol that revealed Rahab's great faith was the scarlet cord she hung from her window over the wall of Jericho. Verses 17-20 record how the two spies promised her safety if she would display that cord in her window. They vowed that everyone in the house would survive if the red cord were in place. Rahab's faith invited their saving work. Verse 21 says she replied, "'Agreed. . . . Let it be as you say.' So she sent them away and they departed. And she tied the scarlet cord in the window."

Recent scholarship has suggested that the scarlet rope may have been the mark of a prostitute and that Rahab lived, so to speak, in the "red rope" district. It is also noted that since the Hebrew word for "rope" is the same word for "hope" — and most often means "hope" — there may be an intentional pun here: the "rope" is the prostitute's "hope" for customers! But now that Rahab has confessed Jehovah as God, her scarlet "rope" signified a new kind of "hope" — that of deliverance by God.[6]

Be that as it may, the scarlet cord tells us that Rahab's faith, though incipient and uninformed, was *completely trusting*. If the Israelites failed to return and conquer the city, she would soon be found out. The gathering of her family into her home would be interpreted for what it was, someone would talk, and she and her kind would go down to their graves in terrible agony. But Rahab completely believed that judgment was coming and that salvation awaited her. So she let down the scarlet cord in profound trust.

Here, a word about the scarlet cord is in order. Too much has been made of it typologically, as the history of interpretation reveals. Some of the church fathers, such as Clement of Rome, thought the red cord was a symbol of the blood of Christ and that Rahab was a symbol of the Church because through it she obtained safety for her family.[7]

This type of allegorization is still quite popular. A member of my family recalls listening to a flannelgraph story in which the spies were depicted as escaping down the red cord! Following this, the teacher stretched out a red cord as a symbol, not only of the blood, but of the bloodline of Christ.

Having said this, I would like to suggest there is a direct connection with the Passover, which had occurred forty years earlier. Then, you will remember, the Israelites were commanded to gather all their family into the house (just as Rahab did) and paint lamb's blood around the door, so that when the death angel came and saw the blood, all inside would be spared (Exodus 12:21-23). What happened with Rahab parallels this closely, and it seems likely that the spies (though not Rahab) were quite aware of the symbolism. In both cases the red upon the door or the window evidenced the faith of those inside. Francis Schaeffer explains further: "When the children of Israel were about to leave Egypt, they were given the blood of the Passover Lamb under which to be safe. When the people were about to enter the land, they were met by a different, but parallel sign — a red cord hanging from the window of a believer."[8]

What great trust flowed from Rahab's faith. Rahab's sequestering of her family and patiently awaiting the outcome showed her trust. She stood alone against the whole of her culture, something few of us in our contemporary culture have had to do. She, like Moses before, saw the unseen when no one else did (cf. 11:27). Oh, did she believe!

Faith's Work

The Apostle James, in the second chapter of his letter, tells us that true faith produces works, and he gives two examples — first Abraham and then Rahab. He presents them as parallels. Of Abraham he says, "Was not our ancestor Abraham considered righteous for what he did when he offered his son Isaac on the altar?" (2:21). Of Rahab he then says, "In the same way, was not even Rahab the prostitute considered righteous for what she did when she gave lodging to the spies and sent them off in a different direction?" (2:25).

James's point in these two examples is the same. Abraham demonstrated his faith at great cost. He willingly offered up his own son. Rahab's faith was likewise costly. She risked everything. Faith is not a barren intellectual process. True faith issues in action — even when it costs! Is our faith real? Can it be seen in our actions? Are we willing to let it cost us something? We can, and will, if it is real. Rahab's faith was salted with sin. She did not understand everything. But she trusted God — and her faith worked as she sent out the spies and lowered the scarlet cord. True faith works!

FAITH'S FORMATION

We wonder at such great faith, and we wonder where Rahab got it. Abraham Kuyper, the great Biblical scholar who delivered one of the most brilliant of the Stone Lectures at Princeton, and who also served as Prime Minister of the Netherlands from 1901-1905, explains:

> The people who in Rahab's time most frequently used such houses of prostitution were the traveling merchants. From them she had repeatedly heard of the marvelous nation which was approaching from Egypt, and of the God of Israel who had perfected such striking miracles.[9]

Rahab heard that there was only one God, Jehovah. She heard bits and snatches about Israel's destiny. She heard, perhaps derisively, of the nation's high ethical and moral code. Perhaps she had become disillusioned with the culture around her. She was treated as chattel. She had seen life at its worst. All of this together made her open to truth and faith. No doubt, fear contributed to the formation of her faith. Fear is an inevitable and natural consequence of sensing that God's justice leaves us in the wrong. Rahab knew she was a sinner. She was ready for faith. The testimony of the spies opened her to faith. Rahab would immediately have sensed the difference between the Israelite visitors and the clients who normally frequented her house. The spies were not sensualists but holy men of impeccable morals. She had never seen this before. They were sure of their God. Their ethos confirmed the reality of what she had been hearing from the merchants. She was spiritually enticed.

These inner workings coalesced with her disillusionment and fear to produce faith. Rahab's speech in Joshua 2:9-11 is a grand song of belief in the one God:

I know the Lord has given this land to you and that a great fear of
you has fallen on us, so that all who live in this country are melting
in fear because of you. We have heard how the Lord dried up the
water of the Red Sea for you when you came out of Egypt, and what
you did to Sihon and Og, the two kings of the Amorites east of the
Jordan, whom you completely destroyed. When we heard of it, our
hearts melted and everyone's courage failed because of you, for the
Lord your God is God in heaven above and on the earth below.

Jericho had stood for hundreds of years. Today it is still the earliest fortified town known to scholarship.[10] Its inhabitants thought it invincible. But
Rahab heard God's word, and though she was encased by her ancient pagan
culture, which appeared to be eternal, she believed! That is why her faith has
been immortalized. "By faith the prostitute Rahab, because she welcomed
the spies, was not killed with those who were disobedient."

Truly, we can never tell where faith will be found. And Rahab's example tells us there is hope for people where we would never dream of it. When
Jesus came, he said to the Pharisees, "I tell you the truth, the tax collectors
and the prostitutes are entering the kingdom of God ahead of you. For John
came to you to show you the way of righteousness, and you did not believe
him, but the tax collectors and the prostitutes did" (Matthew 21:31, 32).

There is no one who is too bad or too ignorant to be saved! Some are
not only doing drugs but dealing them — dealing death to others. Some have
prostituted their sexuality — doing anything with anyone. But anyone can
come to faith, like Rahab in her bordello, and be saved. Rahab's story means
there is hope for all us sinners with our incipient, imperfect, stumbling, self-
ish faith. This ought to cause us to shout for joy!

FAITH'S REWARD

Rahab's faith garnered three rewards.

Encouragement

First, Israel was encouraged — "Then the two men started back. They went
down out of the hills, forded the river and came to Joshua son of Nun and
told him everything that had happened to them. They said to Joshua, 'The
Lord has surely given the whole land into our hands; all the people are melting in fear because of us'" (2:23, 24). The children of Israel were encouraged through Rahab's great confession of faith (Joshua 2:9-11). They were
uplifted by the positive report that the spies brought back, and they were
strengthened by the miraculous deliverance given to the two spies through
the prostitute.

Salvation

The second reward of Rahab's faith was her own salvation. This came initially as physical salvation, as 6:22-25 records:

> Joshua said to the two men who had spied out the land, "Go into the prostitute's house and bring her out and all who belong to her, in accordance with your oath to her." So the young men who had done the spying went in and brought out Rahab, her father and mother and brothers and all who belonged to her. They brought out her entire family and put them in a place outside the camp of Israel. Then they burned the whole city and everything in it, but they put the silver and gold and the articles of bronze and iron into the treasury of the Lord's house. But Joshua spared Rahab the prostitute, with her family and all who belonged to her, because she hid the men Joshua had sent as spies to Jericho.

Rahab did not initially have saving faith in the spiritual sense, but as she joined with Israel she completely believed and became a full member of God's covenant people. Ultimately, Rahab's faith saved her in every way.

Glorification

The third reward of Rahab's faith may be spoken of as her "glorification." Here her story becomes lyrical — an "impossible dream." Not only did Rahab live in Israel the rest of her life, but she married an Israelite and became an ancestor of Jesus Christ. Matthew's genealogy of Jesus bears out the incredible truth: ". . . and to Ram was born Amminadab; and to Amminadab, Nahshon; and to Nahshon, Salmon; and to Salmon was born Boaz by Rahab; and to Boaz was born Obed by Ruth; and to Obed, Jesse; and to Jesse was born David the king" (Matthew 1:4-6, NASB). And Christ came from David's lineage!

Nahshon, Rahab's father-in-law, was one of the twelve princes who made a special offering at the raising of the Tabernacle. Numbers 7:12 (NASB) says, "Now the one who presented his offerings on the first day was Nahshon . . . of the tribe of Judah." Nahshon was a great prince of Judah, and so was his son Salmon, who married Rahab.

How unutterably beautiful! The Amorite prostitute became a believer and then the wife of a prince of Judah. Rahab was a princess and ancestor of Christ!

Predictably, but nevertheless amazing, some have been uncomfortable with Rahab's being in the genealogy of Christ. Josephus tried to make her out to be an "innkeeper" (*Ant.* V. 1:2, 7), and some have referred to her as a "landlady" or "formerly a fallen woman." As we have seen, she was a *pornee* and nothing else. I think it is wonderful that she belongs to Christ's blood-line. In fact, it fits perfectly, for the whole human race is guilty of spiritual prostitution! Furthermore, all of us have had our lapses. Jesus did not come from a sinless human line. Every person in it was a sinner in need of salvation, including Rahab and the Virgin Mary!

Anyone who looks down on Rahab had better beware, for it is obvious that such a person has a defective doctrine of sin and does not understand the depth of human iniquity or heights of the grace of God. All of us stand in Rahab's place in front of a holy God. And many of us are worse, because she had such little knowledge. We must at least be as wise as Rahab, who though she understood little did understand that she was under God's judgment and sought redemption.

Hebrews 11:31 cites Rahab as an example of one who was saved by faith. James 2:25 says she was saved by works. There is no contradiction, for Rahab was saved by a faith that produced works. There is eternal wisdom for us here in Rahab's faith — especially from the enlightening angles from which we have considered it.

CONCLUSIONS

Faith comes to us in response to God's Word — "faith comes from hearing the message" (Romans 10:17). On this point, we have incredible advantage over Rahab. We have the whole Bible, not just a fragmentary story from the lips of traveling merchants. And the message we hear is not just of judgment but of love and salvation — "For God so loved the world that he gave his one and only Son, that whoever believes in him shall not perish but have eternal life. For God did not send his Son into the world to condemn the world, but to save the world through him" (John 3:16, 17).

Also unlike Rahab, we are surrounded by people of faith who have trusted Christ and can lead us in the way everlasting. There are people who will pray for us, counsel us, even give of their resources to help us grow in faith. The quality of their lives alone draws us upward. Our advantages in forming faith are huge.

Further, God does not expect perfection from us. He knows how weak we are. He forbears with us. But he does expect us to act on our faith — even if it is one step at a time — even if it is a stumbling faith. He expects us to hang the scarlet cord in our windows, announcing our faith in this dark world, and to trust him alone for our salvation. He expects a faith that works.

Regarding reward, I would mention only this: we become not only beneficiaries of Christ's atoning blood, but part of his bloodline as members of his mystical body — we are "in Christ" (a term used no less than 168 times in the New Testament). He calls us brothers and sisters and himself our "elder brother" (cf. 2:11). We have been made royalty and will reign with him forever and forever!

And what more shall I say? I do not have time to tell about Gideon, Barak, Samson, Jephthah, David, Samuel and the prophets, who through faith conquered kingdoms, administered justice, and gained what was promised; who shut the mouths of lions, quenched the fury of the flames, and escaped the edge of the sword; whose weakness was turned to strength; and who became powerful in battle and routed foreign armies. Women received back their dead, raised to life again. Others were tortured and refused to be released, so that they might gain a better resurrection. Some faced jeers and flogging, while still others were chained and put in prison. They were stoned; they were sawed in two; they were put to death by the sword. They went about in sheepskins and goatskins, destitute, persecuted and mistreated — the world was not worthy of them. They wandered in deserts and mountains, and in caves and holes in the ground. These were all commended for their faith, yet none of them received what had been promised. God had planned something better for us so that only together with us would they be made perfect. (11:32-40)

14

Triumphant Faith

HEBREWS 11:32-40

As we now come to the end of the Hall of Faith, we see that it has been a consistent exposition of what faith is, as was defined in the opening verse of chapter 11: "Now faith is being sure of what we hope for and certain of what we do not see." Therefore, faith is a *dynamic certainty* made up of two certitudes: a *future certitude* that makes one sure of the future as if it were present, and a *visual certitude* that brings the invisible within view. One hears God's Word and so believes it that its future fulfillment becomes subjectively present and visible to the spiritual eye.

This grand certainty characterized each of the sixteen heroes thus far presented and was the ground of their triumphs. By faith the heroes of old were enabled to live so as to deserve the testimony that they were "righteous" (v. 4), that they "pleased God" (v. 5), and that they were people of whom God was "not ashamed" (v. 16). And all of them experienced triumphs over great difficulties.

This chapter was composed by the preacher/writer with the hope of steeling the tiny, expatriate Hebrew church against the persecution that was mounting against them and was soon to fall in the genocidal waves of horror orchestrated by the mad emperor Nero. And, indeed, those who did persevere did so because of their profound faith in the promises of God's Word. So we must understand that Hebrews 11 was not just an entertaining and inspiring aside, but was essential life-and-death teaching for the Hebrew church. It may well be the same for us and our children.

Recent history has again reminded us that no dictatorship or democracy is eternal. Freedom, and especially religious freedom, is fragile. Moreover, dark forces are at work in our culture to the extent that it has become politically correct to call "evil good and good evil" (Isaiah 5:20). A case in point is homosexual "marriages" and "families," ideas which received extensive uncritical positive coverage in the *Chicago Tribune* in a recent article entitled *"The Gay Baby Boom."*[1] It is also a matter of record that the New York City schools include in the teachers' resource books for first-graders (the "see Jane go to school, see Jane read" level) that approvingly portray homosexual "marriages" and "families" ("Meet Johnny's parents, Dave and Lance").

To the purveyors of this approved cultural agenda, Judeo-Christian morality is reactionary. And if any of us think that being reactionary is a safe thing, consider what the social engineers have done to reactionaries in the twentieth century. There is only one unforgivable sin in the eyes of the popular moral pundits, and that is intolerance. "The one thing we will not tolerate is intolerance. It is un-American. In fact, it is un-Christian," goes the specious logic. But Jesus was intolerant — and his followers must humbly follow his loving example. It is more than possible — it is highly probable — that the church, once pampered, may become the church persecuted.

Is everything, then, hopeless? No, not at all. A church that lives in the *dynamic certitude* that comes from believing God's Word can have a profound effect on culture — as salt and as light. So the church that is sure of God and sure of his Word will foster great hope. But even if culture proceeds down its neo-pagan path, even if it becomes Neronian in its treatment of the church, there remains substantial hope for those who possess Hebrews 11 faith — for they will be empowered to persevere and will sometimes experience astounding victories.

The preacher concludes chapter 11 with a dazzling rush of encouragement as he quickly describes the empowerment that comes through faith to believers who are either winners or even apparent losers in this life.

EMPOWERED FOR TRIUMPH (vv. 32-35a)

The Empowered

The writer begins by listing half a dozen obvious winners who were empowered for victory: "And what more shall I say? I do not have time to tell about Gideon, Barak, Samson, Jephthah, David, Samuel and the prophets" (v. 32).

At God's direction *Gideon* underwent a remarkable divestment of power in preparation for his phenomenal victory over the Midianites. Obediently he reduced his troops from 32,000 to 10,000 to 300. Then the

300, armed with trumpets and pitchers that concealed torches, routed the Midianites whose "camels could no more be counted than the sand on the seashore" (Judges 7:12). Gideon's feat was a stupendous act of faith.

Likewise, *Barak*, obeying God's word as given through Deborah, sallied forth to meet the great army of Sisera with its 900 chariots of iron and myriads of troops, Barak himself having only 10,000 men drawn from just two of Israel's tribes, Naphtali and Zebulun (Judges 4:6). But his token army was victorious. Once again faith carried the day.

Normally, we do not think of *Samson* as a man of faith, but rather a great dunce whose moral brain waves had gone flat! But there was a subterranean substance of faith in Samson. He knew God had given him power to deliver his people from the Philistines — though he frittered it away. But once blinded, he regained his spiritual perspective, and in a great act of faith he prayed and received strength to avenge himself (Judges 16:25-30).

Neither would we imagine *Jephthah* as a man of faith because of his infamous and foolish vow to sacrifice his own daughter (Judges 11:30-39). Nevertheless, this illegitimate son, this outcast Hebrew Robin Hood, was called back to save Israel — which he did through his faith in God. He conquered because of his faith — notwithstanding that his raw uninformed faith tragically was perverted so that it became the source of his rash and wrongful vow to sacrifice "whatever comes out of the door of my house to meet me" (Judges 11:31).

King *David*, on the other hand, is well-known for his acts of faith, not the least of which was his challenge and defeat of Goliath, to whom he cried, "It is not by sword or spear that the Lord saves; for the battle is the Lord's, and he will give all of you into our hands" (1 Samuel 17:47). Towering faith!

The prophet *Samuel* had lived a life of faith since he was a little "boy wearing a linen ephod" (1 Samuel 2:18), serving Eli in the house of the Lord. Through faith he fearlessly delivered God's word to anyone anywhere at anytime — even the sinning King Saul (1 Samuel 15:22, 23). This faithful proclamation was the hallmark of all true prophets.

Viewed together, this dynamic half-dozen bore remarkable similarities to one another. Each lived in a time when faith was scarce — definitely the minority position. During the days of the judges, everyone did "what was right in his own eyes" (Judges 21:25, RSV), and this ethic was very much alive during the transfer to the monarchy. From Gideon to David, each battled overwhelming odds — Gideon with his 300 against an innumerable host — young David against the giant. Each stood alone *contra mundum*. And most significantly, perhaps, each of these heroes had a flawed faith. John Calvin remarked:

> There was none of them whose faith did not falter. Gideon was slower than he need have been to take up arms, and it was only with

difficulty that he ventured to commit himself to God. Barak hesitated at the beginning so that he had almost to be compelled by the reproaches of Deborah. Samson was the victim of the enticements of his mistress and thoughtlessly betrayed the safety of himself and of all his people. Jephthah rushed headlong into making a foolish vow and was over-obstinate in performing it, and thereby marred a fine victory by the cruel death of his daughter.

And to this we could add that David was sensuous (2 Samuel 11:1ff.), and Samuel lapsed into carelessness in domestic matters (1 Samuel 8:1ff.). Calvin concludes:

> In every saint there is always to be found something reprehensible. Nevertheless although faith may be imperfect and incomplete it does not cease to be approved by God. There is no reason, therefore, why the fault from which we labour should break us or discourage us provided we go on by faith in the race of our calling.[2]

How encouraging! There is hope for every man, woman and child of us. Faith's empowerment is not beyond any of us. As believers we have untapped faith capacities that will surprise not only others but, most of all, ourselves. We each possess interior spiritual nitroglycerin that faith can detonate.

The Empowerments

To further strengthen his argument regarding the power that faith brings to life, the preacher lifts his focus from the empowered to the empowerments that they and others experienced. He lists nine empowerments grouped in three successive groups of three.[3]

The first three give the broad *empowerments* of authentic faith: "who through faith conquered kingdoms, administered justice, and gained what was promised" (v. 33a). This was not only the corporate experience of the half-dozen, but the general experience of the preceding sixteen members of the Hall of Faith.

The second trio lists some of the forms of personal *deliverances* that they experienced: "who shut the mouths of lions, quenched the fury of flames, and escaped the edge of the sword" (vv. 33b, 34a). Samson, David and Beniah all shut the mouths of lions through physical force. Samson, barehanded, took a charging lion by the jaws and ripped it apart. David grabbed a sheep-stealing lion by the beard and thrust it through. Beniah descended into a pit on a snowy day and dispatched another king of the beasts. But Daniel is the preeminent example, through his faith and prayer (Daniel 6:17-22). Shadrach, Meshach and Abednego trusted God, and thus coolly conversed in a blazing furnace while the awe-struck king looked on (Daniel 3:24-27). King David, as well as the prophets Elijah and Elisha, escaped the sword, as did many others (1 Samuel 18:10, 11; 1 Kings 19:8-10; 2 Kings 6:31, 32; Psalm 144:10).

The third triad tells about the astounding *power* that came by faith: "whose weakness was turned to strength; and who became powerful in battle and routed foreign armies. Women received back their dead, raised to life again" (vv. 34b, 35a). Elijah stretched himself out three times on the dead form of the son of the widow of Zarephath and cried to God for his life — and then carried the child alive down to his distraught mother (1 Kings 17:17-24). Elisha, his understudy, accomplished a similar feat for the Shunammite woman's son — "mouth to mouth, eyes to eyes, hands to hands . . . the boy's body grew warm" (2 Kings 4:34).

Three triads — nine empowerments — what power comes through faith! This was important to know and believe under the darkening skies of Nero's impending pogrom. The examples of the empowered six and the litany of the triads of empowerments that have come to the church ought to make one thing very clear: God delights to effect mighty triumphs through people of faith. Faith pleases God — and faith empowers.

God can deliver the faithful anytime he wants from anything! Noah's family was delivered from a flood that drowned all the rest of the human race. Moses and Israel walked through the Red Sea. Joshua and Israel crossed the flooded Jordan. Rahab survived the fallen walls. Gideon prevailed while outmanned a thousand to one. God can deliver us triumphantly from anything if he so pleases — sickness, professional injustice, domestic woe, the growing oppression of a neo-pagan culture — *whatever!* And he will do it again and again and again. But remember, it is always "by faith" in his Word.

But the parallel truth is, God has not promised wholesale deliverance *in this life* for his people at all times and in every situation. Not all of us will be "winners" in this life. From the world's point of view some people of faith are huge "losers."

EMPOWERED FOR PERSEVERANCE (vv. 35b-39)

Now to balance the record, the writer changes the emphasis by showing that faith also provides a different empowerment — the power to persevere to the end.

Perseverance in Persecution

The switch comes abruptly in the middle of verse 35 and on through 36 where the writer describes the power to persevere in persecution: "Others were tortured and refused to be released, so that they might gain a better resurrection. Some faced jeers and flogging, while still others were chained and put in prison." The apparent reference here is to the Maccabean persecution because the word for "tortured" has etymological reference to the *tympanum*, a large drum or wheel on which Maccabean victims were stretched and beaten or even dismembered. Second Maccabees details the gruesome torture of a ninety-year-old priest, Eleazar, who refused to eat swine's flesh (6:18-31), and then goes on to recount the even more revolting accounts of the systematic torture of seven brothers for the same reason (7:1-42).

Each of them could have been released if they had compromised, but each categorically refused — the reason being, as our text explains, "so that they might gain a better resurrection" (v. 35b). Better? How can one resurrection be "better" than another? Is one slow and another like a rocket launching? What is meant here? It is a "better resurrection" because it is a resurrection not just back to life on this earth, as happened to women's sons mentioned in verse 34, but a resurrection to everlasting life in the world to come.

Significantly, the Maccabean accounts of the torture of the seven brothers carry the words of heroic encouragement by their mother based on her hope of the resurrection:

> I do not know how you came into being in my womb. It was not I who gave you life and breath, nor I who set in order the elements within each of you. Therefore the Creator of the world, who shaped the beginning of man and devised the origin of all things, will in his mercy give life and breath back to you again, since you now forget yourselves for the sake of his laws. (2 Maccabees 7:22, 23)

The point of these macabre examples is that through faith God's children can experience triumphant perseverance — even preferring torture to compromise and release.

Perseverance to Death

The preacher moves on to explicitly remind his little church that some of the faithful persevered even to death: "They were stoned; they were sawed in two; they were put to death by the sword" (v. 37a). Since stones are plentiful in Palestine, they were often the murderous weapons of choice against the prophets. Jesus mourned this fact, crying out: "O Jerusalem, Jerusalem, you who kill the prophets and stone those sent to you, how often I have longed to gather your children together" (Matthew 23:37).

As to being sawed asunder, there is no record of this happening to a martyr in the Bible. However, the writer here draws on a non-Biblical *haggadah* in *Ascension of Isaiah*, which asserts that the prophet Isaiah was sawn in two by the false prophets of Manasseh, who stood by "laughing and rejoicing," and that "he neither cried aloud nor wept, but his lips spake with the Holy Spirit until he was sawn in twain" (5:1, 2, 14).[4]

And, of course, untold numbers of the faithful were devoured in a more conventional manner by the sword. So we see that although some "escaped the edge of the sword" through faith (v. 34), others, equally faithful, suffered its pain. But through faith they persevered to death whether stoned or sawed or stabbed. What power!

Perseverance in Deprivation

Lastly, there were those of the faithful who knew deprivation: "They went about in sheepskins and goatskins, destitute, persecuted and mistreated — the world was not worthy of them. They wandered in deserts and mountains, and in caves and holes in the ground" (vv. 37b, 38). The calculated irony here is that the world has rejected such people, and yet the world does not deserve to have them even if it were to accept them.

So much for the prosperity gospel! Here are saints who are so holy and so full of faith that the world is not worthy to contain them, and yet they are called to persevere in persecution, deprivation, and death. Not only that, but the reason they are able to persevere *is* their great faith! Christians under the oppressive old paganism of Roman culture were to take note, and so must we in the darkening neo-paganism of our day.

Now, what was the result for those who were faithful in persecution, deprivation, and death? Beautifully, it was and is the same as for those who experienced great public triumphs in their lives (the Noahs and Moseses and Gideons).

First, they "were all commended for their faith" (v. 39a). This is the way the chapter began — "Now faith is being sure of what we hope for and certain of what we do not see. This is what the ancients were commended for" (vv. 1, 2) — and this is how it ends. All the faithful (the known and unknown, the famously triumphant and those who anonymously persevered in suffering) were "commended for their faith." God forgets no one who loves and serves him! It is his great pleasure to commend faith!

The second result is that "none" — that is, none of the great triumphant members of the Hall of Faith or those who persevered without earthly triumphs — "none of them received what had been promised" (v. 39b). Although many promises had been given and fulfilled in their lifetimes, they did not receive the great promise — namely, the coming of the Messiah and salvation in him. Every one of the faithful in Old Testament times died before Jesus appeared. They entered Heaven with the promise unfulfilled.[5]

Why is this? The answer is given in our final verse: "God had planned something better for us so that only together with us would they be made perfect" (v. 40). No one was "made perfect" under the Old Covenant, because Christ had not yet died. They were saved, but not until Jesus' work on the cross was complete could salvation be perfect. Their salvation looked ahead to what Christ would do. Ours looks back to what he has done — and ours is perfect.

The surpassing excellence of this is that the faithful of all the ages would not be made perfect apart from Christians. As Leon Morris says:

> Salvation is social. It concerns the whole people of God. We can experience it only as part of the whole people of God. As long as the believers in Old Testament times were without those who are in Christ, it was impossible for them to experience the fullness of salvation. Furthermore, it is what Christ has done that opens the way into the very presence of God for them as for us. Only the work of Christ brings those of Old Testament times and those of the new and living way alike into the presence of God.[6]

All the faithful of all the ages are made perfect in Christ. We are all in it together — from Abel to Rahab — from Paul to Billy Graham.

And the message to the embattled little church, and to us, is: *how great our advantage!* Right here, while we walk on earth, we have the perfection of Christ. And it is so much better under the New Covenant. We now have a high priest who has offered a perfect sacrifice for our sins once and for all. Our Savior/priest sits at the right hand of the Father and prays for us. We have, then, a better hope!

How much easier it is for us to walk in faith — even if the walk is down the shadowy roads of neo-pagan culture. We are called to a *dynamic certainty* on the basis of God's Word. It is a *future certainty* that makes the future as if it were present. It is a *visual certainty* that brings the invisible into view.

This is survival truth! We must not succumb to the delusion that gentle rain and sunshine will continue to fall on the church in America as the culture sinks further into neo-paganism. What foolishness! How ahistorical. What ego! What hubris to imagine that the church will sail untouched through the bloody seas.

Those who have ears, let them hear God's steeling Word through the saints of old!

Therefore, since we are surrounded by such a great cloud of witnesses, let us throw off everything that hinders and the sin that so easily entangles, and let us run with perseverance the race marked out for us. Let us fix our eyes on Jesus, the author and perfecter of our faith, who for the joy set before him endured the cross, scorning its shame, and sat down at the right hand of the throne of God. Consider him who endured such opposition from sinful men, so that you will not grow weary and lose heart. (12:1-3)

15

Consider Him

HEBREWS 12:1-3

On a Sunday morning during my first year as pastor of College Church (in Wheaton, Illinois), as I stood in the pastors' room before the first service going over the notes of a sermon I was not very confident about, the chief elder burst into the room, flushed with enthusiasm. "Pastor, I have the most wonderful thing to tell you — Alan Redpath is in the congregation this morning, sitting there with Stephen Olford!" Both men are famous British preachers who had pastored here in America — Dr. Redpath at Moody Church in Chicago and Dr. Olford at Calvary Baptist in New York City. Both these men had been held up as paragons of pulpit excellence in my seminary homiletics classes. I responded disingenuously with something like, "Oh, that's . . . wonderful" — and then began to pore even more nervously over my notes.

Now, I always prepare as thoroughly as possible and have always tried to do my best regardless of the situation; but I do remember consciously crossing and dotting my homiletical "t's" and "i's" that morning — though it is to be feared that my sermon was eminently forgettable! But my point is, the presence of notable witnesses is motivating, whatever one's activity may happen to be.

On an earlier occasion during my seminary years, when I was working a swing-shift in a factory in Los Angeles, I made the acquaintance of a law student who played tennis, and Larry King and I talked a lot of tennis during breaks. Soon we began to exchange a little tennis "trash" about who was the best, which after some weeks eventuated into a casual "we'll find out" tennis match. And the game was fairly casual until Larry's wife, Billy Jean King, showed up and began to do a little of her own talking. She was not impressed. Predictably, our shots became crisper, and we began to sweat more — all, of course, with a conscious male "who cares!" casualness! Wimbledon champion Billy Jean's presence definitely elevated the game.

Golfers, think what would happen to your concentration if Arnold Palmer joined your foursome! Or imagine the adrenaline if while shooting some hoops, Michael Jordan appeared saying, "Mind if I join you?" Every ounce of "wanna be" in our mortal bodies would suddenly be on the court! The presence of the pros, the Hall of Famers, is innately elevating.

On a far more exalted level the truth also obtains, for the author of Hebrews paints an awesome picture of one's spiritual observers in an attempt to motivate and instruct his faltering little church to persevere.

The scene is a great coliseum. The occasion is a footrace, a distance event. The contestants include the author and the members of his flock and, by mutual faith, *us*. The cloud of witnesses that fills the stadium are the great spiritual athletes of the past, Hall of Faith members — every one a Gold Medal winner. They are *not* live witnesses of the event, but "witnesses" by the fact that their past lives bear witness to monumental, persevering faith that, like Abel's faith, "still speaks, even though he is dead" (11:4).[1]

Everywhere one looks in the vast arena, there is a kind face nodding encouragement, saying, "I did it, and so can you. You can do it. You have my life for it!" Moses strokes his long beard and smiles. Rahab winks and gives a royal wave.

Your heart is roundly pumping. You are afraid. And with all your being you want to do well. What to do? Our text eloquently answers with a challenge that can be summarized in four succeeding imperatives.

DIVEST! (v. 1a)

The call to divestment is clearly spelled out in the opening line: "Therefore, since we are surrounded by such a great cloud of witnesses, let us throw off everything that hinders and the sin that so easily entangles" (v. 1a). The divestment here, the throwing off of everything, has reference to the radical stripping off of one's clothing before a race, as in the Greek custom of the day. And the writer orders a double divestment — first, of all hindrances, and second, of sin.

Divest Sin

The sin that we are especially commanded to cast off is described as "the sin that so easily entangles," which is an apt description of what sin repeatedly does. A phenomenon of nature, repeated billions of times, provides an ongoing allegory of sin's billion-fold pathology. Perhaps you have seen it yourself while lying on the grass by a sundew plant when a fly lights on one of its leaves to taste one of the glands that grow there.[2] Instantly, three crimson-tipped, finger-like hairs bend over and touch the fly's wings, holding it firm in a sticky grasp. The fly struggles mightily to get free, but the more it struggles, the more hopelessly it is coated with adhesive. Soon the fly relaxes, but to its fly-mind "things could be worse," because it extends its tongue and feasts on the sundew's sweetness while it is held even more firmly by still more sticky tentacles. When the captive is entirely at the plant's mercy, the edges of the leaf fold inward, forming a closed fist. Two hours later the fly is an empty sucked skin, and the hungry fist unfolds its delectable mouth for another easy entanglement. Nature has given us a terrifying allegory.

But the most sobering thing we see here is that "*the sin* which so easily entangles" us refers to the specific sin(s) each of us, individually, is most likely to commit — a "besetting sin" as it is termed in the older translations. We each have characteristic sins that more easily entangle us than others. Some sins that tempt and degrade others hold little appeal for us — and vice versa. Sensuality may be the Achilles' heel for many men, but not all. Another who has gained victory over such sin may regularly down jealousy's deadly nectar, not realizing it is rotting his soul. Dishonesty may never tempt some souls, for guile simply has no appeal to them, but just cross them and you will feel Satan's temper!

What sin is it that so *easily* entangles you or me? Covetousness? Envy? Criticism? Laziness? Hatred? Lust? Unthankfulness? Pride? Whatever sin it is, it must be stripped off and left behind.

Divest Hindrances

Our divestment must go even further as we "throw off everything that hinders" — literally, "the weight that hinders." Not all hindrances or weights are sin, however. In fact, what is a hindrance to you may not be a hindrance in any way to someone else. A hindrance is something, otherwise good, that weighs you down spiritually. It could be a friendship, an association, an event, a place, a habit, a pleasure, an entertainment, an honor. But if this otherwise good thing drags you down, you must strip it away. For example, there may be an ostensibly harmless place (a forest, a store, an apartment, a city) that, because of your past sins, still lures you downward. Such a place must be tossed aside and forgotten.

This image is extreme. If we are to finish well in faith, we must strip our souls naked of "everything that hinders and the sin that so easily entangles" us. The benevolent knowing faces of the witnesses beckon us to do so. We will never run well without doing this. What is called for here, I believe, is a conscious, systematic divestment of all sins and hindrances — a divestment that is regularly performed. Remember, all it takes is *one* sin or *one* hindrance to sabotage the runner's soul!

RUN! (v. 1b)

Properly divested, there remains one great thing to do — and that is run: "and let us run with perseverance the race marked out for us" (v. 1b).

Run the Course

We each have a specific course mapped out for us, and the course for each runner is unique. Some are relatively straight, some are all turns, some seem all uphill, some are a flat hiking path. All are long, but some are longer. But the glory is, each of us (no exceptions!) can finish the race "marked out for us." I may not be able to run your course, and you may find mine impossible, but I can finish my race and you yours. Both of us can finish well if we choose and if we rely on him who is our strength and our guide!

We can experience the same satisfaction the Apostle Paul did as he neared the finish line:

> I have fought the good fight, I have finished the race, I have kept the faith. Now there is in store for me the crown of righteousness, which the Lord, the righteous Judge, will award to me on that day — and not only to me, but also to all who have longed for his appearing. (2 Timothy 4:7, 8)

Is that not a comforting and inviting thought? There is no doubt that we can finish "the race marked out for us" — and finish it with satisfaction.

Run with Perseverance

The secret is to "run with perseverance." Here the example of Bill Broadhurst is instructive. In 1981 Bill entered the Pepsi Challenge 10,000-meter race in Omaha, Nebraska. Surgery ten years earlier for an aneurysm in the brain had left him paralyzed on his left side. Now, on that misty July morning, he stands with 1,200 lithe men and women at the starting line.

The gun sounds! The crowd surges forward. Bill throws his stiff left leg forward, pivots on it as his foot hits the ground. His slow *plop - plop - plop* rhythm seems to mock him as the pack races into the distance. Sweat rolls down his face, pain pierces his ankle, but he keeps going. Some of the runners complete the race in about thirty minutes, but two hours and twenty-nine minutes later Bill reaches the finish line. A man approaches from a small group of remaining bystanders. Though exhausted, Bill recognizes him from pictures in the newspaper. He is Bill Rodgers, the famous marathon runner, who then drapes his newly won medal around Bill's neck. Bill Broadhurst's finish was as glorious as that of the world's greatest — though he finished last. Why? Because he ran with perseverance.

> That determination, unhasting and unresting, unhurrying and yet undelaying, which goes steadily on, and which refuses to be deflected. Obstacles will not daunt it; delays will not depress it; discouragements will not take its hope away. It will halt neither for discouragement from within nor for opposition from without. (William Barclay).[3]

It is quite within the reach of every one of us to manifest positive, conquering patience — putting one heavy foot in front of the other until we reach the glorious end. The race is not for sprinters who flame out after 100 or 200 or 400 meters. It is for faithful plodders like you and me. Fast or slow, strong or weak — all must persevere.

FOCUS! (v. 2)

Focus on Jesus

Now, stripped bare of any weights or sin and running with perseverance, we are given the focus that will ensure our finishing well — and that is, of course, Jesus: "Let us fix our eyes on Jesus, the author and perfecter of our faith" (v. 2a).

By insisting that we focus on Jesus, instead of the name Christ, the writer is calling us to focus on Jesus' humanity as we saw it here on earth. Jonathan Edwards remarked beautifully concerning this that we are to "take notice of Christ's excellence which is a . . . feast."[4] And so it is! We are to focus on him first as "author" (*archegos* — literally, "pioneer") of our faith. Jesus is the pioneer and author of all faith in both the Old and New Testaments. He initiates all faith and bestows it (cf. Ephesians 2:8-10).

But, still more, he is the "perfecter of our faith." His entire earthly life was the very embodiment of trust in God (2:13). He perfected living by faith. He lived in total dependence upon the Father (10:7-10). It was his absolute faith in God that enabled him to go through the mocking, crucifixion, rejection and desertion — and left him perfect in faith. As F. F. Bruce has said, "Had he come down by some gesture of supernatural power, He would never have been hailed as the 'perfecter of faith' nor would He have left any practical example for others to follow."[5] But the sublime fact is, he endured everything by faith, and thus he is uniquely qualified to be the "author and perfecter" of the faith of his followers.

Do we sense the need of faith to run the race? Then we must "fix our eyes on Jesus, the author and perfecter of our faith." That is, as the Greek suggests, we must deliberately lift our eyes from other distracting things and focus with utter concentration on him — and continue doing so.[6] This is fundamental to a life of faith and finishing the race!

Focus on Jesus' Attitude

Along with this we ought to focus on Jesus' attitude — "who for the joy set before him endured the cross, scorning its shame" (v. 2b). Some people wrongly imagine that because Jesus was a divine man, the physical and spiritual sufferings of the cross were somehow "less" for him. What wrongheaded thinking, as John Henry Newman so brilliantly explained:

> And as men are superior to animals, and are affected by pain more than they, by reason of the mind within them, which gives a substance to pain, . . . so, in like manner, our Lord felt pain of the body, with a consciousness, and therefore with a keenness and intensity, and with a unity of perception, which none of us can possibly fathom or compass, because His soul was so absolutely in His power, so simply free from the influence of distractions, so fully directed *upon* the pain, so utterly surrendered, so simply subjected to the suffering. And thus He may truly be said to have suffered the whole of His passion in every moment of it.[7]

So we must let the full force of the text's statement here in Hebrews — he "endured the cross" — sink into our souls. The *physical* pain he endured was absolute. But the spiritual pain was even greater because his pure soul, which knew no sin, became sin for us, inducing a heretofore unknown pain. And we must also absorb the fact that he "endured the cross, scorning its shame." That is, he thought nothing of its shame — he dismissed it as nothing.

How and why could he do this? Because of "the joy set before him" — which was rooted in his coming super-exaltation when he "sat down at the right hand of the throne of God" (v. 2c). His exaltation, with all that it means for his people's *shalom* and for the triumph of God's purpose in the universe, was "the joy set before him." We can list some specific aspects of his joy. There was the joy of his "reunion," as it were, with the Father. What an exalted thought — Heaven's homecoming! Imagine the joy! David's words suggest the idea: "You will fill me with joy in your presence, with eternal pleasures at your right hand" (Psalm 16:11). Then there was the joy of being crowned with honor and glory and having all things put under his feet (2:6-8; cf. Psalm 8:4-6). There was also the joy before him of bringing many sons to glory — making us part of his joy (2:10).

Our blessed and glorious Lord lived his earthly life in faith's *dynamic certitude.* "Now faith is being sure of what we hope for [*future certitude*] and certain of what we do not see [*visual certitude*]." Our blessed Lord fixed his "eyes not on what is seen, but on what is unseen. For what is seen is temporary, but what is unseen is eternal" (2 Corinthians 4:18) — and thus his joy was the "eternal weight of glory" (2 Corinthians 4:17, NASB).

Now on this matter of focus, understand this: even though the great gallery of past saints witnesses to us, our central focus must be Jesus — *sola Jesu*! Focus on him as the "pioneer" and originator of faith. Focus on him as the divine human "perfecter" of faith. Focus on the joy that enabled him to endure the awesome agony of the cross and dismiss as nothing the shame. Focus on his joyous exaltation — and the fact that you are part of the joy.

CONSIDER! (v. 3)

In capping his famous challenge to finish well, the writer gives the idea of focusing on Jesus a dynamic twist by concluding: "Consider him who endured such opposition from sinful men, so that you will not grow weary and lose heart" (v. 3). The phrase "grow weary and lose heart" was sports lingo in the ancient world for a runner's exhausted collapse.[8] Thus, the way for the Christian runner to avoid such a spiritual collapse was to "consider him" — that is, to carefully calculate (we derive our word *logarithm* from the Greek word translated "consider") Jesus and his endurance of opposition from the likes of Caiaphas, Herod and Pilate. We are to remember his confidence and meekness and steel-like strength in meeting his enemies.

No one can miss the superb wisdom of this passage: we must be totally absorbed with Jesus. This requires negation — turning away from those things that distract us — and then the positive act of consciously focusing and meditating on Jesus. This is why we must read and re-read the Gospels. This is why our worship must be Christocentric. This is why *he* must be the measure of all things.

If we are believers, we are in the race, and we are surrounded by a great cloud of lives whose examples call for our best — the *patriarchs* (Abraham, Isaac and Jacob), the *prophets* (Moses, Elijah, Samuel, Daniel, Jeremiah), the *apostles* (Peter, John, Paul), the *martyrs* (Stephen, Polycarp, Cranmer, Elliott, Saint), the *preachers* (Luther, Calvin, Wesley, Spurgeon), the *missionaries* (Carey, Taylor, Carmichael), our *departed family members*, and on and on. Their faces invite us to finish well.

So the imperatives are before us:

- We must *divest* ourselves of all hindrances and sins. Figuratively speaking, if our foot hinders us, we must chop it off; if our eye causes us to sin, we must gouge it out (cf. Matthew 5:29, 30). We will not finish the race apart from radical divestment.
- We must *run* with patient perseverance the race that is marked

out individually for each of us. We must put one foot in front of the other, refusing to quit — unhasting, unresting, constant.

- We must *focus* on Jesus as "the pioneer and perfecter of our faith." Jesus must cover the entire sky. He must be the center and horizons of our sight. Such vision will insure for us faith's beginning and end.
- We must *consider* him and how he lived amidst contradiction and follow his example.

In your struggle against sin, you have not yet resisted to the point of shedding your blood. And you have forgotten that word of encouragement that addresses you as sons: "My son, do not make light of the Lord's discipline, and do not lose heart when he rebukes you, because the Lord disciplines those he loves, and he punishes everyone he accepts as a son." Endure hardship as discipline; God is treating you as sons. For what son is not disciplined by his father? If you are not disciplined (and everyone undergoes discipline), then you are illegitimate children and not true sons. Moreover, we have all had human fathers who disciplined us and we respected them for it. How much more should we submit to the Father of our spirits and live! Our fathers disciplined us for a little while as they thought best; but God disciplines us for our good, that we may share in his holiness. No discipline seems pleasant at the time, but painful. Later on, however, it produces a harvest of righteousness and peace for those who have been trained by it. (12:4-11)

16

Divine Discipline

On August 7, 1954, during the British Empire Games in Vancouver, Canada, one of the greatest mile-run match-ups ever took place. It was touted as the "miracle mile" because Roger Bannister and John Landy were the only two sub-four-minute milers in the world. Bannister had been the first man ever to run a four-minute mile. Both runners were in peak condition.

Dr. Bannister, who is today Sir Roger and master of an Oxford college, strategized that he would relax during the third lap and save everything for his finishing drive. But as they began the third lap, John Landy poured it on, stretching his already substantial lead. Immediately, Bannister adjusted his strategy, increasing his pace and gaining on Landy. The lead was cut in half, and at the bell for the final lap they were even.

Landy began running even faster, and Bannister followed suit. He felt he was going to lose if Landy did not slow down. Then came the famous moment (replayed thousands of times in print and celluloid) as at the last stride before the home stretch the crowds roared. Landy could not hear Bannister's footfall and thus compulsively looked back — a fatal lapse of concentration. Bannister launched his attack, and Landy did not see him until he lost the lead. Roger Bannister won the "miracle mile" that day by five yards.

Landy's lapse serves as a modern visualization of what the writer of Hebrews implicitly warned against in his earlier charge to "run with endurance the race that is set before us, fixing our eyes on Jesus, the author and perfecter of faith" (Hebrews 12:1, 2, NASB). Those who look away from Christ — the end-goal of our race — will never finish well. And this was exactly what was happening to some treading the stormy waters mounting around the early church. They had begun to take their eyes off Christ and to fix them instead on the hardships challenging them.

When these Hebrew Christians first came to Christ, the Savior filled their lives from horizon to horizon. It was a delightful, joyous fixation. But that initial rush of joy began to be assaulted by hardships. Some of their life-long friendships cooled to estrangement. They were no longer welcome in the synagogue. Some lost their jobs as they were squeezed out of the family business. Others were assaulted by domestic stress, as even husband and wife relationships became strained over the matter of Christ. And to boot, their newfound faith did not shield them from the common vicissitudes of life — they suffered reversals, accidents, illness, and death just like everyone else.

As a result, not a few were distracted. Those increasingly longer looks away from Christ left some off-stride. Others stumbled here and there, and tragically a few had quit altogether. They were, in fact, a microcosm of many in the modern church who have lost their focus through hardship — who say, "It all began so well. But I didn't expect this. I had problems before I became a Christian, but nothing like this. Thanks for the offer of the abundant life, but I've got an abundance of problems already! You go ahead. I think I'll take a breather."

The preacher/writer now attempts to encourage people like these.

GENTLE REPROACH FOR FALTERING ENDURANCE (vv. 4-6)

He begins this section with a pair of gentle reproaches. First, he reminds them that life is not as bad as some may suppose. "In your struggle against sin," he says, "you have not yet resisted to the point of shedding your blood" (v. 4). Jesus, of course, had suffered death because of his decision to stay on track — all the way to the cross. And some of the heroes of the faith so memorably praised at the end of chapter 11 had paid the ultimate price as well. But though the Hebrew church had experienced severe persecution early on, under the Emperor Claudius, no one had yet been martyred. The parallels with the modern church in the West are plain to see. The tides of neo-paganism are rising, but none of us have resisted to the point of spilling blood.

Then, like now, was no time to be discouraged — especially considering the great examples of those who have remained steadfast amidst far greater hardships. "Cut the melodrama," the writer seems to be saying, "I don't see any bodies lying around."

The preacher's other reproach was this: they had failed to recall and reassure themselves with God's Word — "And you have forgotten that word of encouragement that addresses you as sons" (v. 5a). Of course, this is an even more common sin of the modern church — which, the pollsters tell us, cannot name the books of the Bible or locate the Ten Commandments or the Beatitudes, much less tell us what they are. This also brings us to the indisputable axiom, *we cannot be profoundly influenced (or encouraged) by that which we do not know.* The comfort and strength of God's Word will avail us not at all if we do not *know* it. Many today do not know enough of God's Word to survive a skinned knee! Knowing God's Word is essential for spiritual survival, as the preacher earlier insisted in his letter: "We must pay more careful attention, therefore, to what we have heard, so that we do not drift away" (2:1).

Having reproached his congregation for forgetting God's Word, the preacher calls for their attention in a special word of encouragement that addressed them specifically as God's children. This is taken from the Greek rendering of Proverbs 3:11, 12. Verse 5 represents verse 11 of Proverbs 3, which clearly warns those undergoing hard times of two opposite pitfalls of *disdain* and *dismay* regarding divine discipline. Regarding the perils of *disdain*, "My son, do not make light of the Lord's discipline" (v. 5b). The fact is, many who experience the unpleasantness of discipline choose to remain indifferent as to its significance. They vaguely intuit that they are experiencing discipline, but refuse to meditate upon what it might mean. They make light of it — they blow it off! It is better not to think too much about one's hardships, they say to themselves, or they might have to do something about them. Better to just ignore them. By refusing to consider their deep waters, their lives remain perpetually shallow.

The other pitfall is *dismay* — "and do not lose heart when he rebukes you" (v. 5c). Far from being indifferent to discipline, there are some who are overwhelmed by it all. They are paralyzed — just as the runners described in verse 3 came to "grow weary and lose heart" and collapsed on the track. Such giving up is inexcusable because none of God's children will ever be tested beyond their strength (cf. 1 Corinthians 10:13).

So we see that when disciplined we must not afford ourselves either the luxury of *disdain* or of *dismay*. Why? Because discipline is the telltale sign of being loved by God and in family relationship to him — "because the Lord disciplines those he loves, and punishes everyone he accepts as a son" (v. 6). In other words, if we cop out in respect to the Lord's discipline either by *disdain* (making light of it) or *dismay* (fainting away), we are turning our back on the personal evidence of his love and relationship to us. Discipline is the divinely ordained path to a deepening relationship with God and a growing love with him. It is the only path! Thus to refuse discipline is to turn our back on growth and love. Therefore we must heed God's words of encouragement to us — especially as they are given in the following verses, which are an elaboration of Proverbs 3:11, 12.

GENTLE CHALLENGE TO SUSTAINED ENDURANCE (v. 7a)

To begin with, the truth of the Proverbs passage elicits a command: "Endure hardship as discipline" (v. 7a). Jesus endured (v. 2), and it is imperative that we endure.

The word "discipline" comes from a root word generally meaning "to teach or instruct as one would a child" (cf. Acts 22:3; 1 Timothy 1:20; Titus 2:12). Often it means "to correct or punish" — as it means here (cf. v. 10; Luke 23:16, 22). Broadly, it signifies much of what we would think of as discipline for the purpose of education. We experience God's education through hardship or affliction.

Significantly, God's discipline of his children never involves his wrath. Every reference in the New Testament on the subject indicates that God's wrath rests upon and is reserved for the unbelieving.[1] God has no such thoughts toward his own — no thoughts of calamity. Theodore Laetsch, the Old Testament scholar, makes a most perceptive comment regarding this:

> His plans concerning his people are always thoughts of good, of blessing. Even if he is obliged to use the rod, it is the rod not of wrath, but the Father's rod of chastisement for their temporal and eternal welfare. There is not a single item of evil in his plans for his people, neither in their motive, nor in their conception, nor in their revelation, nor in their consummation.[2]

So the preacher to the Hebrews, who exhorts his flock to "endure hardship as discipline," is enjoining them to a most positive pursuit that has as its goal the very growth of their souls.

God's discipline takes three distinct forms — namely, corrective discipline, preventative discipline, and educational discipline[3] — though there are surely other distinctives of discipline that extend beyond these classifications.

Corrective Discipline

Sometimes God's children undergo corrective judgment that comes directly from God's love. King David is a prime exhibit here. His adultery and resulting homicide brought down stiff judgment. The son of his illicit union died, and violence attended his home (cf. 2 Samuel 12:10). His son Amnon raped his half-sister Tamar. Absalom murdered Amnon and then, in league with Bathsheba's father Ahithophel, staged a rebellion. This was a stiff corrective, but David did learn from it and grew in grace. Consider Psalm 51, and also the chastened wisdom of Psalm 119:

> Before I was afflicted I went astray
> but now I obey your word. . . .
> It was good for me to be afflicted
> so that I might learn your decrees.
> (Psalm 119:67, 71)

Likewise, in New Testament times the Corinthian church underwent God's corrective discipline when some of its believers suffered illness and even death because they were profaning the Lord's Supper through their greedy, self-centered indulgence and, in some cases, outright drunkenness. Paul explained, "When we are judged by the Lord, we are being disciplined so that we will not be condemned with the world" (1 Corinthians 11:32). Harsh correctives, but they come from a heart of fatherly love.

Preventative Discipline

It is a fact of forestry that very often when small trees are cleared away, some of the big trees will subsequently come down. Why? The smaller trees shielded the larger trees from nature's assaults, and thus the large trees never developed the strength to stand alone. Just so, God regularly allows his children to undergo hardships to prevent their falling.

For example, the Apostle Paul was a humble man. Nevertheless, God gave him a thorn in the flesh to keep him from becoming conceited because of the great revelations God had given him (2 Corinthians 12:7, 8). Paul prayed for it to be removed but later thanked God as he realized how his thorn had protected him.

This same realization enabled D. D. Matheson to pray: "Thou Divine Love, whose human path has been perfected by sufferings, teach me the value of any thorn . . . and then shall I know that my tears have been made a rainbow, and I shall be able to say, 'It was good for me that I have been afflicted.'" Preventative discipline, properly understood, is seen as a substantial grace.

Educational Discipline

A careful reading of the story of Job reveals that his afflictions came not as corrective discipline or preventative discipline, but for his education. This is majestically confirmed by Job's own words at the end of his ordeal: "'Hear, now, and I will speak; I will ask Thee, and you instruct me.' I have heard of Thee by the hearing of the ear; but now my eye sees Thee; therefore I retract, and I repent in dust and ashes" (Job 42:4-6, NASB). Job's afflictions, coupled with his dialogue with God, gave him a stupendous revelation of God far beyond that of his contemporaries. From Job's example we understand that discipline may not come because one is doing poorly, but because he is doing well (cf. Job 1:1)! Job was, in fact, a spiritual athlete. And because of his excellence, God (like a wise coach) brought greater stress and challenge to Job so that he might ascend to undreamed of levels of spirituality.

So we see that all the hardships that come the believer's way are loving discipline and are, in effect, either *corrective* or *preventative* or *educational*. We must remember this! As James Moffatt said, "To endure rightly, one must endure intelligently."[4] If we have an informed, intelligent, Biblical understanding of the afflictions that come our way, and we believe God's Word, we will endure. The *correction* of David, the *prevention* of Paul, the *education* of Job — this is sanctifying grist for the reflective heart.

GENTLE REASONS FOR SUSTAINED ENDURANCE (vv. 7b-11)

From here the writer goes on to provide more reasons for the intelligent embrace of and endurance in affliction.

A Paternal Reason

The primary one is that discipline is a sign of God's paternity — it is evidence that we are his children. "God is treating you as sons," he says, "for what son is not disciplined by his father? If you are not disciplined (and everyone undergoes discipline), then you are illegitimate children and not true sons" (vv. 7b, 8).

John Perkins, the remarkable preacher and social activist, gives a poignant and deeply instructive account in his book *Let Justice Roll Down* of his father's deserting him when he was a boy.

> I knew then that Daddy was going away without me. But I still didn't turn back. So once more he came back and whupped me a last time.
>
> Just then my Auntie came up. She must have missed me and followed after me. I stood there between the two of them, neither one saying anything. Then she took me by the hand and dragged me away, back down the tracks toward home.
>
> I looked back once, but Daddy was already gone. And with him went my newfound joy in belonging, in being loved, in being somebody for just a little while. Years would pass before I would know this joy again.
>
> I cried all the way back to the house, holding tightly to Auntie with one hand and carrying my heart with the other.
>
> What was Daddy really thinking, what was in his mind that day he left me? I never found out. I never ever really had a chance to talk with Jap in the few times I saw him again before he died.
>
> But I do know that, even when he punished me for following him that afternoon, he was admitting we had some sort of *relationship.*[5]

Even in this terribly disordered relationship, a failed father's egregious discipline was a telltale sign of his paternity. The Scriptures affirm this primal impulse: "He who spares the rod hates his son, but he who loves him is careful to discipline him" (Proverbs 13:24). And, "The rod of correction imparts wisdom, but a child left to itself disgraces his mother" (Proverbs 29:15).

The ancient world found it incomprehensible that a father could possibly love his child and not punish him. In fact, a real son would draw more discipline than, say, an illegitimate child for the precise reason that greater honor and responsibility were to be his. The ultimate example of this is, of course, Jesus who as the supreme Son "learned obedience from what he suffered and, once made perfect, he became the source of eternal salvation for all who obey him" (5:8, 9). There is no doubt about it — the hardships and disciplines we endure are signs of our legitimacy and ought to be embraced as telltale signs of grace.

An A Fortiori *Reason*

Another reason we should opt for the intelligent acceptance of enduring hardship as discipline is the *a fortiori* argument from the lesser to the greater: "Moreover, we have all had human fathers who disciplined us and we respected them for it. How much more should we submit to the Father of our spirits and live!" (v. 9). Respect and submission characterized ancients in regard to their *natural* fathers — and it developed a disciplined productive life in the child. But, *a fortiori*, how much more should we submit to our *supernatural* Father and live a life that is life indeed! Submission to the discipline of our *temporal* fathers brought good things, but how much more will come through submission to the discipline of our *eternal* Father. Conscious submission to our divine Father is essential to truly live in the here and now and to have an ever-deepening experience of the abundant life.

Those who live life to the fullest are those who do not buck God's discipline but rather knowingly embrace it. If your spiritual life is static and unfulfilling, it may be because you are consciously or unconsciously resisting God's discipline. If so, God's Word to you is, *submit* to him and begin to truly live!

A Sanctifying Reason

Next, the author argues for our continued endurance of affliction by giving us a sanctifying reason for it: "Our fathers disciplined us for a little while as they thought best; but God disciplines us for our good, that we may share in his holiness" (v. 10). Every earthly father, if he is candid, will admit he has meted out imperfect discipline at best. All fathers have learned by doing. Sometimes we were too severe, other times too lax. Sometimes we showed favoritism. Sometimes we punished the wrong child. Sometimes a child "got it" because the boss had "given it" to us. But God has never made such a mistake. No discipline of his was ever capricious or ill-informed or ill-tempered. None of his discipline has ever been misplaced.

Moreover, all the disciplines of the Heavenly Father have one grand aim, which is nothing less than to make his people like him — holy (cf. Leviticus 19:2; Matthew 5:48; 1 Peter 1:15, 16). In Christ we have been made partakers of the divine nature (2 Peter 1:4), and as partakers, God chastens us so that we will partake even more. The most holy of us are those who have properly endured the most discipline. What a gift, then, discipline is! Jonathan Edwards says of such people:

> They are holy by being made partakers of God's holiness, Heb. xii. 10. The saints are beautiful and blessed by a communication of God's holiness and joy, as the moon and planets are bright by the sun's light. The saint hath spiritual joy and pleasure by a kind of effusion of God on the soul.[6]

What more could we wish in this life?

A Hedonistic Reason

The writer concludes his train of thought by giving a hedonistic, pain/pleasure reason for enduring discipline. First, concerning *pain*: "No discipline seems pleasant at the time, but painful" (v. 11a). That is certainly true whatever the level of discipline — a spanking, a privilege suspended, a possession removed, an injury, an illness, a persecution. Moreover, we would be patently weird if we enjoyed the pain — pious masochists. But eventually there comes the *pleasure*: "Later on, however, it produces a harvest of righteousness and peace for those who have been trained by it" (v. 11b).

Blessed hedonism! A "harvest of righteousness" comes to believers who endure under discipline — not just the objective, imputed righteousness of God (2 Corinthians 5:21), but a subjective, day-to-day righteous life. To the eyes of onlookers the believer's righteous life becomes apparent — as he more and more shows the character of God. But that is just half of the crop, the other half being a "harvest of peace" — *shalom*. As Isaiah wrote, "The fruit of righteousness will be peace; the effect of righteousness will be quietness and confidence forever" (32:17). Peace — *shalom* — means not only quietness of soul but wholeness. As Richard John Neuhaus says: "It means the bringing together of what was separated, the picking up of the pieces, the healing of wounds, the fulfillment of the incomplete, the overcoming of the forces of fragmentation. . . ."[7] It is Heaven's peace experienced now in an unpeaceful world. Some harvest!

This only comes through enduring hardship as discipline. It does not come through fighting the hard things in life, but from accepting them as discipline from God.

Hardships will do one of two things to us. They will *distract* our focus from Christ, forcing us into a spiritual "Landy's lapse" — so that we are slowed down, or even drop out of the race. Or they will *intensify* our focus on Christ, so that we "run with endurance the race that is set before us, fixing our eyes on Jesus the author and perfecter of faith" (Hebrews 12:1, 2, NASB). If we do this, we will neither *despise* the Lord's discipline nor *dismay* and lose heart (cf. v. 3). We will understand that the disciplines we endure are evidences of the love and relationship God has for us (cf. v. 6).

And thus we will do our best to endure, embracing the reasons we ought to endure hardship as discipline.

- We embrace the *paternal reason* because discipline proves that God is our Father and we are his children!
- We embrace the *a fortiori reason* because discipline makes us live life that is life indeed!
- We embrace the *sanctifying reason* because discipline makes us like God — holy!
- We embrace the *hedonistic reason* because though there is pain now, later it produces a double harvest of righteousness and peace!

This is why we keep our eyes on Jesus and keep running!

Therefore, strengthen your feeble arms and weak knees. "Make level paths for your feet," so that the lame may not be disabled, but rather healed. Make every effort to live in peace with all men and to be holy; without holiness no one will see the Lord. See to it that no one misses the grace of God and that no bitter root grows up to cause trouble and defile many. See that no one is sexually immoral, or is godless like Esau, who for a single meal sold his inheritance rights as the oldest son. Afterward, as you know, when he wanted to inherit this blessing, he was rejected. He could bring about no change of mind, though he sought the blessing with tears. (12:12-17)

17

Failing Grace

HEBREWS 12:12-17

Writer and sometimes marathoner Art Carey described in a memorable piece for the *Philadelphia Inquirer* his experience of "hitting the wall" and then going on to finish the Boston Marathon. We pick up his story mid-stride:

By now, the rigors of having run nearly twenty miles are beginning to tell. My stride has shortened. My legs are tight. My breathing is shallow and fast. My joints are becoming raw and worn. My neck aches from all the jolts that have ricocheted up my spine. Half-dollar-size blisters sting the soles of my feet. I'm beginning to feel queasy and light-headed. I want to stop running. I have "hit the wall."

Now the real battle begins. Up the first of many long inclines I start to climb — one-two, one-two, one-two, right-left, right-left, right-left. I keep watching my feet move, one after the other, hypnotized by the rhythm, the passage of the asphalt below . . . shoulder cramps, leaden legs, seething blisters, dry throat, empty stomach, stop — keep moving — must finish. . . . A radio-listening spectator reports that the race is over. Six miles away, Bill Rodgers has won again. His ordeal is done; the most intense of my own is about to begin.

"Heartbreak Hill" — the last, the longest and the steepest, a half-mile struggle against gravity designed to finish off the faint and faltering. Hundreds of people stand along the hill, watching . . . [urging] the walkers to jog, the joggers to run, the runners to speed on to Boston.. . . . Slowly, ever so slowly, the grade begins to level out. . . .

The last four miles are seemingly endless. Some runners, their eyes riveted catatonically to the ground, trudge alone in their bare feet, holding in their hands the shoes that have blistered and bloodied their feet. Others team up to help each other, limping along, arm-in-arm, like maimed and battle-weary soldiers returning from the front.

Finally, the distinctive profile of the Prudential Building looms on the horizon. I begin to step up my pace. Faster, faster . . . smoother, smoother. Suppress the pain. Finish up strong. Careful — not too fast. Don't cramp. . . .

I can see the yellow stripe 50 yards ahead. I run faster, pumping my arms, pushing off my toes, defying clutching leg cramps to mount a glorious, last-gasp kick . . . 40 yards, 30 yards, 20 yards . . . cheers and clapping . . . 10 yards . . . finish line . . . an explosion of euphoria . . . I am clocked in at two hours, 50 minutes and 49 seconds. My place: 1,176. I find the figures difficult to believe, but if they are accurate, then I have run the best marathon of my life.

While times and places are important, and breaking a personal record is thrilling (especially as you grow older), the real joy of the Boston Marathon is just finishing . . . doing what you have set out to do.[1]

According to Holy Scripture, as we have it in Hebrews 12, the marathoner's grit and finishing joy are metaphorical of what we Christians, ancient and modern, are called to in this life. The spiritual life is a long-distance run (vv. 1-3). Though we will "hit the wall" many times, we are called to "tough it out," realizing that the hardships we endure are disciplines that enable us to share in God's holiness (cf. vv. 4-11).

The author's transcending desire is that his flock, and indeed the Church universal, will finish well. So he expounds the metaphor further in verses 12-17 with specific advice on what to do (vv. 12-14) and what to guard against (vv. 15-17) in order to finish well.

FINISHING WELL — WHAT TO DO (vv. 12-14)

Run Tough

The telltale signs of flagging energy are drooping arms, flopping hands, and wobbling knees that reduce the runner's stride to a mincing gait. These signs were proverbial in Biblical culture for mental and spiritual slowdown. Isaiah encouraged his despairing, stumbling people by saying, "Strengthen the feeble hands, steady the knees that give way; say to those with fearful hearts, 'Be strong, do not fear; your God will come'" (35:3, 4). Job was heartened by Eliphaz, the Temanite who reminded him, "Think how . . . you have strengthened feeble hands. Your words have supported those who stumbled; you have strengthened faltering knees" (Job 4:3, 4).

So here the preacher, like an attentive coach, employs the proverbial exhortation, "Therefore, strengthen your feeble arms and weak knees" (v. 12). The command to "strengthen" comes from the word from which we derive our English word *orthopedic*. The sense is, "make upright or straight" — or in modern coaching terms, "Straighten up! Get those hands and feet up! Suck it in!"

Of course, he is not promoting a do-it-yourself, bootstrap Christian life. But Christians must will to tough it out by God's grace. Life for the believer is full of repeated hardships that come as divine discipline. In fact, these disciplines are substantive signs that we are authentic sons and daughters (cf. vv. 7, 8). But they still require grit every bit analogous to the determined marathoners. Muscular Christianity is a must! Run tough!

Run Tough Together

Toughing it out is essential, but there is still more to the idea because this toughness is not meant to be a solo venture. In the next verse the writer alludes to Proverbs 4:25-27 as he calls his people to corporate toughness in helping one another to run well: "'Make level paths for your feet,' so that the lame may not be disabled, but rather healed" (v. 13). Here the NIV translates *orthas*, which normally means "straight," as "level,"[2] but the idea remains clear — to put the paths in better order so as to make the race easier for the lame — "so that the lame may not be disabled" (literally, "put out of joint").[3]

The point is, every consideration should be made to help everyone finish the race. The bloodied, blistered Boston Marathoners teaming up to help each other, limping along arm-in-arm, are a vivid metaphor of this idea. But the church should include not only the weak assisting the weak, but also the strong teaming up with the weak in what Bishop Westcott called "the duty of mutual help."[4]

Hebrews is full of this idea of helping each other make it: "But encourage one another daily, as long as it is called Today, so that none of you may be hardened by sin's deceitfulness" (3:13). "Therefore, since the promise of entering his rest still stands, let us be careful that none of you be found to have fallen short of it" (4:1). "Let us, therefore, make every effort to enter that rest, so that no one will fall by following their example of disobedience" (4:11). "We want each of you to show this same diligence to the very end, in order to make your hope sure" (6:11). "Let us not give up meeting together, as some are in the habit of doing, but let us encourage one another" (10:25).

I believe Art Carey is right in saying, "The real joy of the Boston Marathon is just finishing" — and I am even more sure that the real joy of the race set before us will be in the finishing.

> *When by His grace*
> *I shall look on his face*
> *That will be glory,*
> *Be glory for me.*

But I also believe there is a double joy — and that is finishing together! As we run the race, we must exorcise the wretched curse of American individualism that so hinders the church. Sure, we have to be tough. We have to "gut it out" by God's grace. But we also have to hang tough *together*. The strong among us must hold up the dangling hands and wobbling knees of the weak with our prayers and acts of mercy. Those who are strong must make straight paths for the weak by the exemplary direction of their lives. The lives of the strong must keep the weak on the right road. Their lives must never cause the weak to stumble. We have to run tough, and we have to run together!

Run After Peace and Holiness

As we run we are encouraged to a dual pursuit — namely, peace and holiness: "Make every effort to live in peace with all men and to be holy; without holiness no one will see the Lord" (v. 14). Our experience tells us that though we may have peace with God, we do not always have peace with all men and women. Commitment to Christ incurs the enmity of the world. "If the world hates you," said Jesus, "keep in mind that it hated me first" (John 15:18). If we follow Christ, we must expect conflict. But how unexpected and disheartening it is when conflict is encountered in the church! There is a passage in Tolkien's *The Fellowship of the Ring* in which God-fearing elves join with God-fearing dwarves to oppose the Dark Lord. But immediately they begin to quarrel, calling down plagues on each other's necks. Then one of the wiser of the company, Haldir, remarks, "Indeed in nothing is the power of the Dark Lord more clearly shown than in the estrangement that divides all those who still oppose him."[5]

Conflict in the church brings glory to Satan and disgraces our God. Few things will grieve God more and impede the great race more than conflict in the Body of Christ. In fact, conflict in the church — and the failure to pursue peace — is the most public reason so many never finish. Satan too often infiltrates committees and elders' homes and parsonages, paralyzing those who ought to be setting the pace for others.

So as we run the race we must pursue peace with "all men" — both Christians and non-believers alike. The word "make every effort" or "pursue" is an uniquely aggressive word. It is often used in the sense of "to chase after one's enemies — to persecute."[6] We must chase after peace! Other Scriptures further enjoin the aggressive pursuit of peace, urging us to "make every effort to keep the unity of the Spirit through the bond of peace" (Ephesians 4:3), and to "make every effort to do what leads to peace" (Romans 14:19). Similarly, Romans 12:18 says, "If it is possible, as far as it depends on you, live at peace with everyone." And, of course, there is the grand dominical beatitude, "Blessed are the peacemakers, for they will be called sons of God" (Matthew 5:9). Those who pursue peace *will* to forgive and *will* to forget and *will* to be kind and *will* to be thoughtful and *will* to help others and *will* to pray for their enemies!

The preacher has linked the pursuit of peace with the pursuit of practical holiness (purity of soul) because he sees a logical association between them. Significantly, Jesus made the same association between peace and purity by joining them in successive beatitudes. "Blessed are the pure in heart" is followed by "Blessed are the peacemakers" (Matthew 5:8, 9). Character and peace are woven together as a single garment of the soul. Ultimately, it is holy people who finish the race, for it is they who "will see God" (Matthew 5:8) at his glorious return or in the glory that comes with death.

The application is clear: the way to finish well in life's marathon is to pursue peace and holiness — to give it our best — to "make every effort to live in peace with all men and to be holy." We must learn the "runner's lean," stretching ourselves forward to peace, extending our entire beings toward holiness!

FINISHING WELL — WHAT TO GUARD AGAINST (vv. 15-17)

As the writer continues his advice about finishing well, he turns from the positive charges (regarding running tough, running tough together, and running after peace and holiness) to negative admonitions about what to guard oneself against. The warnings come in three successive clauses.[7]

Gracelessness

The first clause is in verse 15a and warns against what we shall call gracelessness: "See to it that no one misses the grace of God." Grace is the divine attitude of benevolence God has toward his children. The image that helps me to picture this is that of a brimming pitcher in God's hand tilted to pour blessing on us. The Apostle James says essentially this when he declares, "But he gives more grace" (4:6, RSV) — literally, "great grace." Thus we confidently know there is always more grace for the believer. Earlier in 4:16 the preacher/writer urged us, "Let us then approach the throne of grace with confidence, so that we may receive mercy and find grace to help us in our time of need."

The unchanging truth is, we can have no need that outstrips his grace, and we never will! Even if we fall into deep sin, greater grace is available, as Paul said: "But where sin increased, grace increased all the more" (Romans 5:20b). "For daily need there is daily grace; for sudden need, there is sudden grace; for overwhelming need, there is overwhelming grace," wrote John Blanchard.[8]

Because of this, what a tragedy gracelessness is — and hence the warning, "See to it that no one misses the grace of God" (literally, "falls short of the grace of God") — the idea being that of "falling behind, not keeping pace with the movement of divine grace which meets and stirs the progress of the Christian."[9]

And how does this gracelessness come to afflict a child of grace? First and primarily, through unconfessed sin. Lack of confession, in effect, places a hand against the tilted pitcher with a tragic power that omnipotence refuses to overcome.

Secondly, one often misses the grace of God by a self-imposed famine of God's Word. For millennia God has watered the lives of his people with his Word. Those who do not read and meditate on it are self-condemned to a state of spiritual anorexia.

A third way to gracelessness is the absenting of oneself from the fellowship of the church, Christ's Body. The movement of divine grace through Christ's Body is meant to be a corporate experience. A section of Paul's prayer for the church in Ephesians 3:17-19 explains the important truth that it is "together with all the saints" that we "grasp how wide and long and high and deep is the love of Christ" and, indeed, go on to "be filled to the measure of all the fullness of God." Our capacity to understand God's Word and to experience his grace is vitally linked to our participation in church "with all the saints." It is in rich community that we experience grace upon grace.

Beautifully here in our text "See to it" is a plural command, making it everyone's responsibility to make sure no one misses the grace of God. Moreover, "See to it" is an unusual word that bears the sense of oversight (in fact, we derive the word *bishop* from this verb).[10] The idea is: "All of you, act like bishops in seeing that no one succumbs to gracelessness." We are called to some sanctified "meddling" in each other's lives. We must consciously involve ourselves in the Body of Christ, assuming responsibility for seeing others go on in grace, and also humbly receiving their loving care for us. We all need grace to finish the race!

> *'Tis grace hath brought me safe thus far,*
> *And grace will lead me home.*

Apostasy

The next clause calls the church to steel itself against idolatry and apostasy if it is to finish well, warning the believers to beware "that no bitter root grows up to cause trouble and defile many" (v. 15b). The image of idolatry as a bitter root comes from Deuteronomy 29:18, where the Lord formally warned his people against apostasy: "Make sure there is no man or woman, clan or tribe among you today whose heart turns away from the Lord our God to go and worship the gods of those nations; make sure there is no root among you that produces such bitter poison." The phrase in our text that depicts the root's apostatizing growth is freighted with even further insight because it describes a hidden seed that takes root and grows slowly, so that only time reveals what it is.[11] Virtually every church has such bitter roots, and it is the height of arrogance to imagine otherwise.

The call here is for vigilance. Certainly this does not enjoin a "witch-hunt." The Lord specifically warned against such a response because such actions would tear out real wheat with the weeds (Matthew 13:24-30). Nevertheless, we must be alert. Every fellowship of any size has a few "bitter roots" who follow false gods and subtly poison those around them. If we are to run well, the price is vigilance — especially in the good times.

Appetites

The next verse indicates there are two appetites that can torpedo the race — the *sexual* appetite and the *physical* appetite: "See to it that no one is sexually immoral, or is godless like Esau, who for a single meal sold his inheritance rights as the oldest son" (v. 16). Here the writer asserts in clearest terms that Esau was sexually immoral, calling him a *pornos*, from which we get the word *pornography*. Interestingly, the Old Testament does not say he was a fornicator unless it is implied in his marrying the two Canaanite daughters of Heth, who subsequently made life miserable for his parents (cf. Genesis 26:34, 35). Rabbinical tradition, however, both Palestinian and Hellenistic, paints Esau as a man completely subject to his libido.

Philo of Alexandria in his *Questions and Answers on Genesis* made this observation regarding Esau: "The hairy one is the unrestrained, lecherous, impure and unholy man."[12] The Palestinian Targum on Genesis 25:29 describes him as coming home exhausted on the same day he sold Jacob his birthright and saying that on "that day he had committed five transgressions," one of which was adultery with a betrothed maiden.[13]

The indictment from extra-Biblical literature parallels the revelation of Holy Scripture — that Esau was a *pornos* subject to the whims of his tom-cat nature — the archetype of the twentieth-century testosterone man. His essential sensuality made God quite unreal to him — as lust always does.[14]

This goes hand in glove with the text's second assertion that he was "godless," *bebelos*, a man who had no regard for God, whose focus was only on physical pleasures. Calvin says of such that they are:

> ... those in whom the love of the world so holds sway and prevails, that they forget heaven as men who are carried away by ambition, addicted to money and riches, given over to gluttony, and entangled with other kinds of pleasures, and give the spiritual kingdom of Christ either no place or the last place in their concerns.[15]

Remember Esau's story in Genesis 25? He grew up to be a big, hairy, red-headed lout whose focus was *fun* (hunting), *food*, and *females*, as Hebrews here asserts. Big "Red" (for that is what his nickname "Edom" meant) came in from the field hungry after hunting and found Jacob cooking some lentil stew. So he motioned, "Quick, let me have some of that red stew! I'm famished!" (v. 30), to which Jacob made the incredible proposition, "First sell me your birthright" (v. 31), only to be followed by the even more incredible flip response, "Look, I am about to die.... What good is the birthright to me?" (v. 32). Unbelievable! Old sweaty Red chose a cheap meal over the divine promise.

Esau was completely earthbound. All his thoughts were on what he could touch, taste, and suck. Instant gratification was his rule of thumb. He was void of spiritual values. Godless!

Esau was like a living beer commercial — bearded, steroid-macho, with two things on his mind: sexual pleasure and physical pleasure — food, drink, sports and sleep. "Hey, you only go around once. You've got to get it while you can." He was the prototype of modern godlessness — like the forty-five-year old man who had spent all his post-college years devoted to money and when asked, "How is it with your soul?" answered candidly, "My soul? I don't even know whether I have one." Tragic!

In Esau's pathetic case he went on to lose his birthright and blessing (cf. Genesis 27). And there was no remediation, because the text concludes, "Afterward, as you know, when he wanted to inherit this blessing, he was rejected. He could bring about no change of mind, though he sought the blessing with tears" (v. 17). If Esau sought forgiveness (and perhaps he did), God would have given it to him. But there was no way Esau's pleading could undo what was done. He had to live with the consequences. He could never possibly finish as well as he had begun.

God's message to all who are in the race is so clear: Sexual and physical appetites, given free rein, will ruin our race. Sure, we can repent of any sin, but Esau-like sins will leave deficiencies that can never be regained. How tragic, then, that so many today are selling a glorious finish for a cheap meal!

Art Carey's lyrical note on completing the Boston Marathon went like this: "The real joy of the Boston Marathon is just finishing ... doing what you have set out to do. It is like climbing Mount Everest, hitting a home run during the World Series, or scoring a touchdown during the Super Bowl."

And it may well be. But if that is so, can you imagine what it is going to be like, after life's numerous "heartbreak hills" and bloody feet, when we cross the tape having finished well with our eyes fixed on "Jesus, the pioneer and perfecter of our faith" (12:2)?

Do we want to finish well? Then here is what we must do:

- *Run tough* — "Therefore, strengthen your feeble arms and weak knees" (v. 12).
- *Run tough together* — "'Make level paths for your feet,' so that the lame may not be disabled, but rather healed" (v. 13).
- *Run after peace and holiness* — "Make every effort to live in peace with all men and to be holy; without holiness no one will see the Lord" (v. 14).

And here is what we must guard against:

- *Gracelessness* — "See to it that no one misses the grace of God . . ." (v. 15a).
- *Apostasy* — ". . . and that no bitter root grows up to cause trouble and defile many" (v. 15b).
- *Appetites* — "See that no one is sexually immoral, or is godless like Esau, who for a single meal sold his inheritance rights as the oldest son" (v. 16).

The joy of the Christian's marathon will be finishing. May we finish well!

You have not come to a mountain that can be touched and that is burning with fire; to darkness, gloom and storm; to a trumpet blast or to such a voice speaking words that those who heard it begged that no further word be spoken to them, because they could not bear what was commanded: "If even an animal touches the mountain, it must be stoned." The sight was so terrifying that Moses said, "I am trembling with fear." But you have come to Mount Zion, to the heavenly Jerusalem, the city of the living God. You have come to thousands upon thousands of angels in joyful assembly, to the church of the firstborn, whose names are written in heaven. You have come to God, the judge of all men, to the spirits of righteous men made perfect, to Jesus the mediator of a new covenant, and to the sprinkled blood that speaks a better word than the blood of Abel. (12:18-24)

18

Marching to Zion

HEBREWS 12:18-24

As we have seen in the three preced-
ing studies of this chapter, Hebrews 12 presents wisdom for living the
Christian life by employing the metaphor of a long-distance race. Following
Christ of necessity involves enlisting in a lifelong spiritual marathon. Success
in this great race is dependent on the careful cultivation of spiritual athleticism. Verses 1-3 presented the basics — that we must run with perseverance
divested of sin and hindrances and *focused* on "Jesus, the pioneer and perfecter of our faith." Verses 4-11 further advised us regarding how to endure
the race's hardships as spiritual discipline and make the most of it. Verses
12-17 instructed us positively on what to do and negatively on what to guard
against if we wish to finish well.

One of the facts that comes through loud and clear is that marathoning is tough. Spiritual runners experience the spiritual equivalents of what the
Boston marathoner regularly undergoes — bone grinding against raw bone,
searing half-dollar-sized blisters, "hitting the wall" so that each step is like
running through warm caramel. Sometimes, like modern marathoners, they
are encouraged by those along the way, just as the spectators who line
Boston's "Heartbreak Hill" encourage the walkers to jog and the joggers to
run, cheering, "Pick up those feet. You can do it!" Because of such encouragement, runners finish well.

But there is an experience the spiritual runner undergoes that is virtually unknown to those involved in a mere physical race — and that is the jeer-

ing of carping distracters. This was the experience of the early Hebrew church and of virtually all who have subsequently followed in its footsteps. Specifically, in that day Jewish Christians were being taunted by their newly estranged relatives and friends and synagogue officials for leaving the historic Jewish faith. As they followed Christ and attempted to put one foot in front of the other, as they ascended their own spiritual "heartbreak hills," they were hearing discordant voices: "You are on the wrong path. You are headed away from Sinai and Jerusalem. You have left your heritage in Abraham and Moses. You have forsaken your nation that has had the great blessings of God. You will never make it!"

The writer addresses such thinking in verses 18-24 by contrasting where his people have come from with where they have come to and are indeed going. The contrast is between Mounts Sinai and Zion — the Old and New Covenants — terror and joy — distance and closeness.

FROM SINAI'S LAW (vv. 18-21)

Essential to understanding the contrast, we must see that the giving of the Law at Mount Sinai was an awesome *physical* display, as depicted in Exodus 19:16-19, 20:18, 19, and Deuteronomy 4:11, 12. The prelude to the divine fireworks at Sinai involved the people's consecration as directed by God (cf. Exodus 19:10-15). They washed their clothing (vv. 10, 11, 14) and abstained from sexual relations, so as to be ceremonially clean (v. 15). They also observed God's orders that no man or beast touch the mountain on pain of death by stoning or arrows (vv. 12, 13).

The stage remained set for three days. Then on the morning of the third day, the people saw a thick cloud cover the top of Sinai illumined by gold veins of lightning with accompanying thunder rolling down the slopes, plus a deafening trumpet blast that reduced everyone to trembling (v. 16). Whether the trumpet sound was natural or unnatural cannot be determined. Personally, I believe it was supernatural because it was heard by all the million plus in the camp and because the giving of the Law was attended by "myriads of holy ones" (Deuteronomy 33:2). Hundreds of thousands of angels hovered invisibly around and over Sinai, and some, I think were blowing celestial horns.

Whatever the case, Moses led his people from their tents to the foot of the mountain, and this is what they saw: "Mount Sinai was covered with smoke, because the Lord descended on it in fire. The smoke billowed up from it like smoke from a furnace, the whole mountain trembled violently, and the sound of the trumpet grew louder and louder. Then Moses spoke and the voice of God answered him" (Exodus 19:18, 19). Imagine what it must have been like to be there: the ground is unsteady under your feet due to perpetual seismic tremors — the sky is black in deep darkness except for the radiating forks of lightning in the gloom and the fire blazing from the top of Sinai "to the very heavens" (Deuteronomy 4:11) — celestial shofars blare louder and louder in primal moans — Moses speaks, and God answers him with a voice like thunder. The only thing that matches the incredible display you are witnessing is the seismic trauma in your heart!

The people were visibly, physically assaulted with the holiness and majesty of God. This palpable divine display on Sinai communicated far more than any speech or written word ever could — and all Israel, young and old, could understand.

In addition to providing a glimpse of God's holiness, the blazing fire atop Sinai emphasized that his holiness rendered him a judge — "a consuming fire" (cf. Deuteronomy 4:24; Hebrews 12:29). The effect of these physical signs was to display in no uncertain terms the absolute unapproachableness of God. The mountain was so charged with the holiness of God that for a man to touch it meant certain death. Even if an innocent animal wandered to the mountain, it would contract so much holiness that it became deadly to the touch and had to be killed from a distance by stone or arrow.[1]

The salutary effect upon those at the foot of Sinai was substantial — it instilled a proper fear of God. As Moses explained, "God has come to test you, so that the fear of God will be with you to keep you from sinning" (Exodus 20:20). It was patently remedial. To understand that God is holy and that one is a sinner is to stand at the threshold of grace. Moreover, the giving of the Ten Commandments in this awesome context — and Israel's failure to keep them — served to emphasize the people's impotence and doom, which is a further grace, however negative the experience may be.

But this said, the great problem with the trip to Sinai was that while men and women could come to see God's holiness and their sinfulness, the Law provided no power to overcome sin.

> *To run and work the law commands,*
> *Yet gives me neither feet nor hands.*

Understanding this, the writer's explanation that they have come to a better mountain than Sinai makes sense: "You have not come to a mountain that can be touched." Zion, to which they had come, is a spiritual mountain, whereas Sinai was a physical mountain that could be touched only at pain of death.

> You have not come to a mountain that can be touched and that is burning with fire; to darkness, gloom and storm; to a trumpet blast or to such a voice speaking words that those who heard it begged that no further word be spoken to them, because they could not bear what

was commanded: "If even an animal touches the mountain, it must be stoned." The sight was so terrifying that Moses said, "I am trembling with fear." But you have come to Mount Zion. . . ." (vv. 18-22a)

In effect, the writer is admonishing his people as they attempt to run with perseverance the race that is marked out for them to not listen to the voices of their old friends who are still immersed in the futile pursuit of attempting to live up to Sinai, but rather to do everything in their power to maintain a straight path to Zion's grace.

There is an early passage in *Pilgrim's Progress* in which Christian, amidst the difficulties of trying to walk the narrow path to Zion, is lured away by Mr. Worldly Wiseman's counsel and directed toward the futility of Sinai. Bunyan writes:

> So Christian turned out of his way to go to Mr. Legality's house for help; but, behold, when he was got now hard by the hill, it seemed so high, and also that side of it that was next the wayside did hang so much over, that Christian was afraid to venture farther, lest the hill should fall on his head; wherefore there he stood still, and wotted not what to do. Also his burden now seemed heavier to him than while he was in his way. There came also flashes of fire out of the hill that made Christian afraid that he should be burnt: here, therefore, he sweat and did quake for fear. And now he began to be sorry that he had taken Mr. Worldly Wiseman's counsel; and with that, he saw Evangelist coming to meet him, at the sight also of whom he began to blush for shame.[2]

And, of course, Mr. Evangelist got him back on track, and the race continued on to Zion, the heavenly Jerusalem.

Today, few Christians, especially Gentiles, are in danger of turning back to Sinai per se and embracing the Levitical corpus of the Old Testament. Sinai, with its fiery mountain and its code, is simply too daunting. Instead, we fabricate our own mini-Sinais with a series of mini-laws which reflect nothing of the fiery presence and which are, we think, well within the reach of our unaided powers. If one is an evangelical, one's little legalisms reflect something of Biblical ethics, however faintly. If one is liberal, the little legalisms will simply reflect cultural consensus about popular causes.

But whether evangelical or liberal, our legalisms — our mini-Sinais — are always *reductionist*, shrinking spirituality to a series of wooden laws which say, "If you will do those six or sixty or six hundred things, you will be godly." And, of course, legalism is always *judgmental*. How easily our hearts imagine that our lists elevate us, while at the same time providing us with a convenient rack on which to stretch others in merciless judgment.

TO ZION'S GRACE (vv. 22-24)

From Mount Sinai we now switch to Mount Zion and the sublimest description anywhere of what we come to under grace. It is lyrical and has the feel of an early confession regarding the church. Perhaps the little Hebrew church sang or chanted its words in the months that followed as it attempted to run the race amidst the ensuing Neronian persecution. There follows now seven sublimities.

First, we come to the *city of God* — "But you have come to Mount Zion, to the heavenly Jerusalem, the city of the living God" (v. 22a). Mount Zion was the location of the Jebusite stronghold that David captured and made the religious center of his kingdom by bringing to it the golden Ark of God — God's presence with his people. When Solomon built the Temple and installed the Ark, Zion/Jerusalem became synonymous with the earthly dwelling-place of God. In Christ we have come to its *heavenly counterpart*, the spiritual Jerusalem from above. In one sense, this is still to come (cf. 13:14, "but we are looking for the city that is to come"), but we have also already arrived there in spirit.

Christians are *now* citizens of the heavenly city and enjoy its privileges. Paul wrote, "But our citizenship is in heaven. And we eagerly await a Savior from there, the Lord Jesus Christ" (Philippians 3:20). We are in Zion by virtue of our incorporation in Christ, for "God raised us up with Christ and seated us with him in the heavenly realms in Christ Jesus" (Ephesians 2:6).

Sure, the fiery presence is there, but we have the requisite holiness and access of Christ. And what is more, we are in Zion for good. "But you have come to Mount Zion" is in the perfect tense, emphasizing our permanent, continuing state. This is why the seemingly endless miles of life's marathon and the inevitable "heartbreak hills" do not stop us. We are in Zion and marching — marathoning — to Zion!

Second, as the church we meet *angels* — "You have come to thousands upon thousands of angels in joyful assembly" (v. 22b). Moses tells us that "myriads of holy ones" attended the giving of the Law (Deuteronomy 33:2), and from Daniel we hear that "Thousands upon thousands attended him [the Ancient of Days — God]; ten thousand times ten thousand stood before him" (Daniel 7:10). David said, "The chariots of God are tens of thousands and thousands of thousands" (Psalm 68:17). In the church we come to these dizzying thousands of angels.

They are everywhere — mighty flaming spirits, "ministering spirits sent to serve those who will inherit salvation" (1:14), passing in and out of our lives, moving around us and over us just as they did Jacob of old. Sometimes they protect God's elect — for example, the "tall men in shining garments" who surrounded Mr. and Mrs. John G. Paton years ago in the New Hebrides — or the "tall soldiers with shining faces" who protected missionary Marie Monsen in North China — or, on another occasion, the "huge men, dressed in white with flaming swords" who surrounded the Rift Valley Academy — and on another the "hundreds of men dressed in white, with swords and shields" who stood guard over a hut shielding Clyde Taylor, who would one day found the National Association of Evangelicals. Similarly, a missionary from the church I pastor, Carol Carlson, serving in China in 1922, learned why the bandits never attacked her compound — there were "men in white walking up and down the wall."[3]

At other times, angels preside over the apparent earthly tragedy of God's people. Olive Fleming Liefeld in her book *Unfolding Destinies* tells how two young Auca Indians, Dawa and Kimo, heard singing after witnessing the martyrdom of the five missionaries in the jungles of Ecuador: "As they looked up over the tops of the trees they saw a large group of people. They were all singing, and it looked as if there were a hundred flashlights."[4]

But the grand emphasis of our passage is not so much the angels' care of us, but rather our joining them in festal assembly. The word translated "joyful assembly" was used in ancient culture to describe the great national assemblies and sacred games of the Greeks. Whereas at Mount Sinai the angels blew celestial trumpets that terrified God's people, we are to see ourselves on Mount Zion as dressed in festal attire and worshiping in awe side by side with these shining beings!

Third, we come to *fellow-believers* — "to the church of the firstborn, whose names are written in heaven" (v. 23a). Jesus is the firstborn *par excellence*, and by virtue of our union with him *we* are firstborn.[5] All the rights of inheritance go to the firstborn — to us who are "co-heirs with Christ" (Romans 8:17). Bishop Westcott says we are "a society of 'eldest sons' of God."[6] There are no second or third or fourth sons and daughters in the church. We all get the big inheritance!

And there is more. As firstborn, our names are written in Heaven along with the firstborn who are already there. In other words, there is an amazing solidarity between the Church Triumphant in Heaven and the Church Militant here on earth. We are all the Body of Christ! The family is never broken. It simply keeps growing and going on and on — a bulging assembly of rich first sons and daughters.

> *Fading is the world's best pleasure*
> *All its boasted pomp and show;*
> *Solid joys and lasting treasure*
> *None but Zion's children know.*
>
> (John Newton, 1779)

Fourth, we come to *God* — "You have come to God, the judge of all men" (v. 23b). Although the scene in Zion to which we come is a joyous festival, it is not a casual thing. We come to Zion to meet the God of Sinai, who is judge of all. We understand regarding him that "nothing in all creation is hidden from God's sight. Everything is uncovered and laid bare before the eyes of him to whom we must give account" (4:13). We also know that he said, "'It is mine to avenge; I will repay,' and again, 'The Lord will judge his people.' It is a dreadful thing to fall into the hands of the living God" (10:30, 31).

Knowing this, we come before him in awe because he is the Judge. But we do not come in craven dread, because his Son has borne the judgment for us. This is our *highest delight* — to gather before God! It is a miracle of grace.

Fifth, we come to the *Church Triumphant* — "to the spirits of righteous men made perfect" (v. 23c). As we have noted, though they are in Heaven, we share a solidarity with those who have gone before. The same spiritual life courses through us as through them. We share the same secrets as Abraham and Moses and David and Paul. Here is an amazing thing — they died millennia before us, but God planned, according to 11:40, "that only together with us would they be made perfect." They waited for centuries for the perfection we received when we trusted Christ, because that came only with Christ's death — "by one sacrifice he has made perfect forever those who are being made holy" (10:14). Because of Christ's work we are not one whit inferior to the patriarchs, for through Christ we are all equal in righteousness!

Sixth, we come — "to *Jesus* the mediator of a new covenant" (v. 24a). Significantly, Christ's human name, redolent in the Incarnation, is used here because we have come to the man "*like* us, and the man *for us*." Moses was the mediator of the Old Covenant, but as great as he was, he trembled fearfully at Mount Sinai (cf. v. 21). But through Jesus, the mediator of the New Covenant, we draw near with confidence. The promises of the New Covenant are sure, for they are in Jesus. He is the source and dispenser of all for which we hope. He is *in* us, and we are *in* him.

> *Savior, if of Zion's city,*
>   *I through grace a member am,*
> *Let the world deride or pity,*
>   *I will glory in Thy name.*
>
> (John Newton, 1779)

Seventh, we come to forgiveness because of *sprinkled blood* — "and to the sprinkled blood that speaks a better word than the blood of Abel" (v. 24b). Abel's warm blood cried from the ground for vengeance and judgment, but Christ's blood shouts that we are forgiven and have peace with God.

Hallelujah! O, the eloquence of Jesus' blood! It says that what was impossible for us has happened. It says that you and I are forgiven!

As fellow-pilgrims in the great marathon, we must not veer off course toward Sinai, because Jesus has met Sinai's great demands for holiness and perfection at Calvary atop Mount Zion.

> *To run and work the law commands,*
> *Yet gives me neither feet nor hands;*
> *But better news the gospel brings;*
> *It bids me fly, and gives me wings.*

The Scriptures tell us that in the Church "you have come" (*right now!*) to these seven sublime realities:

- To the City of God,
- To myriads of angels,
- To fellow-believers,
- To God,
- To the Church Triumphant,
- To Jesus,
- To forgiveness.

If this does not create a wellspring of thanksgiving in our hearts and make us want to march to Zion, what will?

See to it that you do not refuse him who speaks. If they did not escape when they refused him who warned them on earth, how much less will we, if we turn away from him who warns us from heaven? At that time his voice shook the earth, but now he has promised, "Once more I will shake not only the earth but also the heavens." The words "once more" indicate the removing of what can be shaken — that is, created things — so that what cannot be shaken may remain. Therefore, since we are receiving a kingdom that cannot be shaken, let us be thankful, and so worship God acceptably with reverence and awe, for our "God is a consuming fire." (12:25-29)

19

A Consuming Fire

HEBREWS 12:25-29

During Christianity's second century, a notable heretic by the name of Marcion came to power in Asia Minor. Though he was excommunicated early on, his destructive teaching lingered for nearly two centuries. Marcion taught the total incompatibility of the Old and New Testaments. He believed there was a radical discontinuity between the God of the Old Testament and the God of the New Testament — between the Creator and the Father of Jesus. So Marcion created a new Bible for his followers that had no Old Testament and a severely hacked-up New Testament that consisted of only one Gospel (an edited version of Luke) and ten select and edited Pauline epistles (excluding the Pastorals). His views were spelled out in his book *Antitheses*, which set forth the alleged contradictions between the Testaments. Tertullian in his famous *Against Marcion* wrote a five-volume refutation.

But Marcionism never completely died out, and in the nineteenth century, especially, with the rise of liberalism, it underwent a revival among those who wished to separate what they considered to be the crude and primitive parts of the Old Testament from the New. Friedrich Schleiermacher, the eighteenth- and nineteenth-century father of liberalism, said the Old Testament has a place in the Christian heritage only by virtue of its connections with Christianity. He felt it should be no more than an appendix of historical interest. Adolph Harnack argued that the Reformers should have dropped it from

197

the canon of authoritative writings. Likewise, there are thousands today who have rejected the Old Testament either formally or in practice.

The error of this kind of approach was pointed out by another liberal, Albert Schweitzer, who demonstrated that such thinking amounts to choosing aspects of God that fit one's man-made theology. Men project their own thoughts about God back up to him and create a god of their own thinking. Anyone who is in touch with modern culture knows that this kind of reasoning — Marcionism — is alive and well.

What does this have to do with us who hold both Testaments to be the inerrant, infallible Word of God? Very much! You see, Marcionism is subtly alive in the evangelical enterprise's understanding of God. Of course, it is true that the New Testament gives us a fuller revelation of God and that we do not live under the Old Testament. Nevertheless, the God we worship is still the *same God*. But, sadly, many Christians today are so ignorant of their Bibles, especially the Old Testament, that they have a tragically sentimentalized idea of God — one which amounts to little more than a Deity who died to meet their needs — the sin question is minimized or ignored. The result is the incredible paradox of evangelicals who "know Jesus" but who do not know who God is — unwitting Marcionites!

The remedy for this travesty is the Bible, specifically Sinai in the Old Covenant and Zion in the New Covenant — each of which present a vision or an *aesthetic* for understanding God.[1]

From Mount Sinai we learn, in Moses' words, that God is a consuming fire — "Be careful not to forget the covenant of the Lord your God. . . . For the Lord your God is a consuming fire, a jealous God" (Deuteronomy 4:23, 24). The vision is stupendous — a mountaintop blazing with "fire to the very heavens" (Deuteronomy 4:11) — cloaked with a deep darkness — lightning illuminating golden arteries in the clouds — celestial rams' horns overlaying the thunder with mournful blasts — the ground shaking as God's voice intones the Ten Commandments. God is transcendentally "other," perfectly good and holy. He radiates wrath and judgment against sin. God cannot be approached.

This is the vision for the heart of every believer — "the Lord your God is a consuming fire." It is the corrective so needed in today's church that has shamefully trivialized worship, turning it into a self-assured farce. Here God's divine intention in creating Sinai is obvious because "a picture is worth a thousand words." Flaming Mount Sinai shows us God!

Of course, the other mountain, Mount Zion of the New Testament, completes the picture. There we see God's love as God the Son takes all of his people's transgressions on himself so that he "became sin" (2 Corinthians 5:21; cf. Galatians 3:10,11, 13) — writhing under its load like an impaled serpent (cf. Numbers 21:4-8). There on the cross we see God the Son dying for our sins and extending forgiveness to all who will believe in him, trusting his work alone for salvation. What a vision we are bequeathed from Calvary: God with his arms nailed wide as if to embrace all those who come to him — his blood covering the earth, speaking a better word than the blood of Abel (12:24)— the consuming love of God. Mount Zion, crowned by Golgotha, shows us God!

Both mountains — Sinai and Zion — reveal the true God. Neither can be separated from the other. God is not the God of one hill but of both. Both visions must be held in blessed tension within our souls — consuming fire and consuming love. This will save us from the damning delusion of Marcion!

It is this great twin-peaked God to whom we come as we marathon onward to "Mount Zion, to the heavenly Jerusalem, the city of the living God" (v. 22). The massive dual revelation of the mountains is meant to shape our pilgrimage. The question we must ask is, how then are we to march? What are we to do? The answer? *Obey* and *worship*.

OBEDIENCE (vv. 25-27)

Effectual Word

We ought to obey because God's word is unstoppably *effectual*: "See to it that you do not refuse him who speaks. If they did not escape when they refused him who warned them on earth, how much less will we, if we turn away from him who warns us from heaven?" (v. 25). This is what is called in logic an *a fortiori* argument, an argument that argues that what is true in the lesser case will be even more true in the greater. In the lesser case, God's earthly warning at Sinai first suffered subtle refusal by the Israelites when they "begged that no further word be spoken to them" (v. 19; cf. Exodus 20:19) — though their refusal there at Sinai was more from fear than from outright rejection of God. However, in the years that followed, they explicitly refused God's word by repeated disobedience during the four decades of wandering in the wilderness. So grievous was their disobedience that Numbers 14:29 records that God pronounced judgment in that everyone who was twenty and older would die in the desert. And, indeed, none did escape except faithful Caleb and Joshua. A million plus corpses littered the desert.

Considering the inexorable penalty for disobeying God's earthly message, how much greater will the penalty be in the greater instance of disobeying his heavenly message of grace through his Son? (cf. 1:2). Surely no one will escape! This, of course, has been the writer's message all along. In 2:3a he warned, "How shall we escape if we ignore such a great salvation?" Later in 10:28, 29 he said much the same thing, emphasizing greater punishment:

Anyone who rejected the law of Moses died without mercy on the testimony of two or three witnesses. How much more severely do you think a man deserves to be punished who has trampled the Son of God under foot, who has treated as an unholy thing the blood of the covenant that sanctified him, and who has insulted the Spirit of grace?

The message is so clear: we had better obey God's Word because his threat that no one who disobeys will escape is ineluctably effectual. It is a "done deal." No person will escape who refuses the gospel! God is a relentless "consuming fire."

Final Word

If this is not sufficient reason to obey the God of the two mountains, there is another, and that is that his word is *final*, as the writer goes on to explain: "At that time his voice shook the earth, but now he has promised, 'Once more I will shake not only the earth but also the heavens.' The words 'once more' indicate the removing of what can be shaken — that is, created things — so that what cannot be shaken may remain" (vv. 26, 27).

The initial historical event where God's voice shook the earth was at Mount Sinai when he verbally spelled out the Ten Commandments with a thunderous voice. Imagine how terrifying it was to have the ground under one's feet tremble in response to God's audible word. There were no sleepers in the congregation at Sinai!

But there is an infinitely greater shaking coming, an eschatological cosmic shaking of the whole universe, and it too will be triggered by God's word. Here the writer has quoted God's promise from Haggai 2:6 — "Once more I will shake not only the earth but also the heavens" (v. 26b) — indicating that every created thing will be shaken to utter disintegration. This is in accord with what the Scriptures teach us about the power of God's word. Genesis says he created everything by his word as he spoke the universe into existence. Therefore, one "little word" from him can and will fell creation!

The Psalmist tells us that creation is transitory: "In the beginning you laid the foundations of the earth, and the heavens are the work of your hands. They will perish, but you remain; they will all wear out like a garment" (Psalm 102:25, 26; cf. Hebrews 1:10-12). Isaiah says of the future, "Therefore I will make the heavens tremble; and the earth will shake from its place at the wrath of the Lord Almighty, in the day of his burning anger" (13:13). And Peter identifies it with the day of the Lord: "But the day of the Lord will come like a thief. The heavens will disappear with a roar; the elements will be destroyed by fire, and the earth and everything in it will be laid bare" (2 Peter 3:10). Think of it! All one hundred thousand million galaxies — each containing at least that many stars — each galaxy one hundred light-years across — will hear the word and shake out of existence! Just a little word from God, and it is done.

The reason for this is clearly spelled out: "So that what cannot be shaken may remain" (v. 27b). The people of God, as a part of the order of those things that are unshakable, will survive. But everything else in the universe will be shaken and therefore purged. Everything that is wrong will be eradicated. No sin, no imperfection will remain. Then there will be a blessed reconstruction — "Then I saw a new heaven and a new earth, for the first heaven and the first earth had passed away" (Revelation 21:1).

To those who are obedient this is good news. And the writer means it to be a powerful encouragement to the beleaguered little church to which he writes, in which some feel as though their lives are being shaken to pieces by Rome. "Stand firm amidst the Roman tremors," he seems to be saying, "because the ultimate shaking is coming when Rome, and indeed the entire present evil order will fall into oblivion. And you, as part of the new order, will survive. Take heart!" On the other hand, to those who are ignoring God's word and drifting further away, this was a disquieting revelation and a challenge to obedience.

But to all, including us, there is here a mighty call to obey God's word, because it is *effectual* and *final*. No Israelite who disobeyed God's earthly word survived the desert, and how much more will be the case with those who disobey the heavenly word through Christ. God's word is effectual — it never fails. And God's word is final. It started the universe, and it will stop it! So the command to all us pilgrims in verse 25 comes with great force: "See to it that you do not refuse him who speaks."

Are you refusing God? Has he been speaking to you, but you have been ignoring his word? What folly! His word is *effectual*, and it is *final*.

WORSHIP (vv. 28, 29)

After obedience, the other great "to do" that comes from the two mountains is worship: "Therefore, since we are receiving a kingdom that cannot be shaken, let us be thankful, and so worship God acceptably with reverence and awe, for our 'God is a consuming fire'" (vv. 28, 29). Charles Colson, in his book *Kingdoms in Conflict*, relates:

> In 1896, the . . . planners of St. John the Divine in New York city envisioned a great Episcopal cathedral that would bring glory to God. Nearly a century later, though the immense structure is still under construction, it is in use — in a way that its planners might well have regarded with dismay.
>
> St. John's Thanksgiving service has featured Japanese Shinto priests; Muslim Sufis perform biannually; Lenten services have

focused on the ecological "passion of the earth" . . . St. John the Divine has ceased to be a house of the one God of the Scriptures, and has become instead a house of many gods. Novelist Kurt Vonnegut Jr. wrote for the cathedral's centennial brochure that "the Cathedral is to this atheist . . . a suitable monument to persons of all ages and classes. I go there often to be refreshed by a sense of non-sectarian community which has the best interest of the whole planet at heart. . . ."

Dean James Morton has encountered opposition, but he defends it saying: . . .

"This cathedral is a place for people like me who feel con-stricted by the notion of excluding others. What happens here — the Sufi dances, the Buddhist prayers — are serious spiritual experi-ences. We make God a Minnie Mouse in stature when we say these experiences profane a Christian church."[2]

The Scriptures, however, would argue that it is Dean Morton who has made the great God of Sinai and Zion into a mousy deity whose only "virtue" is sub-Biblical toleration. It is difficult to conceive how much far-ther one could depart from the awesome God of the Scriptures — a God who tolerates no other gods before him, who forbids idolatry and demands the holiness of his people. Instead of giving his people a golden calf, the cathe-dral dean has given them a Mickey-Mouse reflection of popular culture — a profoundly vapid idolatry.

Note our text well! It says that "our 'God is [not was!] a consuming fire.'" The God of Zion is the same God as the God of Sinai. God has not changed. To some of us, the troubles faced by some of the great religious tra-ditions may seem far removed. But the truth is, similar problems are com-mon in the more independent, evangelical traditions. One Sunday morning a friend of mine visited a church where, to his amazement, the worship pre-lude was the theme song from the Paul Newman/Robert Redford movie *The Sting*, entitled (significantly, I think) "The Entertainer." The congregation was preparing for divine worship while cinematic images of Paul Newman and Robert Redford in 1920s garb hovered in their consciousness! Absurd!

And that was just the prelude, for what followed was an off-the-wall service that made no attempt at worship, the "high point" being the announcements when the pastor (inspired, no doubt, by the rousing prelude) stood unbeknownst behind the unfortunate person doing announcements making "horns" behind his head with his forked fingers and acting Bozo-like for the congregation. This buffoonery took place in a self-proclaimed "Bible-believing church" that ostensibly worships the holy Triune God of the Bible!

But what was in the pastor's and people's minds? What did they really think of God? How could anyone do such things and understand who God is? The answer is, they were modern evangelical Marcionites whose ignorance of Holy Scripture had so edited God that divine worship had become man-centered vaudeville — and poor slapstick at that!

Granted, Christians ought to laugh — they ought to have the best sense of humor on this planet. And Christians ought to enjoy life. But they must also know and understand that God remains a "consuming fire" and that acceptable worship takes place when there is authentic "reverence and awe." This is God's Word!

When we come to worship, we must keep both mountains in view — the approachable Zion with its consuming love, and the unapproachable Sinai with its consuming fire — and then come in reverent boldness.

Everything depends on how we see God. If we see him Scripturally we will experience awe and reverence — and there will be times when we are overwhelmed with the numinous as our souls are engaged by God. Our heart's desire for ourselves and those around us ought to be that: 1) they be regenerated, 2) they have a radical Biblical vision of God, a sense of his holiness and transcendence, and 3) this will inform all of life — their worship, their sense of mission and evangelism, their stewardship, their affirmation and delight in creation, their relationships, their sexual ethics — everything!

We members of the unshakable Kingdom are meant to worship with thankful hearts. Our pulses should race with thanksgiving — "Thanks be to God for his indescribable gift!" (2 Corinthians 9:15). Whatever we do or wherever we go, we must be "always giving thanks to God the Father for everything, in the name of our Lord Jesus Christ" (Ephesians 5:20).

It is so easy to succumb to focusing on one mountain at the expense of the other. But theological balance is the key. Our God is both unapproachable and approachable.

The twin peaks of our spiritual life demand two things as we march to Zion: *obedience* and *worship*. Let us obey his Word implicitly, for it is *effectual* — it never fails, and it is *final* — it will shake the whole universe. Let us worship him with reverence and awe and thanksgiving!

Keep on loving each other as brothers. Do not forget to entertain strangers, for by so doing some people have entertained angels without knowing it. Remember those in prison as if you were their fellow prisoners, and those who are mistreated as if you yourselves were suffering. (13:1-3)

20

Ecclesial Ethics

HEBREWS 13:1-3

Much of the New Testament, especially the epistles, follows the common pattern of giving theological instruction followed by practical application — *theology*, then *practicality*. The change can be expressed in many ways — from *exposition* to *exhortation*, from *creed* to *conduct*, from *doctrine* to *duty*, from the *indicative* to the *imperative*. This characteristic movement took place in Hebrews in the shift between chapters 11 and 12 where the writer began to exhort his people regarding their duty to run the great race marked out for them.

Yet, while the continental divide in Hebrews is between chapters 11 and 12, there are numerous mini-divides that follow the theology-to-practicality pattern. One such divide follows closely in the switch from chapter 12 to chapter 13. Chapter 12 builds to an intensely theological crescendo with the statement that "God is a consuming fire," which is then met by the intensely *practical* command that opens chapter 13 — namely, to "keep on loving each other as brothers." So now we move from *fire* to *function* — from *vertical* to *horizontal* — from *love for God* to *love for the church*.

The implication is clear: what we think about God has everything to do with our relationship to each other and with the world. For example, this logic is built into the very structure of the Ten Commandments. The first four are intensely vertical and theological, followed by six that are intensely horizontal and ethical. This is why worship is so important — because a proper grasp of God will guide our footsteps in the world.

So the question that our text answers is this: understanding that God is both the consuming fire of Mount Sinai and the consuming love of Mount Zion, how ought we to live — especially in the church? What ought our ecclesial ethics to be?

VOLITIONAL LOVE (v. 1)

The answer begins with the command given in verse 1: "Keep on loving each other as brothers."

There had been an evident flagging of brotherly affection among the members of the tiny Jewish congregation as it rode the increasingly hostile seas of Roman culture. History and experience show that persecution and the accompanying sense of dissonance with pagan and secular culture can bring two opposite effects. One is to draw God's people together, but the other is to promote disaffection. For example, in the 1830s two New York Christians, Reverend John McDowall and Mr. Arthur Tappan, were drawn together in their battle against the abuse of women fallen to prostitution, and the two men formed the Magdalen Society. But when their work began to probe too close to the heart of New York society, both found that they could, "scarcely go into a hotel, or step for a moment on board a steamboat, without being annoyed by . . . angry hissing."[1] This, along with threats from Tammany Hall and derisive newspaper coverage that branded Mr. Tappan as "Arthur D. Fanaticus," brought immense stress upon the two men, which served to exacerbate their differences and finally ended their friendship.[2]

I have witnessed the same phenomenon when ministering in Europe at a conference attended by some expatriate Eastern Europeans who under lengthy persecution had become increasingly rigid, legalistic and judgmental. I learned then that persecution can definitely have a spiritual downside.

The structure of the command here to "Keep on loving each other as brothers" (literally, "Let the brotherly love *remain*") suggests that the brotherly and sisterly bonds in the little church were dangerously frayed among some of the members.[3] This was not the way they had begun because initially the fresh experience of salvation in Christ had brought with it the discovery of a shared paternity, the joyous sense of being brothers and sisters with the same Father, and the experience of *philadelphia* — the word used here, meaning "brotherly love."

At first, this love had come to those new believers as naturally as one's first steps, very much like Paul's allusion to the similar experience of the Thessalonians: "Now about brotherly love [*philadelphia*] we do not need to write to you, for you yourselves have been taught by God to love each other" (1 Thessalonians 4:9). For these new Christians, loving other believers was as easy as "falling off a log." They could not wait to get to church where they could drink in the fellowship of the godly. The fellowship of their new brothers and sisters was delectably mysterious to them, and they rejoiced in plumbing the depth of each other's souls.

Indeed, their brotherly love was a telltale sign of their salvation. As the Apostle John would later write: "We know that we have passed from death to life, because we love our brothers" (1 John 3:14). Their impulse to brotherly love provided a sweet, inner self-authentication. It also announced to the world that their faith was the real thing, for Jesus had said, "All men will know that you are my disciples if you love one another" (John 13:35).

What a glorious phenomenon brotherly love is — a sense of the same paternity (a brotherly and sisterliness taught by God, a desire to climb into each other's souls), a sweet inner authentication, and the sign of the real thing to the world.

But it had been waning in the little house-church with the years of stress and uncertainty. Some of the brethren had grown weary of each other. And a few actually seemed to exchange mutual hatred.

What to do? The answer given here is utterly volitional — they were to *will* to practice brotherly love! Inwardly, this requires that we will to consider the stupendous implications of our shared generation — that we truly are "brothers" and sisters (the terms are not merely sentimental but are objective fact) — that though we are millions, we share only one Father — that we will still be brothers and sisters when the sun turns to ice — that God is pleased when brothers and sisters dwell together in unity (cf. Psalm 133 and John 17).

Outwardly, we must will to say and do only those things that will enhance our *philadelphia*. To paraphrase Will Rogers, we must so order our lips that we would not be afraid to sell the family parrot to the pastor — or to any other Christian friend.

We must will to love one another. George Whitefield and John Wesley did this even though they disagreed in matters of theology. Whitefield's words say it all:

> My honored friend and brother . . . hearken to a child who is willing to wash your feet. I beseech you, by the mercies of God in Christ Jesus our Lord, if you would have my love confirmed toward you. . . . Why should we dispute, when there is no possibility of convincing? Will it not, in the end, destroy brotherly love, and insensibly take from us that cordial union and sweetness of soul, which I pray God may always subsist between us? How glad would the enemies of our Lord be to see us divided. . . . Honored sir, let us offer salvation freely to all by the blood of Jesus, and whatever light God has communicated to us, let us freely communicate to others.

The will to let brotherly love remain — this is a divine duty.

VOLITIONAL HOSPITALITY (v. 2)

In March 1990 Clark and Ann Peddicord, Campus Crusade for Christ representatives in Germany, gave this report in a personal letter:

> Last week the former communist dictator, Erich Honecher, was released from the hospital where he had been undergoing treatment for cancer. There is probably no single person in all of East Germany that is more despised and hated than he. He has been stripped of all his offices and even his own communist party has kicked him out. He was booted out of the villa he was living in; the new government refused to provide him and his wife with accommodation. They stood, in essence, homeless on the street. . . . It was Christians who stepped in. Pastor Uwe Holmer, who is in charge of a Christian help-center north of Berlin, was asked by Church leaders if he would be willing to take them in. Pastor Holmer and his family decided that it would be wrong to give away a room in the center that would be used for needy people, or an apartment that their staff needed; instead, they took the former dictator and his wife into their own home. It must have been a strange scene when the old couple arrived. The former absolute ruler of the country was being sheltered by one of the Christians whom he and his wife had despised and persecuted. In East Germany there is a great deal of hate toward the former regime and especially toward Honecher and his wife, Margot, who had ruled the educational system there for 26 years with an iron hand. She had made sure that very few Christian children were able to go on for higher education. There are ten children in the Holmer family and eight of them had applied for further education in the course of the past years: all had been refused a place at college because they were Christians, in spite of the fact that they had good or excellent grades in school. Pastor Holmer was asked why he and his family would open their door to such detestable people. . . . Pastor Holmer spoke very clearly, "Our Lord challenged us to follow him and to take in all who are weary and heavy laden — both in soul and in body. . . ."[4]

The story is a miracle, for no one, apart from the grace of God and the example of Christ and the instruction of the New Testament, would stoop to do such a thing. Pastor Holmer was certainly informed by God's Word, and perhaps even the teaching here of Hebrews 13:2 — "Do not forget to entertain strangers, for by so doing some people have entertained angels without knowing it."

We may wonder, why this teaching on hospitality, and what motivated it some 2,000 years ago? For starters, inns were proverbially miserable places from earliest antiquity on. In Aristophanes' *The Frogs*, Dionysus asks Heracles if he can tell him which inn has the fewest fleas. Plato, in *The Laws*, instances an innkeeper keeping his guests hostage. And Theophrastus puts innkeeping on the level of running a brothel.[5]

Thus inns were not congenial or healthy places for Christians. This, coupled with the fact that many Christians had suffered ostracism by both society and family, necessitated Christian hospitality — which was happily provided by brothers and sisters who could do so. Predictably, such hospitality was sometimes abused. The first-century pagan satirical writer Lucian describes how his Elmer Gantry-like protagonist Proteus Peregrinus took advantage of naive Christians, reporting that "he left home, then, for a second time, to roam about, possessing an ample source of funds in the Christians, through whose ministrations he lived in unalloyed prosperity" (*The Passing of Peregrinus*, 16)[6]

Significantly, such abuses became so common that the *Didache*, an early Christian handbook, gave this advice:

> Let every Apostle who comes to you be received as the Lord, but let him not stay more than one day, or if need be a second as well; but if he stays three days, he is a false prophet. And when an Apostle goes forth let him accept nothing but bread till he reach his night's lodging; but if he ask for money, he is a false prophet." (11:4-6)[7]

The effect of all this was that some Christians had noticeably cooled in their hospitality. As the country song says: "Fool me once — shame on you! Fool me twice — shame on me!"

To counter this destructive trend among his congregation, the writer again frames his advice as a command: "Do not forget to entertain strangers" (v. 2a) — or more exactly, "Do not forget to show love to strangers." In the Greek there is even a beautiful assonance between the words for brotherly love (*philadelphia*) and love for strangers (*philozenia*). The writer has phrased his language for maximum impact.

To him, hospitality was so important that he tantalized his people with an enchanting possibility — "for by so doing some people have entertained angels without knowing it" (v. 2b). The primary reference here was no doubt to the cheerful hospitality Abraham extended to three strangers who unbeknown to him were angels — one of whom was no less than Jehovah himself (Genesis 18)! The Hebrew mind would recall a chain of similar encounters — perhaps Gideon's encounter with the angel under the oak in Ophrah (Judges 6:11ff.), or Manoah's unstinting hospitality to the "angel unaware" who then announced that he and his wife would give birth to Samson (Judges 13).

By presenting the delectable possibility of hosting a real angel, the preacher was not promoting hospitality on the chance that one might "luck out" and get an angel, but was simply saying that the possibility of its happening indicated how much God prizes hospitality in his people.

The fact is, some of us have entertained angels! Hebrews 12:22 says that in coming to Zion, "You have come to thousands upon thousands of angels in joyful assembly." That hasty hamburger topped with raw onions and served to a hungry stranger may have rested in a celestial stomach — and with no heartburn! Bishop Westcott was right: "We only observe the outside surface of those whom we receive. More lies beneath than we can see."[8]

The Scriptures consistently place a high premium on hospitality. Paul says, "Share with God's people who are in need. Practice hospitality" (Romans 12:13). Peter choruses, "Offer hospitality to one another without grumbling" (1 Peter 4:9). No one must ever think for a moment of being a Christian leader but not practicing hospitality — "Now the overseer must be above reproach . . . self-controlled, respectable, hospitable . . ." (1 Timothy 3:2; cf. Titus 1:8).

Why this great premium on opening one's home and life to others? There is a reason beyond meeting each other's occasional material needs — it is in each other's homes that we really get to know one another. In fact, you can never really know another person without being in his or her abode. In one's home, over the table, relaxed amidst the decor and accoutrement of one's persona — that is where exchange is naturally enhanced and brotherly love elevated. Sharing a blessed meal at the family table can be quasi-sacramental. It binds us together in the reality that everything comes from Christ.

And finally, there is another reason for hospitality — sharing love with strangers who do not know Christ. East German dictator Eric Honecher was no angel, that is for sure! But I think some angels dropped in to Pastor Holmer's home. I also believe that if Eric and Margot Honecher ever become Christians, the primary earthly medium will have been humble Christian hospitality! The writer's unadorned point stands firm: we must *will* to be hospitable.

VOLITIONAL EMPATHY (v. 3)

Herman Melville in his novel *White Jacket* has one of the ship's sailors became desperately ill with severe abdominal pain. The ship's surgeon, Dr. Cuticle, waxes enthusiastic at the possibility of having a real case to treat, one that challenges his surgeon's ability. Appendicitis is the happy diagnosis. Dr. Cuticle recruits some other sailors to serve as his attendants.

The poor seaman is laid out on the table, and the doctor goes to work with skillful enthusiasm. His incisions are precise, and while removing the diseased appendix he proudly points out interesting anatomical details to his seaman-helpers who had never before seen the inside of another human. He is completely absorbed in his work and obviously a skilled professional. It is an impressive performance, but the sailors — without exception — are not impressed but are rather appalled. Why? Their poor friend, now receiving his last stitch, has long been dead on the table! Dr. Cuticle had not even noticed.[9] Cold Dr. Cuticle — a man with icewater in his veins — was insensitive and void of empathy.

But such is never to be the case with Christians, as the writer to the Hebrews further commands: "Remember those in prison as if you were their fellow prisoners, and those who are mistreated as if you yourselves were suffering" (v. 3). In this respect, the little Jewish church had earlier excelled, as the preacher averred in 10:32-34:

> Remember those earlier days after you had received the light, when you stood your ground in a great contest in the face of suffering. Sometimes you were publicly exposed to insult and persecution; at other times you stood side by side with those who were so treated. You sympathized with those in prison and joyfully accepted the confiscation of your property, because you knew that you yourselves had better and lasting possessions.

And how important their sympathetic caring had been, because those suffering the abuse of prison were virtually dependent on the church for survival.

The early church had a remarkable reputation in the pagan community for caring for its own. Lucian, again, has his bogus Christian, Proteus Peregrinus, tossed into prison, and, satirical as Lucian was, the sympathetic care of Christians shines. Says Lucian, the Christians

> . . . left nothing undone in the effort to rescue him. Then, as this was impossible, every other form of attention was shown him, not in any casual way but with assiduity; and from the very break of day aged widows and orphan children could be seen waiting near the prison, while their officials even slept inside with him after bribing the guards. The elaborate meals were brought in, and sacred books of theirs were read aloud. (*The Passing of Peregrinus*, 12)[10]

Similarly, *The Apology of Aristides* describes Christians' care for the incarcerated, saying:

> If they hear that any of their number is imprisoned or oppressed for the name of their Messiah, all of them provide for his needs, and if it is possible that he may be delivered, they deliver him. If there is

among them a man that is poor or needy, and they have not an abundance of necessaries, they fast two or three days that they may supply the needy with their necessary food.[11]

How beautiful the church had been and would continue to be!

But here we see the preacher giving his people a profound prod to a sublime empathy — an empathy so deep that they would will to project themselves into the inner life of those suffering mistreatment and imprisonment. The unadorned empathy commanded here was not based on the esoteric truth that Christians are members of each other in Christ, but rather on the truth of shared humanity. Project your humanity into the place where their humanity now is — in suffering or in prison.

This call is especially relevant to us modern Christians who have had our empathizing faculties increasingly dulled by the electronic media that assaults us daily with images of suffering narrated with the professional, detached nonchalance of the network anchors.

We must *will* to identify with the imprisoned and mistreated. None of us can excuse ourselves by rationalizing that we are not empathetic by nature. We are to labor at an imaginative sympathy through the power of God!

In summary, we are to stand at the foot of the two mountains and gaze reverently at God's consuming fire and consuming love. We are to drink it in with all its mysterious paradox — for in it lies the vision of God.

But having gazed upward we turn from the *vertical* to the *horizontal*, from the *indicative* to the *imperative* — the ethics of a life aglow with God. And here we must will to obey the imperatives — God's commands.

- We must will to practice brotherly love, *philadelphia* : "Keep on loving each other as brothers" (v. 1). We must will to contemplate the fact of our mutual generation, its profundity and eternity. Our words and actions must be committed to enhancing brotherly love.
- We must will to practice love of hospitality, *philozenia* — a love for strangers: "Do not forget to entertain strangers, for by so doing some people have entertained angels without knowing it" (v. 2). Open hearts and open houses are the Christian way. Hospitality builds the Body of Christ and opens the door to a lost world.
- We must will to be empathetic, to be imaginatively sympathetic: "Remember those in prison as if you were their fellow prisoners, and those who are mistreated as if you yourselves were suffering" (v. 3). The will to imaginative sympathy will make our hearts like that of the Master and will encourage an authentic Christian walk.

Marriage should be honored by all, and the marriage bed kept pure, for God will judge the adulterer and all the sexually immoral. Keep your lives free from the love of money and be content with what you have, because God has said, "Never will I leave you; never will I forsake you." So we say with confidence, "The Lord is my helper; I will not be afraid. What can man do to me?" (13:4-6)

21

Personal Ethics

HEBREWS 13:4-6

From the beginning to the end of Hebrews, the abiding concern of the author has been to so instruct the tiny Hebrew church that it would stay afloat on the increasingly hostile seas of first-century Roman culture. Their ship was a microscopic dot on the massive billows of the official pagan/secular enterprise — and eminently vulnerable. It appeared to outside eyes that the external forces could sink it at will.

But the author knew that the internal threat to the church was far more deadly. In fact, he knew that it could ride out any storm if things were right on the inside. That is why, in our preceding study (vv. 1-3), the preacher so strongly emphasized ecclesial ethics, instructing his people on how to treat those on board the ship — the church. Specifically, he advised, first, brotherly love, then hospitality, and then the necessity of sympathetically identifying with those in the church who were undergoing suffering.

Now in the present text, verses 4-6, he becomes even more intimate in his advice, giving very personal ethical directives about *marriage*, *money*, and one's *mind-set*. He knows that nothing will sink a church faster than moral wavering in respect to sex, materialism, or mental outlook. Here is intimate advice regarding how to keep our ship afloat. It is so essential that any church that ignores it will founder and possibly even sink.

215

ADVICE ABOUT MARRIAGE (v. 4)

The advice about marriage is direct and unequivocal: "Marriage should be honored by all, and the marriage bed kept pure, for God will judge the adulterer and all the sexually immoral" (v. 4).

Marriage and Honor

Here the command to honor marriage is directed at those who dishonored it in two opposite ways — *asceticism* and *libertinism*. Some first-century Christian ascetics considered "virginity as necessary to Christian perfection."[1] This later developed in the second century into the Montanist movement, which later spawned celibate monasticism. To such, those who choose marriage choose inferior spirituality. Marriage was thus implicitly dishonored. But the greatest assault on marriage's honor came from the libertines who saw marriage as irrelevant as they pursued unbridled sexual fulfillment.

These first-century extremes foreshadowed the modern contempt for marriage. For example, Count Leo Tolstoy embraced a perverse marital asceticism late in life, claiming that the responsibilities of marriage impeded his progress in moral perfection. Since he had a large family, this was a remarkable assertion. In an outburst to his daughter Tanya written in 1897 he said:

> I can understand why a depraved man may find salvation in marriage. But why a pure girl should want to get mixed up in such a business is beyond me. If I were a girl I would not marry for anything in the world. And so far as being in love is concerned, for either men and women — since I know what it means, that is, it is an ignoble and above all an unhealthy sentiment, not at all beautiful, lofty or poetical — I would not have opened my door to it. I would have taken as many precautions to avoid being contaminated by that disease as I would to protect myself against far less serious infections such as diphtheria, typhus or scarlet fever.[2]

Tolstoy's wide acceptance, and his radical chic style, gave his ideas unusual weight among the avant-garde culture-shapers of the early twentieth century and ultimately provided grist for subsequent secular attacks by both heterosexuals and homosexuals on marriage. Today radical secular wisdom claims that marriage impedes self-actualization — an unforgivable sin in modern eyes.

However, the main attacks today are mostly libertine. For many, "marriage" is at best a provisional arrangement between two people (sexual orientation is irrelevant) that can be dissolved whenever one wishes, for any reason. To be sure, conventional attitudes toward marriage are not as extreme, though there is a growing skepticism regarding love and marriage. As one person sarcastically put it, "Love: temporary insanity curable by marriage."

But for those of us who live under the authority of God's Word, marriage is an ordinance of God. Genesis proclaims, after God gave Eve to Adam, "For this reason a man will leave his father and mother and be united to his wife, and they will become one flesh" (2:24). Marriage is patently heterosexual and indissoluble. As Jesus said, "Therefore what God has joined together, let man not separate" (Matthew 19:6). Jesus honored marriage by performing his first miracle at a wedding (John 2:1ff.). The Holy Spirit further honored it in Ephesians 5 by using it to portray the relationship of Christ and his church (vv. 23-32).

Therefore, in the words of our text, "Marriage should be honored by all" — or more literally, "Let marriage be precious to all of you." As Christians we celebrate marriage. We joyfully surround a couple as out of their depth they make those wild sacred promises to each other. And we celebrate the mystery with ancient invocations and feasting. Marriage is divinely given and deserves our greatest honor!

Marriage and Purity

Indispensable, of course, to the honor of marriage is purity, and thus the text adds, "and the marriage bed kept pure" (v. 4b). "Bed" is used here as a euphemism for sexual intercourse, and in demanding that it be kept "pure" "our author is referring in sacrificial terms to married chastity."[3] The bed — the sexual relationship — is an altar, so to speak, where a pure offering of a couple's lives is made to each other and to God.

This was radical stuff in the pagan context — and Christians lived it out. When Pliny was sent by the Roman Emperor Trajan to govern the province of Bithynia and looked for charges against the Christians, he had to report back that on the Lord's Day, "They bound themselves by oath, not for any criminal end, but to avoid theft or adultery, never to break their word. . . ."[4] Christian sexual morality was unique in the pagan world and a source of wonder. And it has become increasingly so today in a world that considers adultery irrelevant, purity abnormal, and sex a "right" (however and with whomever one may get it) and that has invented the egregious term "recreational sex."

We Christians are called to be outrageously pure — to be a source of wonder and even derision to this glandular world.

Marriage and Judgment

That we are called to radical purity is nothing to trifle with because the call concludes, "for God will judge the adulterer and all the sexually immoral" (v. 4c). This means that everyone — ostensible Christians and non-Christians alike — will be judged for adultery (extramarital sexual relations) and sexual immorality (other illicit sexual relations, including perversions). Further, those who have taken up adulterous lifestyles and remain unrepentant will suffer ultimate judgment and damnation, for despite their insistence that they are "Christians," they are self-deceived. God's Word is terrifyingly clear:

> Do you not know that the wicked will not inherit the kingdom of God? Do not be deceived: Neither the sexually immoral nor idolaters nor adulterers nor male prostitutes nor homosexual offenders . . . will inherit the kingdom of God. (1 Corinthians 6:9, 10)

> For of this you can be sure: No immoral, impure or greedy person — such a man is an idolater — has any inheritance in the kingdom of Christ and of God. Let no one deceive you with empty words, for because of such things God's wrath comes on those who are disobedient. (Ephesians 5:5, 6)

> It is God's will that you should be holy; that you should avoid sexual immorality. . . . The Lord will punish men for all such sins, as we have already told you and warned you. For God did not call us to be impure, but to live a holy life. (1 Thessalonians 4:3-7)

> But the cowardly, the unbelieving, the vile, the murderers, the sexually immoral, those who practice magic arts, the idolaters and all liars — their place will be in the fiery lake of burning sulfur. This is the second death. (Revelation 21:8; cf. 22:15)

All who are living in serial adultery or fornication and are unrepentant are under God's wrath and ultimate judgment regardless of what they assert about a salvation experience.

The judgment God metes out has both a future and a present reality. In the future, unbelieving sensualists will stand before the Great White Throne and be judged accordingly (cf. Revelation 20:11ff.), and Christians will stand before the Judgment Seat of Christ where their works will be judged (cf. 2 Corinthians 5:10; 1 Corinthians 3:11-15).

Nothwithstanding the inexorable coming of the future judgment, the fact remains that infidelity and its attendant sexual immoralities also regularly inflict judgment in the present. Significantly, Paul tells us, "Flee from sexual immorality. All other sins a man commits are outside his body, but he who sins sexually sins against his own body" (1 Corinthians 6:18). *Physical* misery grimly follows immorality in the present epidemics of herpes and AIDS. *Mental* firestorms afflict millions in the form of guilt, self-hatred and ego disintegration. *Relational* wars are the proverbial result of sensuality —

alienation, estrangement, hatred and sometimes murder. *Societal* degradation follows — jungle ethics, brutalization, illegitimate children, abortion. Anyone who imagines that unrepentant adultery and sexual immorality will go unpunished is in La-la Land. It is happening right now from every angle, and in addition a terrible judgment awaits, for all unrepentant sinners will stand before God, who is a "consuming fire" (cf. 12:29; 10:27).

But what does this have to do with the survival of the church? Everything! I can think of no more efficient way to sink that ship than through adultery and sexual immorality. The reasons are elementary. Immorality perverts theology. I have seen this time and time again with preachers — famous and unknown. They become involved in a secret affair (perhaps several) and yet keep on preaching. But over time an amazing phenomenon takes place — they unconsciously detach themselves from truth. Like the ancient Averroists, they divide truth, so that there is a truth for them and another truth for others. They may not articulate this, but they become practical relativists, and their relativism so eats away at their belief that many, after the trauma of discovery, leave the faith. Tragic shipwreck!

The damage to the church is immense. Preachers caught in such sins suffer a reduction in spiritual ethos. They increasingly sound like old-time railroad conductors who loudly invite people to embark to destinations they themselves have never visited and to which they are incapable of traveling. Powerlessness becomes the hallmark of their rhetoric.

And, of course, they discredit the Word. I can think of no better way to damn the soul of a junior-higher who is just beginning to experience spiritual stirrings than through the fall of a pastor, Sunday school teacher, or other spiritual leader. There can be no more efficient way to dampen the spiritual aspiration of a young family man than adulterous leaders. Because such sin is a particularly lethal sin against the church, I have at times prayed this with my ministerial colleagues: "Lord, if adultery would lie in the future for any of us should we continue to live — then take us home now." Better dead than damage the church!

So, if we want to keep the ship afloat, we must hear and heed God's Word: "Marriage should be honored by all, and the marriage bed kept pure, for God will judge the adulterer and all the sexually immoral" (v. 4).

ADVICE ABOUT MONEY (v. 5)

The second corresponding part of the writer's advice for keeping the church shipshape has to do with money: "Keep your lives free from the love of money and be content with what you have, because God has said, 'Never will I leave you; never will I forsake you'" (v. 5). The author knew that those who loved the world would not stand firm in a storm — that those with the greatest affection for wealth would be the first to turn aside when they understood that losses and crosses would come from sailing with Christ.

Not Covetousness . . .

Covetousness is plainly forbidden here and elsewhere in the Scriptures. "Keep your lives free from the love of money," begins the command. The Scriptures present a desire for wealth as a danger. After Jesus' encounter with the rich young man, Mark tells us:

> Jesus looked around and said to his disciples, "How hard it is for the rich to enter the kingdom of God!" The disciples were amazed at his words. But Jesus said again, "Children, how hard it is to enter the kingdom of God! It is easier for a camel to go through the eye of a needle than for a rich man to enter the kingdom of God." The disciples were even more amazed, and said to each other, "Who then can be saved?" Jesus looked at them and said, "With man this is impossible, but not with God; all things are possible with God." (10:23-27)

Jesus' point was that it is impossible for a man who trusts in riches to get into Heaven, because a rich man trusts in himself! However, by the grace of God it is possible. God's grace can change hearts. At the end of the Sermon on the Mount Jesus recommended:

> Do not store up for yourselves treasures on earth, where moth and rust destroy, and where thieves break in and steal. But store up for yourselves treasures in heaven, where moth and rust do not destroy, and where thieves do not break in and steal. For where your treasure is, there your heart will be also. (Matthew 6:19-21)

Miserly hoarding casts a metallic, lifeless heart. A few verses later Jesus concludes, "No one can serve two masters. Either he will hate the one and love the other, or he will be devoted to the one and despise the other. You cannot serve both God and Money" (Matthew 6:24).

Wealth has its disadvantages. It is difficult to have it and not trust in it. Material possessions tend to focus one's thoughts and interests on this world alone. It can enslave so that one becomes possessed by possessions, comforts, and recreations. Jesus said, "The deceitfulness of wealth and the desire for other things come in and choke the word" (Mark 4:19).

Though wealth has its intrinsic disadvantages, the preacher here is not forbidding wealth but "the love of money." In one sense, such love is no respecter of persons. It can equally afflict a homeless man sleeping on a grate or the man occupying the penthouse sixty stories above him. But, this said, it is difficult not to love what you have spent your life collecting. Paul warned

Timothy, "For the love of money is a root of all kinds of evil. Some people, eager for money, have wandered from the faith and pierced themselves with many griefs" (1 Timothy 6:10).

The warning stands for all of us to hear, for we are rich people. It is a special warning for the captains or helmsmen of the church — those who are to pilot others through the storms. "Now the overseer must . . . not [be] a lover of money" (1 Timothy 3:2, 3). Do not even entertain the tiniest thought of church leadership if you are a lover of money.

. . . But Contentment

The covetous, those who love money, will never be content. The author of Ecclesiastes informs us, "Whoever loves money never has money enough; whoever loves wealth is never satisfied with his income" (5:10). Our hearts resonate with the wisdom of these ancient words. C. H. Spurgeon amplifies this thought:

> It is not possible to satisfy the greedy. If God gave them one whole world to themselves they would cry for another; and if it were possible for them to possess heaven as they now are, they would feel themselves in hell, because others were in heaven too, for their greed is such that they must have everything or else they have nothing.[5]

A story received from ancient times tells of a king who was suffering from a certain malady and was advised by his wise men that he would be cured if the shirt of a contented man were brought to him to wear. The search began for a contented man, but none could be found. So emissaries were sent to the edge of the realm, and after a long search a man was found who was truly content. But he had no shirt! The consensus of enduring wisdom is that contentment comes from a source other than things or possessions.

The Christian knows that true contentment comes from resting in God's care, and this is evident when we follow the flow of verse 5: "And be content with what you have, because God has said, 'Never will I leave you; never will I forsake you'" (v. 5c). In other words, "Christians, be content because you have God — and he will never forsake you!"

Where in the Old Testament did God say he would never leave us or forsake us? Only occasionally explicitly, but everywhere implicitly! God told Jacob as he fled from Esau to Bethel, "I am with you. . . . I will not leave you" (Genesis 28:15). Moses encouraged the Israelites, "Be strong and courageous. Do not be afraid or terrified because of them, for the Lord your God goes with you; he will never leave you nor forsake you" (Deuteronomy 31:6, cf. vv. 7, 8). When Joshua was called to take over Moses' leadership, God said, "I will be with you; I will never leave you or forsake you" (Joshua 1:5).

David instructed Solomon, "Do not be afraid or discouraged, for the Lord God, my God, is with you" (1 Chronicles 28:20).

In no situation will God leave us, nor for any reason will he leave us. He will not leave us even for a little while. He may seem to hide his face, but he will not leave us.

> *The soul that on Jesus hath lean'd for repose,*
> *I will not, I will not, desert to his foes;*
> *That soul, though all hell should endeavour to shake,*
> *I'll never, no never, no never forsake.*
>
> (*Rippon's Hymns*, 1787)

We will be content if we truly embrace the fact that we have God! The Apostle Paul was content. Destitute of worldly possessions, Paul sublimely speaks of himself as "having nothing, and yet possessing everything" (2 Corinthians 6:10). "I know what it is to be in need," he told the Philippians, "and I know what it is to have plenty. I have learned the secret of being content in any and every situation" (Philippians 4:12). And then to Timothy, he gave this jewel: "But godliness with contentment is great gain. For we brought nothing into the world, and we can take nothing out of it. But if we have food and clothing, we will be content with that" (1 Timothy 6:6-8).

A boatload of discontented materialists — lovers of money — will not do well in the coming storms. Those who always want more will turn away from God when their Christianity brings material subtraction rather than addition. On the other hand, those who are content — who have found their ultimate treasure in the unflagging presence and care of God — will sail on!

Today only those who adopt a head-in-the-sand/Pollyanna view will doubt that the tides of secular culture are becoming increasingly hostile and restless. Right now, traditional Judeo-Christian sexual morality regarding marriage, fidelity, sexual orientation and unborn life is considered reactionary by the dominant culture-shapers. The day is fast approaching when those who hold to Christian sexual ethics will be social pariahs.

Heavy seas are ahead, and there are two things that could keep the church from riding the storm — wrong thinking on *sex* and on *money*. It is of the greatest importance that we honor marriage as God's divinely given ordinance. It is imperative that we keep the marriage bed pure so we will not undergo judgment and lose our authenticity and power. Having refused sensual seduction, we must also resist the vacuous seduction of money. Our contentment must announce to our fellow-Christians and the world that Christ is with us and for us — and that he is enough!

Furthermore, our mind-set must be crowned with matchless confidence: "So we say with confidence, 'The Lord is my helper; I will not be afraid. What can man do to me?'" (v. 6). This is the mind-set that will ride the waves no matter what — just as Chrysostom did when he was brought before the Roman emperor and was threatened with banishment:

> "Thou canst not banish me for this world is my father's house." "But I will slay thee," said the Emperor. "Nay, thou canst not," said the noble champion of the faith, "for my life is hid with Christ in God." "I will take away thy treasures." "Nay, but thou canst not for my treasure is in heaven and my heart is there." "But I will drive thee away from man and thou shalt have no friend left." "Nay, thou canst not, for I have a friend in heaven from whom thou canst not separate me. I defy thee; for there is nothing that thou canst do to hurt me."[6]

Remember your leaders, who spoke the word of God to you. Consider the outcome of their way of life and imitate their faith. Jesus Christ is the same yesterday and today and forever. Do not be carried away by all kinds of strange teachings. It is good for our hearts to be strengthened by grace, not by ceremonial foods, which are of no value to those who eat them. We have an altar from which those who minister at the tabernacle have no right to eat. The high priest carries the blood of animals into the Most Holy Place as a sin offering, but the bodies are burned outside the camp. And so Jesus also suffered outside the city gate to make the people holy through his own blood. Let us, then, go to him outside the camp, bearing the disgrace he bore. For here we do not have an enduring city, but we are looking for the city that is to come. Through Jesus, therefore, let us continually offer to God a sacrifice of praise — the fruit of lips that confess his name. And do not forget to do good and to share with others, for with such sacrifices God is pleased. (13:7-16)

22

Sustaining Wisdom

HEBREWS 13:7-16

When I first met Joe Bayly it was late in his life and early in my ministry — a number of years ago when I was called to pastor College Church in Wheaton, Illinois, a church of which Joe had been a member for over twenty years. My first glimpse of Joe was as he sat Quaker-bearded with his wife, Mary Lou, on the front pew smiling benignly (like the face on the oatmeal box) and listening to my forgettable candidating sermon. How would I fare, I wondered, with this imposing personality, the author of the sometimes acerbic *Eternity Magazine* column "Out of My Mind"?

Happily, I learned the smile was real and that Joe Bayly cared little about where I came from, though he was concerned about who I was. Indeed, among the first things he said to me was in reference to the church's highly educated congregation: "Just remember, Pastor, we all slip our trousers on one leg at a time." Joe was put off by anyone and anything that smacked of condescension — especially smarmy, condescending preachers! He was, in fact, a spiritual populist because he truly believed that he could learn from everyone — and so he treated all his acquaintances with equal respect.

As it turned out, Barbara and I became close friends of Joe and Mary Lou, so that in addition to our occasional meals together, our family was regularly included in the Bayly family gatherings during the holidays and such memorable events as sipping apple cider while Joe sat in his rocking chair and read aloud Truman Capote's haunting *A Christmas Memory*.

225

But what stands out most about the Bayly get-togethers was the conversation between Joe and his grown children and anyone else at the table. Joe had brought his children up to reason Biblically and logically about everything, so conversation was always laced with spirited, cheerful family forthrightness. If you had the temerity to state your viewpoint, you had better be ready to defend it. "You believe that?" No quarter was extended, especially to Joe himself.

Joe was profoundly Biblical in his thinking. And, of course, this is one of the reasons Joe was something of a gadfly to the evangelical enterprise. No bromides, trendy or conventional, ever fell from Joe Bayly's pen because he was rigorously orthodox and Biblical and therefore gloriously radical!

Joe Bayly was a prophet — a voice of sanity in an upside-down world. His writings were always penetrating, whether humoring us to greater idealism and faith as he did in *I Saw Gooley Fly* or steeling us for the future with the Orwellian chill of *Winterflight*. Where principle was involved, Joe was a straight shooter and a fighter. And this left him with his share of enemies. But agree or disagree — like him or not — he was never equivocating or disingenuous. His trademark — clarity and economy of expression — left no doubt about where he stood.

He personally made us feel safe. Amidst the confusion, there was always Joe Bayly, who rejected weak-minded reasoning and would think things through, kindly telling us what he thought — right or wrong. Joe's bracing effect was to make us stand up for what we believed.

As his pastor, I witnessed firsthand his belief in the church. For years, he team-taught the Covenant Class, a transgenerational Sunday school class of grandparents, parents, their college-age children, and singles, including unmarried, divorced, and widowed. The Bayly home regularly hosted numerous singles. Though super-busy, Joe also served as prophet, writer, poet, preacher, business executive, and elder.

Joe Bayly always brought with him a sense of the numinous — that life is supernatural and that there is always more. To be sure, this had much to do with the early death of three of his children. But it was also due to his radical Biblical mind-set, for he volitionally set his mind on things above. I remember hearing him say in his final sermon at College Church, "Oh, God, burn eternity into my eyeballs. Help me to see all of this life through the perspective of eternity." God used Joe Bayly to do this for thousands of us.

Perhaps once a month I say to my wife, "I miss Joe Bayly," and we smile and agree that no one has come to replace him — at least for us.

REMEMBER SPIRITUAL LEADERS (v. 7)

Why this consciously sainted biographical memory? The reason is to draw our attention to the indispensable wisdom enjoined in the opening verse of our text: "Remember your leaders, who spoke the word of God to you. Consider the outcome of their way of life and imitate their faith" (v. 7). From this we see that my memory of Joe Bayly is not only a Biblical exercise but is divinely commanded. Why? Because considering Joe Bayly's life and its outcome and humbly attempting to imitate it will encourage me to straighten up and sail right! His conscious commitment to point his ship into the winds of culture, if that is where Scripture points, puts steel in my walk. His sailing style, the trim of his sails, the tilt of his vessel are all salutary to my soul.

Significantly, this is beautifully consistent with the purpose of chapter 13, which is to strengthen the little Hebrew church so it will ride out the coming storms of persecution. A church that adequately recalls its godly leaders and considers the outcome of their way of life and attempts to imitate that way of life will sail well! Remembering, considering, and imitating the virtues of departed believers is of greatest spiritual importance both to one's family and to the broader family of the Body of Christ. Doing so will certainly help keep the boat afloat.

REMEMBER JESUS CHRIST (v. 8)

Departed saints, of course, bless the memory of those who have known them, but they are no longer available for counsel. I cannot talk to Joe Bayly! But Jesus Christ is always available, for as the writer adds in what is perhaps the most famous verse in Hebrews, "Jesus Christ is the same yesterday and today and forever" (v. 8).

What a contrast with the changeableness of us humans and of life here on earth. The cycle from birth to death is a testament to our human mutability. The supple, sweet flesh of a newborn prospers like a flower and then fades and wrinkles and is finally cast off in death. Human personality never ceases changing. Some freshen with time, others sour, most do a little of both. Relationships wax and wane. To meet one twenty years from now may be to meet another person. Forests rise and stand for a millennium — and fade into deserts. Rivers cut canyons and disappear. Newtonian physics, with its straight lines and right angles, is replaced by Einstein's elegant curves of relativity.[1] The only thing that is sure is change! We humans appear for a little while to laugh and weep and work and play, and then we are gone. This is a melancholy thought at best. Our souls long for something solid.

But the great truth is, God does not change, and neither does the Holy Spirit or the Son, Jesus Christ. In fact, the very same Old Testament Scriptures and wording that describe God the Father's immutableness are applied directly to Christ (cf. Psalm 102:27 and Hebrews 1:12; Isaiah 48:12 and Revelation 1:17). This means that though the Savior has ascended into Heaven and dwells in that splendor, he is the same! He is the same in his wrath and his love and mercy and compassion and tenderness as he was here on earth. *Yesterday* Jesus "offered up prayers and petitions with loud cries and tears to the one who could save him from death" (5:7). *Today* he is a high priest before the Father who is able to sympathize with our weakness because he "has been tempted in every way, just as we are — yet was without sin" (4:15). And *forever* this same Jesus "always lives to intercede for them" (7:25).[2] Our priest is eternally the same and eternally contemporary. We need not fear opinion changes or mood swings in Jesus!

> *I stay myself on Him who stays*
> *Ever the same through nights and days.*[3]

No matter what lies ahead in this always-changing world with its drifting continents and fading suns — no matter what the seas may bring, we must sustain ourselves with this double-focus — remembering those who have gone before and focusing on Jesus Christ, our eternal, unchangeable contemporary. Those who truly do this will navigate the roughest seas.

A SUSTAINING UNDERSTANDING (vv. 9-14)

The little Jewish church was not only harried by the imminent threat of persecution, but was also assailed within by the succumbing of some in the congregation to a strange teaching that combined esoteric eating practices with their Christian faith. No one knows exactly what the practices were, though we do know that some held that their sacred menu would make them better Christians.

Understanding Christ's Nourishment

To such the writer/preacher warns, "Do not be carried away by all kinds of strange teachings. It is good for our hearts to be strengthened by grace, not by ceremonial foods, which are of no value to those who eat them. We have an altar from which those who minister at the tabernacle have no right to eat" (vv. 9, 10). Those who imagined that spiritual growth came through a special menu had not only become ignorant of the necessity of grace for growth, but they actually blocked strengthening grace by their proud little rules.

Grace, like the earth's water system, operates on gravity — the spiritual "gravity of grace." Just as the waters of Niagara roll over the falls and plunge down to make a river below, and just as that river flows ever down to the even lower ranges of its course, then glides to still more low-lying areas where it brings life and growth, so it is with God's grace. Grace's gravity carries it to the lowly in heart, where it brings life and blessing. Grace goes to the humble.

This is the spiritual law behind Proverbs 3:34, which James 4:6 quotes: "'God opposes the proud but gives grace to the humble.'" The unbowed soul

228

standing proudly before God receives no benefit from God's falling grace. It may descend upon him, but it does not penetrate, and drips away like rain from a statue. But the soul lying before God is immersed — and even swims — in a sea of grace. So while there is always more grace, it is reserved for the lowly and the humble. Legalisms, even "little" ones such as dietary rules, impede grace. Humility invites the elevating weight of grace!

Actually, the grace we imbibe comes directly from the cross of Christ, for in verse 10 the preacher adds, "We have an altar from which those who minister at the tabernacle have no right to eat," referring to the cross because in a Christian context the sacrifice must be on the cross — the sacrificial altar of our faith.[4] Our spiritual food is nothing less than the life of Christ!

The force of these thoughts is phenomenal. Jesus Christ is eternally the same and eternally contemporary. Therefore, do not get mixed up with strange teaching such as that leading to spiritual diets. Our nourishment comes from grace, which comes directly from the altar — the cross of Christ. This meal goes to the humble!

Understanding Christ's Accessibility

The meal, the work of the cross, also goes only to those "outside the camp" — those who do not subscribe to the old Jewish system. Here the preacher uses a very Hebrew argument to make his point: "The high priest carries the blood of animals into the Most Holy Place as a sin offering, but the bodies are burned outside the camp. And so Jesus also suffered outside the city gate to make the people holy through his own blood" (vv. 11, 12).

The logic goes like this: the sacrifices offered on the Jewish great Day of Atonement were a prophetic type for the sacrifice of Christ, the Lamb of God who takes away the sin of the world (John 1:29). On the Day of Atonement a bull was slain to atone for the sins of the priest and his family, and a lamb likewise was sacrificed for the sins of the rest of the people. The blood of these sacrifices was taken into the Holy of Holies, but both the carcasses were taken outside the camp and burned up (Leviticus 16:27). Therefore, those under the old sacrificial system could not partake of this great offering as a meal.

But Jesus, the ultimate atoning lamb, was sacrificed outside the camp — outside Jerusalem's walls, on Golgotha — as an offering to God. This means two great things: 1) All those who remained committed to the old Jewish system were excluded from the benefit of partaking of Christ's atoning death. And, 2) Jesus' death outside the camp means that he is accessible to anyone in the world who will come to him. Jesus planted his cross in the world so all the world could have access. And there he remains permanently available!

There thus remains only one thing to do, and so the writer exhorts us: "Let us, then, go to him outside the camp, bearing the disgrace he bore. For here we do not have an enduring city, but we are looking for the city that is to come" (vv. 13, 14). The cities of the earth — all earthly institutions — will fall apart. Only the heavenly Zion will remain. We must go, flee to him outside the camp, and willfully embrace his "disgrace," for such an act is worth doing a million times over! Thus Jesus Christ, who is "the same yesterday and today and forever," becomes our constant meal — our food, our drink, our life — and we will receive from him grace upon grace upon grace. And because he is outside the camp, he will always be accessible. In fact, he is with us, in us, and coming to us! This understanding that he *nourishes* us and is *accessible* to us will help us keep on course.

A SUSTAINING LIFESTYLE (vv. 15, 16)

There is one final thing that will sustain us, and that is how we live — our lifestyle — specifically, *worship* and *work*. Or as Coventry Patmore put it, to be "Mary in the house of God/A Martha in our own."

Worshiping Christ

We must make worship the first priority of living: "Through Jesus, therefore, let us continually offer to God a sacrifice of praise — the fruit of lips that confess his name" (v. 15). We all need to be like Mary — at Jesus' feet looking up so that he fills the whole horizon. She worshiped him "in spirit" (John 4:23, 24) because her whole being was passionately engaged in giving him worth. In fact, in a sublime moment she gave her very best for him as *snap!* went the alabaster flask, and she poured her fortune onto Jesus. Jesus said, "She has done a beautiful thing to me" (Mark 14:6).

Here our text is very specific about what he wants. It is a sacrifice — "a sacrifice of praise — the fruit of lips that confess his name." He wants us to say it. He wants to hear us verbally praise him.

> *O God, I love Thee, I love Thee —*
>> *Not out of hope of heaven for me*
> *Nor fearing not to love and be*
>> *In the everlasting burning.*
> *Thou, Thou, my Jesus, after me*
>> *Didst reach Thine arms out dying,*
> *For my sake sufferedst nails and lance,*
>> *Mocked and marred countenance,*
> *Sorrows passing number*
>> *Sweat and care and cumber,*
> *Yea and death, and this for me,*
>> *And Thou couldest see me sinning:*

> *Then I, why should not I love Thee;*
> *Jesus so much in love with me?*
> *Not for heaven's sake; not to be*
> *Out of hell by loving Thee;*
> *Not for any gains I see;*
> *But just that Thou didst me*
> *I do and I will love Thee:*
> *What must I love Thee, Lord, for then? —*
> *For being my King and God. Amen.*

(O Deus Ego Amo Te, Gerard Manley Hopkins)

Working for Christ

Mary must be balanced by Martha in our souls: "And do not forget to do good and to share with others, for with such sacrifices God is pleased" (v. 16). True worship always involves giving ourselves in the service of Christ and others (cf. Romans 12:1; James 1:27; 1 John 3:17, 18). We may participate in an elegant call to worship and prayer, heartily sing the *Gloria Patri*, solemnly repeat the Apostles' Creed, join together in a grand hymn, reverently pray the Lord's Prayer, and attentively listen to the Word, but if we do not do good to others and share what we have, none of it gives pleasure to God. But worship coupled with work — this brings God's pleasure and the winds of the Holy Spirit to our sails so we can ride the most daunting waves.

Sustaining power for the storms of life? How to keep the Good Ship Grace seaworthy?

- First, we must have a sustaining *memory* of two things: 1) a considered memory of the Joe Baylys in our lives and a resolve to humbly imitate their virtues by God's grace; and even more, 2) the measured memory that "Jesus Christ is the same yesterday and today and forever" — that his sustaining love for us will never ever vary. These dual memories will help us stay on course.
- Second, we need a sustaining *understanding* of the nourishment and access Christ provides us. He nourishes us from the cross, resulting in grace and more grace. And he remains outside the camp — in the world — perpetually accessible and inviting.
- Third, there must be a sustaining *lifestyle* that worships like Mary and works like Martha.

These are the keys to safe navigation in a dangerous world!

Obey your leaders and submit to their authority. They keep watch over you as men who must give an account. Obey them so that their work will be a joy, not a burden, for that would be of no advantage to you. Pray for us. We are sure that we have a clear conscience and desire to live honorably in every way. I particularly urge you to pray so that I may be restored to you soon. (13:17-19)

23

Responsibility Toward Leadership

HEBREWS 13:17-19

In 1987 Barbara and I coauthored a book entitled *Liberating Ministry from the Success Syndrome*, targeted to encourage fellow-ministers and Christian workers in their labors for Christ, especially those ministering in less visible places. The book chronicled our early struggle in a small church and how we came to grips with "success," first Biblically and then practically. The result was a surprising flood of letters and phone calls asking for prayer and advice and also invitations to speak. So over the last five years we have spoken to numerous denominational conferences and gatherings of pastors, both old-line and independent, from Maine to California.

In our travels we discovered this: pastors as a group are one of the most hurting and abused segments of our society. This is not an isolated observation. Bill Waldrop, executive director of Advancing Churches and Missions Commitment (ACMC), and his wife, Doris, in their wide travels on behalf of church missions have witnessed the same thing. The four of us have shared our observations at some length. Perhaps the reason we see this so much is that as interlopers we are "safe" to talk to. We are not a part of our listeners' denominations, we do not run in their circles, we have few mutual acquaintances, and best of all, we will be gone shortly afterwards! So, very often

233

after a few congenial remarks a pastor and wife will ask to "talk," and we hear it all — and much of it would tax the credulity of the uninitiated.

Why such pain for so many in ministerial leadership experience? Here are a few reasons:

Christian media. Millions of Christians spend hours daily listening to Christian radio where they hear a top handful of Christian preachers and teachers giving their best stuff, edited and packaged with artistically interspersed background music. Though once isolated, farmers today plow their fields tuned in with headphones while their wives listen to the same programs one after another — sometimes for eight hours a day as they go about their household duties. When they come to church on Sunday they find the fare to be pedestrian and dull in comparison. So at the door the pastor hears things like: "That was interesting, pastor . . . Eh . . . I have a tape by Dr. Frank Lee Terrific that is along the same line. I think you should listen to it. In fact, here it is." The pastor smiles and says, "Thank you." He gets the message but also senses a reduction of his esteem and authority.

Big business mentality. Another source of abuse of those in ministry is a rung-dropping, business-world mentality that divides its world into big fish and small-fry. This mind-set regards the captains of, say, the food industry as fit subjects for veneration, whereas the proprietors of a mom-and-pop grocery store are scarcely worthy of notice. The result in such minds is that the proprietors of a mom-and-pop church are, well, shall we say, lightweights.

American individualism and subjectivism. American individualism is proverbial. And millions of Christians are afflicted with an underlying attitude that imagines we can each go it alone — without the church or anyone else. If we have the Lord, we need nothing else. In fact, this line of thinking can even conclude that bowing to any human spiritual authority will result in a reduction of one's own spirituality. This reaches its destructive apex when a person says, "Well, that's what you think, pastor. But my opinion is as good as yours." The truth is, one's opinion may be even better than the pastor's. But the appeal to the magisterium of one's subjective opinion is a specious appeal. One's opinion is only as good as or better than another's if it is supported by Scripture and rigorous logic. Pastoral authority evaporates where individualism and subjectivism reign.

So, we see that leadership is difficult in the modern church because the ever-present radio has inbred in some an implicit disregard for local pulpits. The disregard has been further fed by a worldly business mentality that regards bigger as worthy of more respect. Mix in the anti-authoritarian strain of American individualism and subjectivism, and it all adds up to a leadership crisis for the modern church and an entire generation of beat-up clergy. No wonder that in so many places the church is awash, drifting aimlessly, and at the mercy of the hostile seas of neo-pagan culture.

What is the answer? Helpfully the essential remedy is provided in verses 17-19, where the preacher/writer gives instruction about the church's responsibility toward leadership. Although the specific dynamics of the early church's anti-authoritarian mind-set differed from ours, the writer gives principles that are relevant to today's church. His advice helped keep the early church afloat, and it will do the same now for those wise enough to take heed.

OBEDIENCE (v. 17)

Obedience Commanded

The writer's wisdom was two-fold, the first being an admonition to obedience: "Obey your leaders and submit to their authority. They keep watch over you as men who must give an account. Obey them so that their work will be a joy, not a burden, for that would be of no advantage to you."

Clearly, all Christians are called to obedience and submission to authority — a call that demands careful definition. We must understand that this does not mean unqualified blanket obedience — the kind that made it possible for Jim Jones to murder 800 of his followers by ordering them to drink poisoned Kool-Aid. Neither does it provide the basis for authoritarian churches, like some of the contemporary house-churches whose members submit virtually every decision of their lives to the elders. I have seen this type of authoritarianism take the most draconian forms, as in one instance the leader ordered all members of the church to cease wearing any modern blend of fabrics, such as dacron and cotton or wool and rayon, because Leviticus 19:19 ordered the Israelites, "Do not wear clothing woven of two kinds of material." "About that shirt, Brother Hughes . . . let's see the tag."

Of course, this call to obedience was never meant to entice anyone to contradict Biblical morality or individual conscience. It was, instead, a call to an obedient heart, as we shall see.

Why Obedience?

But before we consider that, it is helpful to consider the reason for this emphasis on obedience. The answer, first, is that leaders are accountable to God — "They keep watch over you as men who must give an account" (v. 17b). The sense here is that "they and no other keep watch over your souls."[1] In addition, the words "keep watch" literally mean "to keep oneself awake." So the idea may well mean that some of the leaders had lost sleep over certain people in the church.[2] Thomas Aquinas cited the shepherds in the Nativity story as an illustration of such care — "keeping watch over their flocks at night" (Luke 2:8).[3] The pastors to which the writer calls his people to submit were good, energetic, conscientious, caring shepherds.

Moreover, their watching over their people was motivated by the awareness that they "must give an account" to God for the way they care for the flock. The sobering fact is, spiritual responsibility brings with it a higher level of responsibility and judgment. As James wrote, "Not many of you should presume to be teachers, my brothers, because you know that we who teach will be judged more strictly" (James 3:1).

How and why do teachers incur greater judgment? The answer is, if we claim to have an informed knowledge of God's Word for God's people, and further claim that we are charged to deliver it, we are more responsible to deliver it clearly and to obey it. I, by virtue of my professed calling and study of God's Word, will undergo a stricter judgment than many Christians. Increased responsibility means increased accountability. Jesus followed up the Parable of the Foolish Manager by saying, "From everyone who has been given much, much will be demanded; and from the one who has been entrusted with much, much more will be asked" (Luke 12:48).

Every one of us — no exceptions — will stand before the *Bema*, the Judgment Seat of Jesus Christ. The Bible is clear that while believers will *not* stand in judgment for their sin (Romans 8:1), and salvation is a free gift (Ephesians 2:8, 9), the works of believers will nevertheless be judged. "For we must all appear before the judgment seat of Christ" (2 Corinthians 5:10). "So then, each of us will give an account of himself to God" (Romans 14:12). The picture the Bible gives of this judgment is one of individual believers presenting their lives' works to Christ in the form of buildings. The eternal foundation of each building is Christ, but the structures vary. Some are made totally of wood, hay, and straw. Others are of gold, silver, and precious stones. Still others are composite structures of all the elements. Each life will be publicly subjected to the revealing torch of Christ's judgment, and with the flames will come the moment of truth:

> If any man builds on this foundation using gold, silver, costly stones, wood, hay or straw, his work will be shown for what it is, because the Day will bring it to light. It will be revealed with fire, and the fire will test the quality of each man's work. If what he has built survives, he will receive his reward. If it is burned up, he will suffer loss; he himself will be saved, but only as one escaping through the flames. (1 Corinthians 3:12-15)

While all Christians will be at the *Bema*, professed leaders and teachers of the church will undergo a stricter judgment. Leaders will answer for their care of souls.

So we see that the rationale for obedience was very clear for the Hebrew church. 1) Their leaders were so committed to watching over the souls under their care that they lost sleep. And 2) they were doing this with the powerfully motivating knowledge that they would answer to God for how well they did it. Such care invites obedience from God's people.

And if that is not sufficient reason, the author gives another, which is that obedience will make life better for all concerned: "Obey them so that their work will be a joy, not a burden, for that would be of no advantage to you" (v. 17c). The fact is, leadership can be a pain. The words "not a burden" literally read, "not a groaning."[4] I am sure Moses groaned over the disobedience of his people when after the Exodus he brought them to Rephidim where, being out of water and supplies, they began to rebel (cf. Exodus 17:1-7). But forty years later when the *same thing* happened at Kadesh so that the people seemed to be lip-syncing their earlier rebellion — "Why did you bring the Lord's community into this desert, that we and our livestock should die here?" (Numbers 20:4) — his old bones must have really groaned!

All leaders know this pain. Phillips Brooks, one-time Episcopal Bishop of Boston, said:

> To be a true minister to men is always to accept new happiness and new distress. . . . The man who gives himself to other men can never be a wholly sad man; but no more can he be a man of unclouded gladness. To him shall come with every deeper consecration a before untasted joy, but in the same cup shall be mixed a sorrow that it was beyond his power to feel before.[5]

A heart that can know and accept such pain is a glory to God.

> *O give us hearts to love like Thee,*
> *Like Thee, O Lord, to grieve*
> *Far more for others' sins than all*
> *The wrongs that we receive.*[6]

But along with the pain comes joy from obedient charges. "Obey them so that their work will be a joy." The Apostle John wrote, "I have no greater joy than to hear that my children are walking in the truth" (3 John 4). Paul expressed much the same when he encouraged the Philippians to live for Christ in this world "in order that I may boast on the day of Christ that I did not run or labor for nothing" (Philippians 2:16). Later in the same book he referred to them as "my joy and crown" (4:1). Ministry can be a pain — but its pleasures are incredible.

Of course, obedience is good for the people as well, as is implicit in the writer's negative understatement regarding disobedience: "For that [i.e., being a groaning disobedient burden] would be of no advantage to you." It would not be an advantage in this life because the strife that comes to the church through disobedience would not only impede the leaders, but *everyone's* spiritual growth. And at the Judgment Seat of Christ the disadvantage would be monumental!

So the reasons to submit to spiritual authority are substantial: 1) God-appointed leaders are fulfilling the high charge of watching over their congregation's souls. 2) Such leaders must answer to God at the Judgment Seat for their work. And, 3) believers' obedience will bring joy instead of pain — and will work to preserve their soul's advantage. Slavish, blind obedience is not called for here, but a respectful, submissive spirit is. Christians are to be discerning in their hearing of God's Word. They must never accept something as true just because a preacher or leader says it. At the same time, they are to be eager to obey and to submit to authority. Such ought to be one's first impulse when the leader and the people are right with God. Such churches will sail well, because all hands will be coordinated to point the ship in a single direction.

PRAYER (vv. 18, 19)

Prayer Commanded

From the necessity of obedience the author naturally switches to the command to pray: "Pray for us. We are sure that we have a clear conscience and desire to live honorably in every way" (v. 18). The writer's conscience is clear because he has performed well in his spiritual duties toward his friends. His conscience has made him confident toward both men and God. Similarly, Paul could write, "Now this is our boast: Our conscience testifies that we have conducted ourselves in the world, and especially in our relations with you, in the holiness and sincerity that are from God" (2 Corinthians 1:12). And, "By setting forth the truth plainly we commend ourselves to every man's conscience in the sight of God" (2 Corinthians 4:2). What a boon a clear conscience is! When the conscience is clear, one can ask wholeheartedly for the prayers of all the saints.

The preacher's specific request — "I particularly urge you to pray so that I may be restored to you soon" (v. 19) — reflects his simple faith in prayer. If they fail to pray, his return to them may be slowed or possibly never take place. But if they pray, he expects that their prayers will speed his restoration, just as Daniel's prayers brought the return of the angel Gabriel to aid him (cf. Daniel 10:12-14). He believed in prayer!

We are to pray for our leaders. It is recorded that D. L. Moody, founder of Moody Bible Institute, repeatedly appropriated the wisdom of this command. For example, during his great turn-of-the-century evangelistic endeavors he often wired R. A. Torrey at the school asking for prayer, and in response the faculty and students would pray late into the evening and sometimes all night — bringing great power to Moody's faraway ministries.[7] After Moody's death, Torrey himself preached in many countries backed up by an immense chain of prayer. In Australia, 2,100 home prayer groups met for two weeks before he arrived. As a result, there was great power in his preaching and many lives were changed.[8]

Charles Haddon Spurgeon, the peerless Victorian preacher of London, told his vast congregation as he concluded his sermon delivered May 27, 1855:

> My people! shall I ever lose your prayers? Will ye ever cease your supplications? . . . Will ye then ever cease to pray? I fear ye have not uttered so many prayers this morning as ye should have done; I fear there has not been so much earnest devotion as might have been poured forth. For my own part, I have not felt the wondrous power I sometimes experience.[9]

If we desire power in our lives and in our churches, we must pray. Likewise, if we desire our or others' preaching to be more than exegesis and rhetoric, we must pray.

How different the modern church would be if the majority of its people prayed for its pastors and lay leadership. There would be supernatural suspensions of business-as-usual worship. There would be times of inexplicable visitations from the Holy Spirit. More laypeople would come to grips with the deeper issues of life. The leadership vacuum would evaporate. There would be more conversions.

Will we commit ourselves to pray for our pastors and their colleagues and their layleaders — especially those who chair the boards and committees and teach children in Sunday school and lead other important ministries? I suggest three headings for your prayers: 1) devotional, 2) domestic, and 3) professional. This single commitment could ensure ongoing vitality for our churches. No doubt about it!

It is an indisputable fact — pastors as a group are one of the most abused and hurting segments of modern society. Admittedly, sometimes the misery is self-inflicted due to sloth and ineptness. But more often it comes from the factors previously considered.

And this personal *angst* of the clergy is superseded by an even greater tragedy — the mournful fact that tens of thousands of churches are not sailing well. Many are listing dangerously, some are dead in the water, and the skeletal remains of some rest on the bottom. What is the answer? The writer has not given us all of it, but he has given two huge pillars of support.

- *Obedience.* We are to obey our leaders — "Obey your leaders and submit to their authority. They keep watch over you as men who must give an account. Obey them so that their work will be a joy, not a burden, for that would be of no advantage to you" (v. 17). Slavish, unthinking obedience? No! Rather, the *will* to obey, to be respectful, to be supportive — to be a cheerful team player.

- *Prayer.* This obedience is to be oiled by prayer — "Pray for us. We are sure that we have a clear conscience and desire to live honorably in every way. I particularly urge you to pray so that I may be restored to you soon" (vv. 18, 19).

What power this will bring! As Paul said, "On him we have set our hope that he will continue to deliver us, as you help us by your prayers. Then many will give thanks on our behalf for the gracious favor granted us in answer to the prayers of many" (2 Corinthians 1:10b, 11).

May the God of peace, who through the blood of the eternal covenant brought back from the dead our Lord Jesus, that great Shepherd of the sheep, equip you with everything good for doing his will, and may he work in us what is pleasing to him, through Jesus Christ, to whom be glory for ever and ever. Amen. Brothers, I urge you to bear with my word of exhortation, for I have written you only a short letter. I want you to know that our brother Timothy has been released. If he arrives soon, I will come with him to see you. Greet all your leaders and all God's people. Those from Italy send you their greetings. Grace be with you all. (13:20-25)

24

Soaring Benedictions

HEBREWS 13:20-25

The book of Hebrews closes with one of the most exquisite and soaring of all Scriptural benedictions. Multiple millions of worshipers have been dismissed with the pastor's upraised hand and the sonorous words that begin, "May the God of peace . . ."

In its original setting it was especially appropriate for the expatriate Hebrew church as it battened down its hatches, trimmed its sails, and pointed its prow into the ominous rising seas of Roman persecution that would explode full-fury under Nero's infamy. Its appropriateness comes from the fact that the benediction and doxology of verse 21 flows from a grand foundational statement in verse 20 regarding what comes from the God they serve — namely, his *peace*, his *eternal covenant*, and his *risen Shepherd*. So we will do a little digging into the foundation, and then explore the benediction that rises from it.

FOUNDATION OF THE SOARING BENEDICTION (v. 20)

His Peace

Peace is intrinsic to the character and existence of God. God is called "the God of peace" at least five other times in the New Testament (Romans 15:33; 16:20; 2 Corinthians 13:11; Philippians 4:9; 1 Thessalonians 5:23). These citations, along with the opening invocation of our text, "May the God of peace . . .," reference two marvelous aspects of that peace. First, we see his divine tranquility — the eternal repose in God's being. And secondly, it references his *shalom*. God's peace is more than the absence of conflict, it is more than tranquility. It is completeness, soundness, welfare, well-being, wholeness.

Invoking God as "the God of peace" is parallel to Jeremiah 29:11, which reads literally, "'For I know the plans I am planning for you,' declares the Lord, 'plans for *shalom* and not for calamity, to give you a future and a hope'" (based on NASB). Significantly, this promise of *shalom* was given to God's covenant people at the beginning of the Babylonian captivity when it appeared that the seas of the Gentile world had inundated God's people for good.

Therefore, the title "the God of peace" at the end of Hebrews comes as a consciously appropriate benediction to fearful, restless hearts — "Your God is a God of peace, and he will pick up the pieces no matter what happens — he will heal your wounds and fulfill what is lacking. No storm will sink you!" He gives us *his peace* — *his peace*. Jesus said, "Peace I leave with you; my peace I give you. I do not give to you as the world gives" (John 14:27a). He gives us his repose of soul. Are we flirting with fantasy to make such a dazzling assertion? Absolutely not! The promise of Jesus' peace came from his own lips. Notice also that after promising his peace he said, "Do not let your hearts be troubled and do not be afraid" (John 14:27b).

What a salve to the harried church!

The truth for all of us who are his children is that our God is "the God of peace," and his plans for every one of us are for *shalom*, well-being. None of his children are an exception and never will be!

His Eternal Covenant

The second component is his eternal covenant/promise, referenced in the qualifying phrase that follows: "who through the blood of the eternal covenant . . ." Specifically, the foundation for our highest dreams is the everlasting, unbreakable New Covenant promise earlier quoted in 8:10 where God says, "I will put my laws in their minds and write them on their hearts. I will be their God, and they will be my people" (cf. Jeremiah 31:31-34). The promise is nothing less than a renewed heart and a personal relationship with God through the atoning work of God the Son and the indwelling of God the Holy Spirit. We have his word for it that all this is ours if we come to him!

And this covenant, this promise, is eternal. It will never be replaced by another as it once replaced the Old Covenant. It was established by the blood of the ultimate Lamb of God, whose atoning death was ratified and verified by his resurrection. The writer's friends were being encouraged to remember that whatever came, no matter how high the seas, his New Covenant promise would never change or fail. The eternal covenant granted them eternal life.

The stars shine over the mountains,
The stars shine over the sea,
The stars look up to the mighty God.
The stars shall last for a million years
A million years and a day,
But God and I will live and love
When the stars have passed away.
When the stars are gone.

(Robert Louis Stevenson)

His Risen Shepherd

We have seen, as we move toward the great benediction, that we have God's peace and God's eternal promise. The remaining element is his risen Shepherd. The final clause of verse 20 tells us that God "brought back from the dead our Lord Jesus, that great Shepherd of the sheep." The shepherd metaphor is one of the most spiritually sumptuous in all of God's Word. It reveals volumes about us (the sheep) and about the Lord (our Shepherd). As to our "sheepness," Dr. Bob Smith, long-time philosophy professor at Bethel College in Minnesota, used to humor his point home regarding our human state by insisting that the existence of sheep is *prima facie* evidence against evolution. Sheep are so unintelligent and obtuse and defenseless, they could not have possibly evolved — the only way they could have survived is with shepherds!

Certainly we must admit that we are sheep. But even more, we must note that Jesus took up the term *shepherd* and applied it to himself (cf. Mark 14:27). Jesus' shepherd heart welled with compassion, for Mark tells us, "When Jesus . . . saw a large crowd, he had compassion on them, because they were like sheep without a shepherd" (Mark 6:34). Even more, his good shepherd's heart caused him to give everything: "I am the good shepherd; I know my sheep and my sheep know me — just as the Father knows me and I know the Father — and I lay down my life for the sheep" (John 10:14, 15).

But here our writer tells us that he is not only a "good shepherd" — he is also, the "great Shepherd of the sheep." Why? Because he is a risen Shepherd — "brought back from the dead." As the great risen Shepherd, his compassion and protection are mediated from a position of an unparalleled display of power! He, our Shepherd, is exalted at the right hand of the Father. All other shepherds pale by comparison. There is none like our "great Shepherd." Our risen Shepherd lives not only to give us life, but to tend us so that we will be sheep who bring him glory. This means that our grandest spiritual desires are never audacious and that any spiritual aspirations less than the loftiest are not grand enough. What security and what challenge the fact of our risen "great Shepherd" brings to our souls.

Now reflect for a moment on the richness of our foundation from God: 1) We have his peace/*shalom*. 2) We have his unbreakable, immutable eternal promise. And, 3) we have his risen Shepherd's care. We have his peace, his promise, his care. This grand foundation can now bear the weight of the loftiest benedictions of his people and the ascription of glory to God.

EXPRESSION OF THE SOARING BENEDICTION (v. 21)

His Equipping

The writer's petition is richly phrased and to the point: "[May God] equip you with everything good for doing his will" (v. 21a). The richness of this request is in the word "equip," which can mean "to perfect," "to make good," or "to mend." According to Montefiore, "There is a flavour of all these meanings here."[1]

My three grandsons, who are between the ages of three and six, and I have experienced the idea lodged in this word on our occasional fishing trips. Excited little hands and fishing reels often do not mix very well. The result is predictably a tangled line that looks like a bird's nest. To little eyes and hands it looks impossible. But an experienced grandfather has found over the years that a little probing and pulling can almost always fix the worst tangles. Just what the doctor ordered for an aging grandfather's ego! "There we are, son. Now let's catch some fish!"

That is the idea here — to repair things so they can be useful. Matthew uses the word to describe fishermen "mending their nets" (Matthew 4:21, NASB). Paul uses it in Galatians 6:1 regarding "restoring" a brother — that is, putting him back in place. It was used in classical Greek for setting a bone.

So the prayer here is a beautiful request that God mend and perfect his children with everything good, thus equipping them to do God's will. We may sense that we are out of joint, or that life is a bird's nest. But this prayer is built on the idea that God can and does equip us with everything good to do his will — and our experience confirms the truth of this.

The relevance of this closing prayer for the church on troubled seas is obvious: God can put you back together so you can do his will, no matter what. Can you hear the prayer as its benediction lingered over the beleaguered congregation with its sweet, healing hope?

His Enabling

The prayer moves very naturally from equipping to enabling: "And may he work in us what is pleasing to him, through Jesus Christ" (v. 21b). The Scriptures tell us that all creation and all God's works in the world are through Jesus Christ. He not only created everything — he preserves it: "For by him all things were created: things in heaven and on earth, visible and

246

invisible, whether thrones or powers or rulers or authorities; all things were created by him and for him. He is before all things, and in him all things hold together" (Colossians 1:16, 17). So we should have no trouble believing his statement that "apart from me you can do nothing" (John 15:5). This is ontologically true, for we would not even exist apart from him. But the emphasis of Jesus' word in John is upon bearing spiritual fruit: "I am the vine; you are the branches. If a man remains *in me* and *I in him*, he will bear much fruit; apart from me you can do nothing" (italics added).

But gloriously, as believers we are by definition spiritually "in him." According to the famed Greek scholar Adolf Deissman, the term "in Christ" or "in Christ Jesus" occurs some 169 times in Paul's writings.[2] Perhaps the most famous of Paul's "in Christ" statements is 2 Corinthians 5:17 — "Therefore, if anyone is in Christ, he is a new creation; the old has gone, the new has come!"

It follows that once we are in Christ, we can do works through him which please him: "For we are God's workmanship, created in Christ Jesus to do good works, which God prepared in advance for us to do" (Ephesians 2:10). So in Christ each of us has an eternally-designed job description which includes the task, ability and place to serve. And whatever the task to which he has called us, we will be equipped for it as surely as a bird is capable of flight. And in doing the works that he has called us to do, we will be more and more his workmanship and more and more our true self.

Thus the prayer here in Hebrews — "and may he work in us what is pleasing to him, through Jesus Christ" — is eminently do-able!

It is an immutable fact that the power to do what is pleasing to God will always be given to us through Jesus Christ — if we want it! But some of us live as if that is not true. The real question is, Do we want it? Do we desire it? Do we expect it? Do we desire it! Then pray for it!

The foundation we all share is truly monumental. We have *God's peace*, his own *shalom*. His plans for us are only for our wholeness, our well-being, our completeness. We have *his eternal covenant*, the New Covenant in his blood and the promise of a new heart and new relationship. This great promise will never change. We have *his risen Shepherd* who cares for souls with the compassion and power in keeping with his great exaltation at the right hand of God. He is our "great Shepherd."

Having, therefore, the foundation of his *peace*, his *eternal covenant*, and his *great Shepherd*, we pray for ourselves and for our churches. We pray for his *equipping* "with everything good for doing his will" — and thus we find him mending us and putting us right so we can do it! We pray for his *enabling* — "may he work in us what is pleasing to him, through Jesus Christ" — and so find ourselves living under his pleasure and power.

We are, through prayer, equipped and enabled to serve, and our souls soar. Our ship sails well to his glory.

His glory

There is only one thing left to do, and that is to glorify God — "to whom be glory forever and ever. Amen."

- Glorify him for his peace, for it is his nature and his desire for his people. He has only thoughts of peace for us. Approach him with holy delight!
- Glorify him for his eternal covenant. What an amazing thing that God should enter into a covenant with us! Adore him for his blood, which sealed it. Bless him for our new hearts.
- Glorify him for giving us our "great Shepherd," for though we were all going our own way, he sent his Son to save us with his Lamb's blood, and then to shepherd us. Magnify him for his shepherd's compassion and care.
- Glorify him that he has equipped us and enabled us to do his will and to please him — even in the storms!

Glory be to the Father, and to the Son, and to the Holy Spirit. Amen!

Soli Deo gloria!

Notes

CHAPTER ONE: COVENANT AND PERFECTION

1. William Barclay, *The Letter to the Hebrews* (Philadelphia: Westminster, 1957), p. 125.
2. F. F. Bruce, *The Epistles to the Colossians, to Philemon, and to the Ephesians* (Grand Rapids, MI: Eerdmans, 1984), p. 230.
3. C. S. Lewis, *Letters to An American Lady* (Grand Rapids, MI: Eerdmans, 1967), p. 38.
4. G. Abbott-Smith, *A Manual Greek Lexicon of the New Testament* (New York: Charles Scribner's, n.d.), p. 427 defines the Greek *suneidesis* of verse 2 as "consciousness" — "In an ethical sense, innate discernment, self-judging consciousness, *conscience*."
5. Bruce, *The Epistles to the Colossians, to Philemon, and to the Ephesians*, p. 232 explains: "The Greek translator evidently regarded the Hebrew wording as an instance of *pars pro toto*; the 'digging' or hollowing out of the ears is part of the total work of fashioning a human body."
6. Charles Williams, *The Descent of the Dove* (London: The Religious Book Club, 1939), pp. 39, 40.
7. Leon Morris, *The Expositor's Bible Commentary*, Vol. 12 (Grand Rapids, MI: Zondervan, 1981), p. 99 explains:

   We should notice a difference between the way the author uses the verb "to sanctify" (NIV, "made holy") and the way Paul uses it. For the apostle, sanctification is a process whereby the believer grows progressively in Christian qualities and character. In Hebrews the same terminology is used of the process by which a person becomes Christian and is therefore "set apart" for God. There is no contradiction between these two; both are necessary for the fully developed Christian life. But we must be on our guard lest we read this epistle with Pauline terminology in mind. The sanctification meant here is one brought about by the death of Christ. It has to do with making people Christian, not with developing Christian character.

8. Bruce, *The Epistles to the Colossians, to Philemon, and to the Ephesians*. p. 241 writes: "Here their character as the people thus set apart is simply indicated in timeless terms, because emphasis is now laid on the fact that by that same sacrifice Christ has eternally 'perfected' His holy people."
9. Donald Grey Barnhouse, *Let Me Illustrate* (Old Tappan, NJ: Revell, 1967), p. 97.

CHAPTER TWO: FULL ACCESS / FULL LIVING

1. Alan F. Johnson, *The Freedom Letter* (Chicago: Moody Press, 1974), p. 136, who

quotes from Henry Hart Milman, *History of Christianity*, Vol. 4 (New York: Crowell, 1881), p. 144.

2. Leon Morris, *The Expositor's Bible Commentary*, Vol. 12 (Grand Rapids, MI: Zondervan, 1981), p. 104.

3. Bertrand Russell, "A Free Man's Worship," in *Mysticism and Logic* (New York: W. W. Norton & Company, Inc., 1929), pp. 47, 48.

4. James S. Hewitt, *Illustrations Unlimited* (Wheaton, IL: Tyndale House, 1988), p. 291.

5. Ray C. Stedman, *What More Can God Say?* (Glendale, CA: Regal, 1974), p. 171.

6. R. Kent Hughes, "The Discipline of Church," in *Disciplines of a Godly Man* (Wheaton, IL: Crossway, 1991), pp. 151-159.

7. Robert G. Rayburn, *O Come, Let Us Worship* (Grand Rapids, MI: Baker, 1984), pp. 29, 30.

8. Oswald Chambers, *My Utmost for His Highest* (Toronto: McClelland and Stewart, n.d.), p. 192.

9. Elisabeth Elliott, ed., *The Journals of Jim Elliot* (Old Tappan, NJ: Fleming H. Revell, 1978), p. 309.

10. *Dynamic Preaching*, Vol. 5, No. 2 (February 1990), p. 8.

CHAPTER THREE: THE PERILS OF APOSTASY

1. Sculley Bradley, ed., *The American Tradition in Literature*, fourth edition (New York: Grosset & Dunlap, 1974), p. 46.

2. David Gooding, *An Unshakeable Kingdom* (Grand Rapids, MI: Eerdmans, 1989), p. 201.

3. Leon Morris, *The Expositor's Bible Commentary*, Vol. 12 (Grand Rapids, MI: Zondervan, 1981), p. 106.

4. Herbert Lockyer, *Last Words of Saints and Sinners* (Grand Rapids, MI: Kregel, 1969), p. 133.

5. *Ibid.*, p. 132.

6. William B. Johnston, ed., *Calvin's Commentaries: The Epistle of Paul the Apostle to the Hebrews and the First and Second Epistles of St. Peter* (Grand Rapids, MI: Eerdmans, 1977), pp. 77, 78.

7. Simon J. Kistemaker, *Exposition of the Epistle to the Hebrews* (Grand Rapids, MI: Baker, 1984), p. 295.

8. Morris, *The Expositor's Bible Commentary*, Vol. 12, p. 107.

9. Kistemaker, *Exposition of the Epistle to the Hebrews*, p. 296, explains:

   This song was well known to the readers because they sang it in their worship services. The wording differs somewhat in the original Hebrew and its Greek translation: therefore, scholars have made the suggestion that "the citation in this form may have been stereotyped by apostolic example in the language of the primitive church." The citation occurs in the selfsame wording in Romans 12:19. We may assume that it circulated in the early church as a proverbial saying.

10. Clarence E. Macartney, *Macartney's Illustrations* (New York: Abingdon, 1946), pp. 163, 164.

11. C. S. Lewis, *Surprised by Joy* (New York: Harcourt, Brace, Jovanovich, 1955), p. 232.

CHAPTER FOUR: KEEP ON!

1. C. H. Spurgeon, *The Metropolitan Tabernacle Pulpit*, Vol. 10, Sermon 580, "God Is With Us" (London: Passmore & Alabaster, 1973), p. 407.

2. George Abbot-Smith, *A Manual Greek Lexicon of the New Testament* (New York: Scribner's, n.d.), p. 432.
3. F. F. Bruce, *The Epistle to the Hebrews* (Grand Rapids, MI: Eerdmans, 1964), p. 270.
4. "Freeze-dried Pets Article Legitimate," *The Bloomington Indiana Herald-Telephone* (December 26, 1985).
5. Warren Bennis and Burt Nanus, *Leaders, the Strategies for Taking Charge* (New York: Harper & Row, 1986), pp. 69, 70.
6. Bruce, *The Epistle to the Hebrews*, pp. 270, 271 explains:

> The word he uses has appeared three times already in this letter; ARV translates it uniformly by "boldness". In Chs. 4:16; 10:19 it is used of the confidence with which Christians may approach the throne of God since Christ is there as their prevailing high priest; in Ch. 3:6 it is used more generally of the courageous confession which Christians should maintain without fail. It is in this last sense that it is used here, with special reference to steadfastness in adverse and disheartening circumstances: "It is, so to say, the content of the Christian attitude in the world, the security of God's salvation and the open confession amidst of opposition." We may think of the "boldness" of Peter and John which made such an impression on the Sanhedrin (Acts 4:13); the forthrightness of their language evinced an inner confidence of heart and life.

7. Simon J. Kistemaker, *Exposition of the Epistle to the Hebrews* (Grand Rapids, MI: Baker, 1984), p. 302.

CHAPTER FIVE: FAITH IS . . .

1. Brooke Foss Westcott, *The Epistle to the Hebrews* (Grand Rapids, MI: Eerdmans, 1967), p. 350.
2. F. F. Bruce, *The Epistle to the Hebrews* (Grand Rapids, MI: Eerdmans, 1964), p. 278 explains:

> This word *hypostasis* has appeared twice already in the epistle. In Ch. 1:3 the Son was stated to be the very image of God's *hypostasis*; in Ch. 3:14 believers are said to be Christ's associates if they hold fast the beginning of their *hypostasis* firm to the end. In the former place it has the objective sense of "substance" or "real essence" (as opposed to what merely seems to be so). In the latter place it has the subjective sense of "confidence" or "assurance." Here it is natural to take it in the same subjective sense as it bears in Ch. 3:14, and so ARV and RSV render it "assurance."

3. William L. Lane, *Hebrews: A Call to Commitment* (Peabody, MA: Hendrickson, 1988), p. 149.
4. William Barclay, *The Letter to the Hebrews* (Philadelphia: Westminster, 1957), p. 145.
5. Daniel J. Boorstin, *The Discoverers* (New York: Vintage Books, 1983), pp. 311, 312.
6. *Leadership Magazine* (Summer 1983), reprinted from the *London Observer*.
7. Bruce, *The Epistle to the Hebrews*, p. 281 explains:

> Thus "the visible came forth from the invisible" (NEB). But how do we know this? By faith, says our author. Greek speculation about the formation of the ordered world out of formless matter had influenced Jewish thinkers like Philo and the author of the book of Wisdom; the writer to the Hebrews is more biblical in his reasoning and affirms the doctrine of *creation ex nihilo*, a doctrine uncongenial to Greek thought. The faith by which he accepts it is faith in the divine revelation; the first chapter of Genesis is probably uppermost in his mind,

since he is about to trace seven living examples of faith from the subsequent chapters of that book.

CHAPTER SIX: ABEL'S FAITH

1. St. Augustine, *The City of God*, Book 15, Chapter 1, in Philip Schaff, ed., *The Nicene and Post-Nicene Fathers*, Vol. 2, trans. Marcus Dods (Grand Rapids, MI: Eerdmans, 1973), p. 284.
2. The deduction that Cain was 129 when he murdered Abel is based on the collation of Genesis 4:25, "Adam lay with his wife again, and she gave birth to a son and named him Seth, saying, 'God has granted me another child in place of Abel, since Cain killed him'" and 5:3, "When Adam had lived 130 years, he had a son in his own likeness, in his own image; and he named him Seth." This deduction, of course, assumes that Seth's birth came soon after Abel's death when God provided a replacement for righteous Abel. But even if there were a decade or two before the advent of Seth, the application still pertains.
3. Franz Delitzsch, *Commentary on the Epistle to the Hebrews*, Vol. 2 (St. Paul, MN: Klock & Klock, 1978), p. 225 says:

   Abel's sacrifice was an expression of heartfelt thankfulness, or, as our author says, tracing the disposition of his mind to its root, an expression of his faith. But inasmuch as the relation between God and man had been disturbed by sin, Abel's faith exhibited itself in recognising and laying hold of the divine mercy in the midst of wrath and judgment, — an aspect of his personal standing with regard to sacrifice, which had its correlative in his offering being of a life and of blood. Even Hofmann recognises in Abel's sacrifice the expression of a need of atonement felt by him.

4. Paul Johnson, *Intellectuals* (New York: Harper & Row, 1988), p. 91.
5. Philip Edgcumbe Hughes, *A Commentary on the Epistle to the Hebrews* (Grand Rapids, MI: Eerdmans, 1977), pp. 454, 455.
6. F. W. Boreham, *The Crystal Pointers* (New York: Abingdon Press, 1925), p. 19.

CHAPTER SEVEN: ENOCH'S FAITH

1. James Trager, *The People's Chronology* (New York: Henry Holt and Company, 1992), pp. 229, 286, 400, 401, 782. Also helpful are: Jerome Burne, ed., *Chronicles of the World* (Mount Kisco, NY: ECAM Publications, 1988); Bernard Grum, ed., *The Timetable of History*, based on Werner Stein's *Kulturfahrplan* (New York: Simon & Schuster, 1991).
2. Philip Edgcumbe Hughes, *A Commentary on the Epistle to the Hebrews* (Grand Rapids, MI: Eerdmans, 1977), p. 457 explains: "The Septuagint, which our author echoes, has 'he pleased God' instead of 'he walked with God'; but this is not to say something different, since only he who pleases God walks with God, that is, enjoys a relationship of harmonious fellowship with him."
3. Warren W. Wiersbe, *Run with the Winners, A Study of the Champions of Hebrews 11* (Wheaton, IL: Tyndale House, 1985), p 44.
4. Annie Dillard, *Teaching a Stone to Talk* (New York: Harper & Row, 1982), p. 69.
5. H. Dermot McDonald, *Commentary on Colossians and Philemon* (Waco, TX: Word, 1990), p. 49.

CHAPTER EIGHT: NOAH'S FAITH

1. Lance Morrow, "Evil," in *Time* Magazine (June 10, 1991), Vol. 137, No. 23, p. 48.

2. Derek Kidner, *Genesis* (Downers Grove, IL: InterVarsity Press, 1975), p. 85 says, "The term for *imagination* (*yēṣer*) is closer to action than the English suggests: it is derived from the potter's verb 'to form' (*cf.* 2:7), and implies design or purpose."

3. Henry M. Morris, *The Genesis Record* (Grand Rapids, MI: Baker, 1976), p. 191 postulates:

A worldwide rain lasting forty days would be quite impossible under present atmospheric conditions; so this phenomenon required an utterly different source of atmospheric waters than now obtains. This we have already seen to be the "waters above the firmament," the vast thermal blanket of invisible water vapor that maintained the greenhouse effect in the ante-diluvian world. These waters somehow were to condense and fall on the earth.

4. Brooke Foss Westcott, *The Epistles to the Colossians, to Philemon, and to the Ephesians* (Grand Rapids, MI: Eerdmans, 1984), p. 356 says: "The faith of Noah was directed to a special revelation which was made known to others also."

5. Leon Morris, *The Expositor's Bible Commentary*, Vol. 12 (Grand Rapids, MI: Baker, 1974), p. 116 says:

In the expression "holy fear" (*eulabētheis*), some put the emphasis on "holy" and some on "fear." While it is true that this verb may convey the notion of fear, it is not easy to see it in this context. The author is not telling us that Noah was a timid type but that he was a man of faith. He acted out of reverence for God and God's command.

6. Philip Edgcumbe Hughes, *A Commentary on the Epistle to the Hebrews* (Grand Rapids, MI: Eerdmans, 1977), p. 464, quoting from *Sibylline Oracles* 1.125ff.

7. Francois Mauriac, *Viper's Tangle* (Garden City, NY: Image Books, 1957), p. 98.

8. The Kingston Trio, "The Merry Melody":

> They're rioting in Africa, they're starving in Spain.
> There are hurricanes in Florida, and Texas needs rain
> The whole world is seething with unhappy souls.
> The French hate the Germans, the Germans hate the Poles.
> The Poles hate the Yugoslavs, South Africans hate the Dutch.
> And I don't like anybody very much.
> But we all should be grateful and thankful and proud,
> That man's been endowed with a mushroom shaped cloud.
> And we know for certain that some lucky day,
> Someone will set the spark off and we'll all be blown away.

CHAPTER NINE: *ABRAHAM'S FAITH*

1. Merrill C. Tenney, ed., *The Zondervan Pictorial Encyclopedia of the Bible*, Vol. 5 (Grand Rapids, MI: Zondervan, 1975), pp. 847, 848.

2. Philo, *The Migration of Abraham*, 43, 44, Vol. 4, trans. F. H. Colson and G. H. Whitaker, The Loeb Classical Library (Cambridge, MA: Harvard, 1985), p. 157:

There is a deliberate intention when his words take the form of a promise and define the time of fulfillment not as present but future. He says not "which I am shewing" but "which I will shew thee" (Gen. xiii.1). Thus he testifies to the trust which the soul reposed in God, exhibiting its thankfulness not as called out by accomplished facts, but by expectation of what was to be. For the soul, clinging in utter dependence on a good hope, and deeming that things not present are beyond question already present by reason of the sure steadfastness of Him that promised them, has won as it [exercised] faith, a perfect good; for we read a little later "Abraham believed God" (Gen. xv.6).

3. Hugh Montefiore, *A Commentary on the Epistle to the Hebrews* (Grand Rapids, MI: Baker, 1984), p. 58.

4. F. F. Bruce, *The Epistle to the Hebrews* (Grand Rapids, MI: Eerdmans, 1984), p. 296 explains:

Our author points out that Abraham did not receive the promise of the inheritance at the time of his first call; the land to which he was directed to go was the "place which he was to receive for an inheritance"; the promise of the inheritance was not given until he had returned from Egypt and Lot had chosen the well-watered circuit of Jordan to settle in (Gen. 13:14ff.); it was reaffirmed to him along with the promise of an heir (Gen. 15:18ff.), and again after the bestowal of the covenant of circumcision (Gen. 17:8). The divine bidding was sufficient for him at his first call, "and he went out, not knowing whither he went." The promise of the inheritance was not in the first instance an incentive to obedience; it was the reward of his obedience.

5. Jaroslav Pelikan, ed., *Luther's Works*, Vol. 29 (Saint Louis: Concordia, 1987), p. 238.

6. Bruce, *The Epistle to the Hebrews*, p. 297, n. 85.

7. Leon Morris, *The Expositor's Bible Commentary*, Vol. 12 (Grand Rapids, MI: Zondervan, 1981), p. 119.

8. Brook Foss Westcott, *The Epistle to the Hebrews* (Grand Rapids, MI: Eerdmans, 1967), p. 360.

9. Bruce, *The Epistle to the Hebrews*, pp. 301, 302.

CHAPTER TEN: ABRAHAM'S AND THE PATRIARCHS' FAITH

1. E. A. Speiser, *Genesis* (New York: Doubleday, 1964), pp. 161, 162.

2. Brooke Foss Westcott, *The Epistle to the Hebrews* (Grand Rapids, MI: Eerdmans, 1967), p. 365 explains: "The time . . . marks the immediate coincidence of the act of obedience with the call for it."

3. *Ibid.*, p. 365 explains: "The first verb expresses the permanent result of the offering completed by Abraham in will; the second his actual readiness in preparing the sacrifice which was not literally carried into effect."

4. G. Abbott-Smith, *A Manual Greek Lexicon of the New Testament* (New York: Scribner's, n.d.), p. 270 indicates that the root idea of *logizomai* is numerical calculation that, of course, came to be used metaphorically without reference to numbers for a reckoning of characteristics or reasons.

5. Paul Hendrickson, *Seminary, a Search* (New York: Summit Books, 1983), p. 313.

CHAPTER ELEVEN: MOSES' FAITH

1. William L. Lane, *Hebrews: A Call to Commitment* (Peabody, MA: Hendrickson, 1988), p. 58.

2. H. St. J. Thackeray, trans., *Josephus Jewish Antiquities* 2.9. 4, Vol. 4 (Cambridge, MA: Harvard, 1978), p. 259.

3. John Brown, *Hebrews* (Edinburgh: Banner of Truth, 1972), p. 539 explains:

We know that, at the time this Epistle was written, it was the common faith of the Jews that such a revelation had been made. Josephus, in his "Antiquities of the Jews," Book ii. chap. v., expressly states, that a divine communication was made to Amram during the pregnancy of Jochebed, that the child about to be born was to be the deliverer of his nation from Egyptian tyranny. There is nothing in Scripture inconsistent with this. Though we have no account in Scripture of an express revelation made as to sacrifice, we conclude, from its being said that it was "by faith Abel offered a more excellent sacrifice than Cain," that such a revelation was made; and on the same principle, I cannot help considering the Apostle as here giving sanction to the commonly received belief of the Jews on this subject and stating that it was the faith of Moses' parents in this revelation that led them to act as they did, in preserving their infant's life at the risk of their own.

See also Warren Wiersbe, *Run with the Winners, A Study of the Champions of Hebrews 11* (Wheaton, IL: Tyndale House, 1985), p. 100.

4. W. B. Johnston, trans., *Calvin's Commentaries: The Epistle of Paul the Apostle to the Hebrews and the First and Second Epistle of St. Peter* (Grand Rapids, MI: Eerdmans, 1963), pp. 175, 176.

5. Simon J. Kistemaker, *Exposition of the Epistle to the Hebrews* (Grand Rapids, MI: 1984), p. 345.

6. Boris Pasternak, *Dr. Zhivago* (London: Collins and Harvill Press, 1958), p. 160.

7. F. F. Bruce, *The Epistle to the Hebrews* (Grand Rapids, MI: Eerdmans, 1964), p. 320.

8. *Ibid.*, pp. 131, 132.

9. Brown, *Hebrews*, p. 218.

CHAPTER TWELVE: JOSHUA'S AND HIS PEOPLE'S FAITH

1. C. F. Keil and F. Delitzsch, *Joshua, Judges, Ruth* (Grand Rapids, MI: Eerdmans, 1963), p. 62.

2. John Calvin, *Commentaries on the Book of Joshua*, ed. Henry Beveredge (Grand Rapids, MI: Baker, 1984), p. 88.

CHAPTER THIRTEEN: RAHAB'S FAITH

1. John J. Davis, *Conquest and Crises, Studies in Joshua, Judges and Ruth* (Grand Rapids, MI: Baker, 1976), n.p.

2. Brooke Foss Westcott, *The Epistle to the Hebrews* (Grand Rapids, MI: Eerdmans, 1967), p. 375.

3. Norman L. Geisler, *The Christian Love Ethic* (Grand Rapids, MI: Zondervan, 1979), pp. 78-80.

4. John Calvin, *Commentaries on the Book of Joshua* (Grand Rapids, MI: Baker, 1984), p.47.

5. W. Robertson Nicoll, *The Expositor's Bible* (A. C. Armstrong and Son, 1903), p. 89.

6. Geoffrey W. Bromiley, ed., *The International Standard Bible Encyclopedia*, Vol. 4 (Grand Rapids, MI: Eerdmans, 1991), p. 34 explains:

The detail about the scarlet cord (*tiqwaṭ hûṭ haššânî*, v. 18) is intriguing. Elsewhere this item seems to have erotic connotations. In Cant. 4:3 the bride is said to have lips like a "scarlet thread" (*hûṭ haššânî*); Jeremiah associated scarlet with Israel's vain beautification (Jer. 4:30); the midwife of Tamar (who had conceived while pretending to be a prostitute; cf. Gen. 28:12-26) used a scarlet thread (*[haš]šānî*, 38:28, 30) to distinguish the newborn twins; and Isaiah linked the color with sin (Isa. 1:18). S. D. Walters has suggested that the scarlet rope may have been the mark of a prostitute — i.e., that she lived in the "red rope" district! Also since *tiqwâh* more commonly means "hope" than "rope," there may be a conscious pun here: the "rope" is the prostitute's "hope" (i.e., for customers); but now, having confessed Yahweh as God, her "rope" betokens a new kind of "hope."

7. Martin H. Woudstra, *The Book of Joshua* (Grand Rapids, MI: Eerdmans, 1983), p. 75.
8. Francis A. Schaeffer, *Joshua and the Flow of Biblical History* (Downers Grove, IL: InterVarsity Press, 1975), p. 78.
9. Abraham Kuyper, *Women of the Old Testament* (Grand Rapids, MI: Zondervan, 1961), p. 69.
10. Trent C. Butler, *Word Biblical Commentary: Joshua* (Waco, TX: Word, 1983), p. 32.

CHAPTER FOURTEEN: TRIUMPHANT FAITH

1. "The Gay Baby Boom," *Chicago Tribune* (September 13, 1992), Section 5, pp. 1, 2.
2. William B. Johnston, trans., *Calvin's Commentaries: The Epistle of Paul the Apostle to the Hebrews and the First and Second Epistles of St. Peter* (Grand Rapids, MI: Eerdmans, 1963), p. 182.
3. Brooke Foss Westcott, *The Epistle to the Hebrews* (Grand Rapids, MI: Eerdmans, 1967), p. 377.
4 R. H. Charles, *The Apocrypha and Pseudepigrapha of the Old Testament*, Vol. 2 (London: Oxford, 1968), p. 162; cf. also TB *Sanhedrin* 103b.
5. Simon J. Kistemaker, *Exposition of the Epistle to the Hebrews* (Grand Rapids, MI: Baker, 1984), pp. 357, 358. See also Leon Morris, *The Expositor's Bible Commentary*, Vol. 12 (Grand Rapids, MI: Baker, 1974), p. 132 who succinctly explains:

> But here it is not a question of "the promises" but of "the promise." God made many promises to his people and kept them. So there were many blessings that they received along the way. But the ultimate blessing (which the author characteristically sees in terms of promise) was not given under the old dispensation. God kept that until Jesus came.

6. Morris, *The Expositor's Bible Commentary*, Vol. 12 (Grand Rapids, MI: Zondervan, 1981), pp. 132, 133.

CHAPTER FIFTEEN: CONSIDER HIM

1. F. F. Bruce, *The Epistle to the Hebrews* (Grand Rapids, MI: Eerdmans, 1965), p. 346 writes:

> But in what sense are they "witnesses"? Not, probably, in the sense of spectators, watching their successors as they in their turn run the race for which they have entered; but rather in the sense that by their loyalty and endurance they have borne witness to the possibilities of the life of faith. It is not so much they who look at us as we look to them — for encouragement.

2. *Webster's Seventh New Collegiate Dictionary* (Springfield, MA: G & C Merriam Co., 1971), p. 881:

> **sun-dew**: any of a genus (*Drosera* of the family Droseraceae, the sundew family) of bog-inhabiting insectivorous herbs having viscid glands on the leaves.

3. William Barclay, *The Letter to the Hebrews* (Philadelphia: Westminster, 1957), p. 196.
4. John H. Gerstner, *The Rational Biblical Theology of Jonathan Edwards*, Vol. 1 (Powhatan, VA: Berea Publications, 1991), p. 418.
5. Bruce, *The Epistle to the Hebrews*, p. 352.
6. Brooke Foss Westcott, *The Epistle to the Hebrews* (Grand Rapids, MI: Eerdmans, 1967), pp. 394, 395.

7. John Henry Cardinal Newman, *The Kingdom Within (Discourses Addressed to Mixed Congregations)* (Denville, NJ: Dimension Books, 1984), pp. 328, 329.
8. Hugh Montefiore, *A Commentary on the Epistle to the Hebrews* (London: Adam & Charles Black, 1964), p. 35.

CHAPTER SIXTEEN: DIVINE DISCIPLINE

1. R. Kent Hughes, *The Eschatological Use of 'ΟΡΓΗ in the New Testament*, a thesis presented to Talbot Theological Seminary, June 1972, pp. 31-60.
2. Theodore Laetsch, *Bible Commentary Jeremiah* (St. Louis: Concordia, 1965), pp. 234, 235.
3. John MacArthur, Jr., *Hebrews* (Chicago: Moody Press, 1983), pp. 385-389. The author explains and amplifies the three types of discipline in greater detail.
4. James Moffatt, *Epistle to the Hebrews* (Edinburgh: T & T Clark, 1963), p. 201.
5. John Perkins, *Let Justice Roll Down* (Ventura, CA: Regal, 1976), p. 31.
6. John H. Gerstner, *The Rational Biblical Theology of Jonathan Edwards*, Vol. 1 (Powhatan, VA: Berea Publications, 1991), p. 423, quoting from *Works* (Worcester reprint), IV, p. 174.
7. Richard John Neuhaus, *Freedom for Ministry* (Grand Rapids, MI: Eerdmans, 1979), p. 72.

CHAPTER SEVENTEEN: FAILING GRACE

1. Art Carey, "Beating Agony and the Marathon," *Philadelphia Inquirer* (April 12, 1978).
2. Leon Morris, *The Expositor's Bible Commentary*, Vol. 12 (Grand Rapids, MI: Zondervan, 1981), p. 139.
3. F. F. Bruce, *The Epistle to the Hebrews* (Grand Rapids, MI: Eerdmans, 1964), pp. 364, 365 explains:

> The verb translated "be . . . turned out of the way" should rather be rendered "be put out of joint" (ARV margin, RSV, NEB); it is dislocation and not deviation that is suggested by the following words, "but rather be healed." Sprains and similar injuries must be bound up, so that the whole community may complete the course without loss.

4. Brooke Foss Westcott, *The Epistle to the Hebrews* (Grand Rapids, MI: Eerdmans, 1967), p. 405.
5. J. R. R. Tolkien, *The Fellowship of the Ring* (New York: Ballantine, 1969), pp. 450, 451.
6. G. Abbott-Smith, *A Manual Greek Lexicon of the New Testament* (New York: Scribner's, n.d.), p. 119.
7. Westcott, *The Epistle to the Hebrews*, p. 406.
8. John Blanchard, *Truth for Life* (West Sussex, England: H. E. Walter, Ltd., 1982), p. 254.
9. Westcott, *The Epistle to the Hebrews*, p. 406.
10. Morris, *The Expositor's Bible Commentary*, Vol. 12, p. 139.
11. Westcott, *The Epistle to the Hebrews*, p. 407.
12. Philo, *Question and Answers on Genesis*, trans. Ralph Marcus, The Loeb Classical Library (Cambridge, MA: Harvard, 1979), p. 494.
13. Bruce, *The Epistle to the Hebrews*, p. 367.
14. Dietrich Bonhoeffer, *Temptation* (London: SCM Press, 1961), p. 33, writes:

> It makes no difference whether it is sexual desire, or ambition, or vanity, or desire for revenge, or love of fame and power, or greed for money, or, finally,

that strange desire for the beauty of the world, of nature. Joy in God is in the course of being extinguished in us and we seek all our joy in the creature. At this moment God is quite unreal to us, he loses all reality, and only desire for the creature is real; the only reality is the devil. Satan does not here fill us with hatred of God, but with forgetfulness of God. And now his falsehood is added to this proof of strength. The lust thus aroused envelops the mind and will of man in deepest darkness. The powers of clear discrimination and of decision are taken from us. The questions present themselves: "Is what the flesh desires really sin in this case?" "Is it really not permitted to me, yes — expected of me, now, here, in my particular situation, to appease desire?" The tempter puts me in a privileged position as he tried to put the hungry Son of God in a privileged position. I boast of my privilege against God. It is here that everything within me rises up against the Word of God.

15. William B. Johnston, trans., *Calvin's Commentaries: The Epistle of Paul the Apostle to the Hebrews and the First and Second Epistles of St. Peter* (Grand Rapids, MI: Eerdmans, 1963), p. 197.

CHAPTER EIGHTEEN: *MARCHING TO ZION*

1. F. F. Bruce, *The Epistle to the Hebrews* (Grand Rapids, MI: Eerdmans, 1964), p. 371.
2. John Bunyan, *The Pilgrim's Progress* (Old Tappan, NJ: Revell, 1987), p. 23.
3. See Chapter 3 for bibliographical information on angel stories.
4. Olive Fleming Liefeld, *Unfolding Destinies* (Grand Rapids, MI: Zondervan, 1990), p. 236.
5. Bruce, *The Epistle to the Hebrews*, p. 377.
6. Brooke Foss Westcott, *The Epistle to the Hebrews* (Grand Rapids, MI: Eerdmans, 1967), p. 415.
7. Raymond Brown, *The Message of Hebrews* (Downers Grove, IL: InterVarsity Press, 1982), p. 245.

CHAPTER NINETEEN: *A CONSUMING FIRE*

1. *Aesthetic* is used here in the original Greek idea of *aisthetikos* — sense perception.
2. Charles Colson, *Kingdoms in Conflict* (New York/Grand Rapids, MI: William Morrow/Zondervan, 1987), pp. 222, 223.

CHAPTER TWENTY: *ECCLESIAL ETHICS*

1. Marvin Olasky, *Abortion Rites* (Wheaton, IL: Crossway Books, 1992), p. 140, which quotes from John McDowall, *Magdalen Facts Number 1* (New York: Magdalen Society, 1832), p. 33.
2. Olasky, *Abortion Rites.*, pp. 140-142.
3. Brooke Foss Westcott, *The Epistle to the Hebrews* (Grand Rapids, MI: Eerdmans, 1967), p. 429 says: "The use of ($\mu\varepsilon\nu\acute{\varepsilon}\tau\omega$) suggests that the bond had been in danger of being severed."
4. Reported by George Cowan to Campus Crusade at the U.S. Division Meeting Devotions, Thursday, March 22, 1990.
5. William Barclay, *The Letter to the Hebrews* (Philadelphia: Westminster, 1957), p. 218.
6. A. M. Harmon, trans., *Lucian*, Vol. 5, The Loeb Classical Library (Cambridge, MA: Harvard, 1972), p. 19.
7. Kirsopp Lake, trans., *The Apostolic Fathers*, Vol. 1, The Loeb Classical Library (Cambridge, MA: Harvard, 1970), p. 327.

8. Westcott, *The Epistle to the Hebrews*, p. 430.
9. Eugene H. Peterson, *Working the Angles* (Grand Rapids, MI: Eerdmans, 1989), p. 74.
10. Harmon, *Lucian*, p. 13.
11. J. Rendel Harris, ed., *The Apology of Aristides*, Vol. 1 of "Texts and Studies," ed. J. Armitage Robinson (Cambridge: The University Press, 1891), pp. 48, 49.

CHAPTER TWENTY-ONE: PERSONAL ETHICS

1. Philip Edgcumbe Hughes, *A Commentary on the Epistle to the Hebrews* (Grand Rapids, MI: Eerdmans, 1977), p. 556.
2. Paul Johnson, *Intellectuals* (New York: Harper & Row, 1988), p. 121 where he quotes Henri Troyat, *Tolstoy* (London, 1968), pp. 525, 526.
3. Hugh Montefiore, *A Commentary on the Epistle to the Hebrews* (London: Adam & Charles Black, 1964), p. 240.
4. William Barclay, *The Letter to the Hebrews* (Philadelphia: Westminster, 1957), p. 221.
5. C. H. Spurgeon, *The Metropolitan Tabernacle Pulpit*, Vol. 24 (Pasadena, TX: Pilgrim, 1972), p. 699.
6. Henry Hart Milman, *History of Christianity*, Vol. 4 (New York: Crowell, 1881), p. 144.

CHAPTER TWENTY-TWO: SUSTAINING WISDOM

1. Paul Johnson, *Modern Times* (New York: Harper Collins, 1991), pp. 1-4.
2. F. F. Bruce, *The Epistle to the Hebrews* (Grand Rapids, MI: Eerdmans, 1964), p. 395, 396.
3. Katherine Tynan, *The Flying Wheel*.
4. Leon Morris, *The Expositor's Bible Commentary*, Vol. 12 (Grand Rapids, MI: Zondervan, 1981), p. 150, and Bruce, *The Epistle to the Hebrews*, pp. 399-401.

CHAPTER TWENTY-THREE: RESPONSIBILITY TOWARD LEADERSHIP

1. Brooke Foss Westcott, *The Epistle to the Hebrews* (Grand Rapids, MI: Eerdmans, 1967), p. 444.
2. F. F. Bruce, *The Epistle to the Hebrews* (Grand Rapids, MI: Eerdmans, 1964), p. 407.
3. Philip Edgcumbe Hughes, *A Commentary on the Epistle to the Hebrews* (Grand Rapids, MI: Eerdmans, 1977), p. 586.
4. Bruce, *The Epistle to the Hebrews*, p. 408.
5. Phillips Brooks, *The Influence of Jesus* (London: H. R. Allenson, 1895), p. 91.
6. Bruce, *The Epistle to the Hebrews*, p. 408.
7. J. E. Rosscup, "The Priority of Prayer in Preaching," Richard L. Mayhue, ed., *The Master's Seminary Journal* (Spring 1991), Vol. 2, No. 1, p. 42.
8. *Ibid.*, p. 42.
9. C. H. Spurgeon, *The New Park Street Pulpit*, Vol. 1 (Pasadena, TX: Pilgrim, 1975), p. 204.

CHAPTER TWENTY-FOUR: SOARING BENEDICTIONS

1. Hugh Montefiore, *A Commentary on the Epistle to the Hebrews* (London: Adam & Charles Black, 1964), pp. 250, 251.
2. John A Mackay, *God's Order* (New York: Macmillan, 1953), p. 99.

Scripture Index

General Index

Index of Sermon Illustrations

275

About the Book Jacket

The design of the book jacket brings together the talents of several Christian artists. The design centers around the beautiful banner created by artist Marge Gieser. The banner is more than eight feet tall and was displayed in College Church throughout Pastor Hughes' series of sermons on Hebrews. It is photographed here on the jacket at about one-twentieth of its original size.

According to Scripture, the veil was a tapestry work — blue, purple, and scarlet wools, with white linen (flax) and golden threads being added. The figures of cherubim were worked into both sides of the material. The veil was the thickness of the breadth of a man's hand. The colors have traditionally symbolized various aspects of the nature of Jesus Christ:

Blue — Son of God.
Scarlet — Servant of the Most High.
Purple — King of kings, Lord of lords.
White — Son of Man.

Other artists contributing their talents to the creation of the jacket include: Bill Koechling, photography, and Mark Schramm, overall design and art direction.